The Logos Life

Adventures in Asia, Cultural Catastrophes, Help and Hope, On-board the World's Largest Floating Book-Fair!

by

Natalie Vellacott

Copyright

Natalie Vellacott 2023
Illustrated by Lauren Densham 2023
All rights reserved.

Contents

Preface 5
Port Schedule of Logos Hope 6
Introduction 9
Ready, Set, Go 12
The Never-Ending Journey 19
Pre-Ship Training; PST Penang 22
Logos Hope 30
Open for Business 34
International Café Mayhem! 40
Hindrance or Help? 45
Store-Keepers Living in Freezers 50
Malaysia Ministry 54
Sometimes It's Wrong! 58
Evangelicals or Catholics? 62
Hopelessness 66
Taming the Tongue 70
We Come Begging .....Swimming 76
Bright Lights, Exciting Sounds and Shopping Malls 79
It's More Fun in The Philippines! 82
Introducing the Street Children 86
Desperately Seeking 89
Children, Children Everywhere 92
Stop the Wedding! 95
Emotionless Police 101
Only in the Philippines 105
Smokey Mountain 108
Faithful in Small Things 113

Spiritual Sight	117
Subic Dry Dock	121
Fitness Fanatics	127
Dasmarinas Challenge Team	130
Welcome to Blessed Church	136
Poisoned	142
Music, Motorbikes and Misunderstandings!	147
One Soul Saved; Kuya (Brother) Danny	151
Learning the Lessons	156
Farewell Blessed Church	160
Dry Dock Takes Its Toll	164
Home of Joy	169
Prison Ministry	175
Help without Hope; The Ultimate Tragedy	178
On-Shore Book-Fair	181
The Bridge	187
Speed vs Detail	193
Book-Fair Administrator	196
Picking up the Pace	199
Project Re-organisation	203
Cautious in Cambodia	206
Worldliness in Thailand	209
Fishport Alliance Church	215
Various Visits	222
Gambling Never Pays	225
Poverty and Ignorance	231
Cultural Oddities	235
Island Adventure	240

Streets Paved with Vice 245

Scared to Skype 249

Winding Down 253

Goodbye Logos Hope 257

Epilogue 263

Farewells and Birthday Wishes 266

Natalie's Story 276

The Wordless Book 278

Preface

OM Ships International (www.omships.org) is the organisation behind Logos Hope. The Ships Ministry began in 1970 as part of the global Christian training and outreach movement, OM International. Since then OM's ships, Logos, Logos II, Doulos and now Logos Hope, have visited over 500 different ports in 151 countries and territories and welcomed over 44 million visitors on board.

Their goal is to bring knowledge, help and hope to the people of the world. They do this by supplying vital literature resources, encouraging cross-cultural understanding, training young people for more effective life and service, providing needed relief, and sharing a message of hope in God wherever there is an opportunity.

The ship visits each port for several weeks and opens the gangways to hundreds and sometimes thousands of visitors each day. On average, over one million visitors have been welcomed on board every year! The floating Book-Fair offers over 5,000 titles, providing many visitors their first ever opportunity to purchase quality educational and Christian literature.

An international crew and staff of volunteers live and work on the ships. Teams from the ship go into surrounding areas to supply aid and community care. In each port, the ship's crew joins local churches to bring hope and show love to people whatever their circumstance, culture or background.

Port Schedule of Logos Hope

Penang	Malaysia	Aug 18th 2011	Sep 27th 2011
Port Klang	Malaysia	Sep 28th 2011	Oct 24th 2011
Kuching	Malaysia	Oct 27th 2011	Nov 15th 2011
Kota Kinabalu	Malaysia	Nov 17th 2011	Dec 13th 2011
Singapore	Singapore	Dec 16th 2011	Jan 4th 2011
Cebu	Philippines	Jan 10th 2012	Feb 14th 2012
Manila	Philippines	Feb 16th 2012	Mar 15th 2012
Subic Bay	Philippines	Mar 16th 2012	Dec 12th 2012
Hong Kong	SAR China	Dec 15th 2012	Jan 29th 2013
Sihanoukville	Cambodia	Feb 3rd 2013	Feb 19th 2013
Bangkok	Thailand	Feb 20th 2013	Mar 13th 2013
Hong Kong	SAR China	Mar 20th 2013	May 21st 2013
San Fernando	Philippines	May 24th 2013	Jun 10th 2013
Subic Bay	Philippines	Jun 11th 2013	Jul 1st 2013
Puerto Princesa	Philippines	Jul 2nd 2013	Jul 8th 2013
Kuching	Malaysia	Jul 11th 2013	Aug 9th 2013
Singapore	Singapore	Aug 11th 2013	Aug 11th 2013
Phuket	Thailand	Aug 14th 2013	Aug 24th 2013
Colombo	Sri Lanka	Aug 29th 2013	Sep 23rd 2013

Logos Life / 7

List of Ports in order of Logos Hope Schedule

1 Penang, Malaysia
2 Port Klang, Malaysia
3 Kuching, Malaysia
4 Kota Kinabalu, Malaysia
5 Singapore, Singapore
6 Cebu, Philippines
7 Manila, Philippines
8 Subic Bay, Philippines
9 Hong Kong, SAR China
10 Sihanoukville, Cambodia
11 Bangkok, Thailand
12 Hong Kong, SAR China
13 San Fernando, Philippines
14 Subic Bay, Philippines
15 Puerto Princesa
16 Kuching Malaysia
17 Singapore, Singapore
18 Phuket, Thailand
19 Colombo, Sri Lanka

LOGOS HOPE SHIP LAYOUT

- **DECK 9** — OPEN DECK
- **DECK 8** — SCHOOL FOR CREW CHILDREN/ MUSIC ROOM/ PLAYGROUND
- **DECK 7** — OFFICES/ LEADER CABINS/ SHIP BRIDGE/ STAFF LOUNGE/ CREW LIBRARY
- **DECK 6** — DINING ROOM AND GALLEY/ LOGOS LOUNGE/ MEETING ROOMS
- **DECK 5** — CREW GANGWAY ENTRANCE/ LOBBY / BUSINESS OFFICES/ CREW & GUEST CABINS
- **DECK 4** — BOOK-FAIR/ INTERNATIONAL CAFE/ JOURNEY OF LIFE/ LIFE EXPERIENCE
- **DECK 3** — BOOK HOLD/ FOOD STORE/ HOPE THEATRE/ CREW CABINS (MALE AND FEMALE)
- **DECK 2** — LAUNDRY/ PRAYER ROOM/ CHARLIE/ GYM/ ADD ENGINE ROOM AREA/ CREW CABINS
- **DECK 1** — ENGINE ROOM (RESTRICTED AREA FOR ENGINE EMPLOYEES)

Introduction

In April of 2011, Operation Mobilisation (OM) officially informed me that the Christian missionary ship, Logos Hope's, next two crew intakes were full. The only alternative presented to me was to head to the war-torn country of Afghanistan. I processed the information calmly as, although I liked the idea of being on the ship, it wasn't a dream for me. I had only known about the ship ministry for a short time and had never really had the travel bug, so it didn't appeal for that reason. I had become more excited after reading some personal accounts of the experiences of former crew members and was looking forward to the adventure. But I honestly just wanted to go where God wanted me and if He was leading me to Afghanistan then so be it.

I didn't have much time to contemplate the new opportunity as, just as quickly as the ship leadership had made their decision, they suddenly reversed it. They decided that, although the ship was technically full, they would make an exception for me - they might need me for a special role due to my police background. The role was called Line Up and involved travelling in a small team ahead of the different countries the ship would be visiting to prepare for the ship's arrival and to prepare the programme of ministry for that port. (As it turned out, I didn't end up in that role, but it was the reason given for my last-minute acceptance.)

Realising that I had only a few months before I was due to leave, I was suddenly aware that I really didn't know enough about the day to day details of the two-year mission. I had been so focused on making sure that I was taking the right path by God that I hadn't considered a lot of the detail. Things like: how I was going to deal with the lack of personal space, what was on the ship's itinerary and where all the countries were, began to register on my horizon largely due to the questions people were asking. However, my lack of investigation and unpreparedness worked out quite well in practice. I was able to tell people truthfully that I was trusting God in those areas and was not worried about them!

One thing I *was* worried about, which slightly overshadowed the whole getting ready experience, was the number of vaccinations I was going to have to have in the space of a few weeks. I had always had a fear of injections, probably dating back to the time a disorganised nurse had asked me to hold the needle in my arm whilst she left the room to get an item she had carelessly forgotten. The travel nurse had calculated that I needed a total of nine injections including typhoid, rabies, yellow fever, meningitis, hepatitis A and swine flu. A small dose of any of those diseases can't be good for anyone, let alone all of them at once. I was very ill, but can't tell you which ones made me sick because I had them all at the same time.

Vaccination drama over and fully recovered by early August of 2011, I found myself saying goodbye to my police colleagues in England for what turned out to be the final time, although officially it was just a two-year career break. Many of my colleagues no doubt thought I was crazy not only for giving up two years' worth of wages but for actually paying an organisation to let me work for them. That was really the hardest thing to explain to non-believers who just couldn't understand why anyone would do that and I found myself at times questioning my own sanity in the process of explaining it to them. The conversations followed this general pattern;

> Random Colleague: "So when are you leaving to go on that cruise ship thing?"
> Me: "You mean the Christian Missionary Ship? It's not really a cruise…"
> Random Colleague: "Yeah that…what will you actually be doing on the ship then?"
> Me: "Well I'm not sure really, we'll be given work assignments when we arrive."
> Random Colleague: "Oh so you'll be working, that's good. How much will they pay you?"
> Me: "Well actually I'm not paid. I'm a volunteer. I'm having a fundraiser next-week, would you like to come?"
> Random Colleague: "Wait, what's the fundraiser for…!?"
> Me: "Well…. actually, I have to pay them to work on the ship…"

Random Colleague: "WHAT?! That's totally illegal...you've been conned. Can't you get out of it?"

In late August, after a lot of packing and repacking, (how do you pack properly for a two-year trip, with no realistic idea of what you might need?) I left England with my parents to begin the long drive to Holland. The ten day Go Conference in Amsterdam was part of the orientation. There would be no visits to England during my two-year commitment as the ship was scheduled to be in South East Asia for the duration and it wasn't exactly a quick hop across the English Channel.

What follows is an honest account of my personal experiences whilst serving on board the Christian missionary ship Logos Hope. Having kept journals on board I had, to date, avoided writing about the ship, despite having the material available, as I had felt that my experiences may come across as having been largely negative. I didn't want to tarnish a Christian ministry or write any type of book that could be seen as an expose. But having moved on a few years I can see that my experiences have been used by God to shape me and change my character for future service. It's time to share them in the hope that you might be encouraged by the stories of ministry, entertained by the many mishaps, cultural and otherwise, challenged by the spiritual lessons and most importantly adequately prepared should you personally enter into missionary service. I hope you will be inspired but that this book will also serve as a warning that, as my Pastor said before I left, "the missionary life is hard." The trials and challenges may not come in the expected form.

My prayer on beginning my journey was that God would use me for evangelism and show me a specific country for future service. I believe that both of those prayers were answered but not necessarily in the way that I was expecting. I really hope you will benefit spiritually from traveling with me through South East Asia on the "World's Largest Floating Book-Fair."

CHAPTER ONE

Ready, Set, Go

Arriving in Amsterdam at the conference venue after a very long drive, I briefly hugged my parents then left them awkwardly standing by their car as I headed in the direction in which everyone else appeared to be going. I felt like I was jumping into the deep end of a swimming pool without knowing how to swim. I really had no idea what to expect and wished I had done more research. At least I was sure that God had led me thus far as the door had swung wide open and everything had fallen into place.

I breathed a sigh of relief as I looked around and recognised two guys that I had met on a preparation weekend at OM's base in England. I joined them and after the necessary chit-chat, we headed towards an area that looked to be populated. I discovered that the conference hosted people that were heading to OM fields all around the world and not just to Logos Hope. The group that was joining Logos Hope was around seventy strong.

I found my dormitory and was introduced to the girls I would be sharing a room with. Not really knowing any Asian people in England and not really understanding anything about the culture or language, I would not have predicted that Mia from China was to become one of my closest friends over the subsequent two years. The other girls, also Asian, kept to themselves although one of them disappeared every night only returning in the early hours, which was a little odd, and annoying as she woke us all up!

I struggled with the conference from the outset as we were encouraged to form close friendships with people we barely knew by "taking off our masks" and revealing intimate personal details. The sessions assumed that everyone was wearing a mask in the first place and that we would be willing to remove it. The people who weren't wearing masks or who were but weren't willing to take them off didn't really fit in. I was the oddball who wasn't wearing a mask but if I had been I wouldn't have been willing to take it off. Confused yet? Don't worry, so was I!

In tandem with the de-masking session, the organisers ran a personality test on each of us to determine if we were Drivers, Motivators, Harmonisers or Detailers. It was all gobbledegook to me and I disliked every second of it. The slight light bulb moment only came towards the end of the class, when the instructor informed us that if we had scored highly in the Driver area of the personality test (I had scored the highest and barely registered in any of the other categories), then we were probably thinking that it was all a load of nonsense and that we couldn't wait for it to be over so that we could leave and do something worthwhile. That was exactly what I was thinking and I wished they could have told us that in advance of the session, or for those of us for whom it was relevant, excused us from it. I breathed a sigh of relief when the session finally concluded thinking I would never have to think about any of it ever again. However, for the next two years on the ship, people frequently referred back to the session, placing themselves into the categories as an excuse for all kinds of behaviour. I guess that's what happens when you put people into a box, they assume that they must somehow fit into that box and behave in the prescribed manner.

Aside from that, we heard some good teaching; some described it as "life-changing and amazing." I wouldn't go that far but it had a good Biblical basis and was definitely preferable to the former sessions. Primarily I remember a Bible teacher called Peter Mead; I recognised him straight away. He had led a session on "Knowing God's will" during a short-term mission in which I had been involved in London about five years previously. He had explained that we are far too obsessed with being in or trying to find the "centre" of God's will. He challenged us to think about what that really meant and pointed out that God's will is not hidden from us and that God actually wants us to find it! He referenced the subject of marriage and questioned whether there was one perfect person out there for everyone or whether it was more a case of making prayerful decisions. He asked what would happen if one Christian didn't find the centre of God's will for marriage and married the wrong person. That would then mean that her would-have-been husband would have to marry the wrong wife thereby creating a chain of erroneous marriages. Before long every Christian in that generation would be out of the centre of God's will, and it would all have been caused by one person making the wrong decision about their marriage partner. The message had stayed with me and helped me not to be afraid when making important decisions, providing I was seeking to do the will of God, was prayerful and took wise counsel in the process.

We also got to know some of the people with whom we would be spending the next few years which was enlightening. I met Frank from Taiwan at that stage. Aged nineteen, relatively short and with short dark hair, he wore a perpetually confused look as he struggled to get a basic grasp of English. We teased him mercilessly, all in good humour of course. He took it well.

On one really weird day of the conference, there were a number of "prayer stations" that had been set up in different areas for us to engage with or explore whilst praying. I guess it was for the creative souls amongst us, but once again the whole idea was lost on me. I just preferred to pray quietly alone and without props. Amongst the stations was a line of chairs which people were encouraged to jump over whilst loudly shouting "hallelujah." The purpose? Your guess is as good as mine. In another area of the same room was a line of white blankets that people had buried themselves inside and were lying like half a dozen corpses, presumably also praying. Every so often someone would emerge from one of the blankets as if rising from the dead. They would then blink as their eyes readjusted to the light before making their way in zombie fashion towards another area. There was also a quiet area for people to pray but it was virtually impossible to concentrate with the other antics occurring around and about. After an hour of complete bewilderment, I left the others to their strange practices and went to my room. I read the Bible for a while and then promptly fell asleep, probably from the exhaustion of my mind working overtime trying to work out what it had all been about.

The best days were definitely those on which we took part in simulations. On one of the days, we experienced going through customs, no doubt to try to make us aware of the potential pitfalls and things to avoid in reality. It definitely took me back to police training school with the fake and unrealistic scenarios, but I enjoyed it nonetheless. Others were totally petrified throughout, seeming not to appreciate that it was just a simulation. I wondered if they should have been allowed to participate, particularly when some of them came from countries where problems at customs may mean a never-ending prison sentence or worse. I'm sure it did nothing to ease their burdens as orders were barked at them by conference staff who were disguised as uniformed immigration officials wearing dark sunglasses and, in one case, smoking a smelly cigar. It was pretty intimidating.

We were told in advance of the simulation to try to give as little detail as was acceptable to the authorities. They purposefully didn't tell us that we had to tell the truth, I think to see what we would do if put under pressure. We were split into travelling groups who would look after each other. What I didn't realise was that a few of us who had appeared over-confident whilst in the queue for the fake customs desk had been specially selected for harsher treatment further down the line. Our papers had been stamped with a barely visible smiley face; I guess it was in an attempt to "break" us. Of course, I was one of those individuals, but not knowing the reason I played perfectly into their hands. I became more and more frustrated as I experienced lengthy delays for seemingly no reason, and in the end my group went ahead without me. I had wanted to complete the scenario faultlessly, but it was not to be.

The most entertaining moment came when our travel group was standing in a line against a wall outside a building waiting to be permitted entry. We were being monitored by two armed guards who were marching up and down and watching us closely. It was really quite unnerving, even for me with a police background. One of the guards asked to see Mia's passport and being from a country where, if the authorities asked you to do something you did it immediately without question, she handed it over straight away. Of course, the guard didn't give it back and Mia was wondering what to do and was starting to become really worried. I decided to intervene on her behalf, confidently asking the guard whether he was going to give it back. He stared at me as if in shock that I had dared to speak to him. He then shouted in my face, but I could feel that I was about to laugh as it was all so ridiculous. The guard saw that I was about to laugh and his face also began twitching as I smothered my giggles and Mia looked bemused. After that, he gave the passport back and quickly moved us on to the next stage in the process. Strike one for me.

Inside the building was a darkened room with benches where we were made to sit until we were called through to the next stage. It was really very dark and a bit claustrophobic as we were herded together like cattle on the benches with little room to move. The guards again marched up and down shouting at us. By that point my new friend Frank was absolutely terrified as he was taking the whole thing far too seriously. He was physically shaking and sweating with eyes as wide as saucers, desperately trying not to do anything that might draw the attention of the guards. I tried to keep him calm reminding him that it was just a simulation but he didn't understand my English so I couldn't reassure him. The situation was very funny for me but obviously not for poor Frank.

When it was my turn to go through to the next room I had no idea what I would encounter. I entered and was immediately forced to stand in front of a uniformed woman who was sitting behind a computer screen. She began asking pointed and direct questions about my intentions on entering the country and my plans whilst I was there. I thought I could get away with being vague, but she asked me personal questions to which she obviously already knew the answers, which freaked me out a little. Then, in response to a hazy answer in relation to my faith, she turned her computer screen around to reveal my Facebook profile page in all its glory which completely contradicted what I had just said. I was stunned, caught in a direct lie and didn't really know where to go from there. I had thought it was probably okay to lie in a simulation but the outcome proved once and for all that lying is never okay! I continued answering her questions truthfully after that and was finally allowed to continue.

Afterwards, we heard hilarious tales of people tying themselves up in knots when being asked what the initials OM (Operation Mobilisation) stood for. One person had said "Oranges and Mangos" and another "Operation Mountain" going on to give a lengthy and convincing description of the fake organisation and what its purposes were. Clearly, the person should have been training for some other profession as their talents were being wasted. Some people even ended up denying their faith completely when they were placed under extreme pressure. I wondered why the conference staff went that far as it didn't seem to achieve anything and definitely didn't make anyone more confident for their actual journey through immigration.

Another group simulation tested our ability to interact with other cultures and people of other faiths. You might think that having been a police officer I would be an expert and would know all the right things to do and say. Sadly not, as I was to discover. Our scenario involved going to dinner in the home of a Muslim family. Perfect, I thought, as I had taken part in short-term outreach to Muslims in the past which had involved training in the basics of Islam. I considered myself to be fairly knowledgeable and was confident that our team would be able to set a good example for that reason. But it was not to be. Unfortunately, not only did I fail to lead the way, but ended up being the culprit who caused our group's downfall in dramatic fashion by making one colossal mistake.

We were eating dinner together with our hosts, sitting on the floor around a very low table. One of our team was involved in an in-depth discussion with the Muslim man about faith. He quoted a Bible verse and I thought to myself that maybe it would be useful for him to have a Bible handy for reference. Not wanting to disrupt the conversation by speaking or handing my small Bible to my team-mate. I casually flipped it across the table towards him. I immediately realised that it was not the thing to have done as everyone fell silent and the Muslim man abruptly stood up. He then dramatically clutched his heart, cried out in pain and carried out a fake death by falling face forward onto the floor. I presumed it was in protest at a Holy Bible having been thrown around in his house. After the initial shock where everyone stared at each other and wondered what to do next, the wife sprang into action swiftly and rudely ushering us out of the house, with a broom as I recall.

Leaving the house, I felt slightly apprehensive as, although it had been a training exercise, no one acknowledged the funny side of what had happened. The rest of my team were worried about the impact on them within the training environment due to their association with me! My reprehensible conduct was highlighted during the conference debrief with everyone present, as an example of how not to behave whilst guests in the home of a Muslim family. I felt severely chastised but again couldn't help but see the amusing side as I recalled the shocked expression on the face of the Muslim man (who I knew was just a conference staff member) just before he clutched his chest and dramatically keeled over, leaving his wife to deal with the aftermath.

The fact that the characters in the simulations were conference staff made things more embarrassing for those of us who had acted up. We ran into the staff after they had morphed back into "themselves" through the remainder of the conference. They knew the silly things we had said or done during our interactions with them whilst they were in character. They milked it for all they were worth; the guy who had shouted in my face during the customs activity insisted on grinning and waving whenever he saw me as I ducked away to try to avoid eye contact. Obviously, he was used to readjusting, probably having done it many times; I was not and was surprised by how uncomfortable I felt afterwards.

CHAPTER TWO

The Never-Ending Journey

The Amsterdam conference eventually came to an end and, for an unknown reason, as I didn't think I had made a great impression by that stage, I was asked to be a co-travel leader of our large group of sixty people and one baby. The journey was from the conference site to Pre-Ship-Training (PST) in Penang, Malaysia. I agreed straight away relishing the idea of a challenge and keen to get on with some actual ministry.

On the day we were leaving we stood around with our luggage, waiting outside the conference venue to get on the buses that would take us to the airport. A baggage weight device was being passed around. I thought I would take the opportunity to double check the weight of my luggage even though I knew it would be fine as it had already been quadruple checked before leaving our house in England. I asked a young friend, Leo from Scotland, to help me lift the bag onto the scale. But then I did a double take as it registered almost double the baggage allowance. Leo thought it was hilarious as I started panicking and wondering what I was going to do with the luggage I would have to leave behind and how I would manage without it. We were moments before leaving the venue so there really wasn't time for any of the confusion. I decided to check the weight again with the help of a slightly older and wiser friend, Brian from Ireland, just in case there had been a mistake. I didn't see how I could possibly have got things that wrong. Brian agreed to help and as the new weight registered on the scale, I breathed a sigh of relief before disappearing to hunt Leo down and give him a piece of my mind. Crisis over, it was time for the buses to leave, so we all piled in.

We were scheduled to take two flights - the first long flight was from Holland to Singapore and the second shorter one from

Singapore to Malaysia. The only problem I could foresee was the ten hour stop-over in between flights which had apparently been unavoidable due to the comparative prices. I didn't think much of it at the time and just thought it would be fine. I was already feeling tired, due to not being able to sleep much during the conference. My co-leader, Patrick from Paraguay, was very laid back and calm, completely the opposite of me, which was maybe why they had chosen us. They probably thought we would balance each other out.

Whilst waiting at the airport we tried to deal with the concerns of those in our group - one guy who needed to take a large quantity of medication with him (a two-year supply) and of course there was Frank, who was by then absolutely terrified about the immigration process. If he hadn't been before, the simulation had certainly done the trick. I accompanied Frank through immigration for the first flight, planning to act as a translator if it all went wrong, but there were no problems at that stage and we all boarded the plane safely.

When we arrived at Singapore I was totally exhausted not having been able to sleep on the plane. There was obviously nowhere designated to sleep in the airport so I eventually lay down on the cold hard floor somewhere that I thought was inconspicuous, and after some time managed to fall asleep. However, I kept getting woken up, initially by security guards because it just wasn't the "done thing" in the middle of such a posh airport, and then by members of our group asking really ridiculous questions, mostly in broken English. Having given up attempting to sleep, I ended up in a really bad mood sitting on the floor with a spare T-shirt over my head covering my face.

Whenever anyone spoke to me, I snapped "Don't ask me any more questions because I don't know the answers."

Brian, on seeing my plight and knowing I was tired came to my rescue after a while. To those who still dared to ask questions, he responded "I don't think Natalie is feeling very well" which, though an understatement, was helpful in the circumstances as it stopped people thinking I was seriously moody.

The best moment occurred when I had been left alone long enough slightly to recover my sense of humour. We were trying to gather everyone together as it was time to head for the boarding gate. We had agreed to meet in a certain location and had left somebody sensible, whose first language was English, at the location to ensure correct onward instructions were given to people as they arrived. But when I arrived at the meeting point I found that our chosen man had for some reason swapped himself with Wonhee from South Korea who, at that stage, didn't speak a word of English. When we asked Wonhee where we should go to catch the plane he beamed at us and then nodded and looked confused. We eventually worked out where everyone was and, due to a slight delay in boarding, managed to get them safely onto the flight which was a miracle in the circumstances.

When we arrived in Malaysia, however, I was so busy assisting the guy with the medicine at immigration that I had forgotten about Frank. His concerns about his country Taiwan's relationship with Malaysia were apparently justified as he ended up being detained. After negotiations, he was granted only a fourteen-day visa instead of the three months that we had all been given. To conclude a truly terrible day, one of my check-in bags containing all of my shoes (amongst other things) was lost at the airport, and I had to leave for the hotel without it. I was so exhausted by that point that I really didn't care. I was relieved when we arrived at the hotel as I knew it wouldn't be long before I could sleep.

CHAPTER THREE

Pre-Ship Training; PST Penang

At the conference, we had been told that we would stay on shore for three weeks of Pre-Ship Training (PST) in Penang, Malaysia, before boarding the ship as there were a lot of things we needed to know. Our collective group was entitled, rather unoriginally, PST Penang and one of our first group tasks was to come up with a team chant. We settled for the very uninspiring "All for one, PST Penang, woo Penang, woo Penang, woo Penang" The idea was that whenever the PST was mentioned by name on the ship, usually by one of the leaders from the stage, all those present from the group would launch into the chant. Our chant was unique as the guys in our group proved by continuing the "woo Penang" for as long as possible on each occasion until those from other training groups groaned with annoyance and told them to "shut up." As you can probably imagine the chanting began very enthusiastically, chiefly amongst the younger people, but by the end of our two-year commitment when many people from our group had already departed, the voice became dimmer and dimmer. Finally, there was usually one lone soul who was either still faithfully chanting or hiding in the audience hoping people wouldn't remember which PST he was from.

On arriving at the luxurious hotel, I was amazed, having prepared for the mission by weaning myself off caffeine and branded shampoo, that these items were readily available. We were warned, however, by our lead trainer, Andy from England, that we should make the most of it as it would be our last taste of luxury for a while. Andy is, amongst other things, remembered for the moments during his training sessions when he seemed to lose his voice mid-sentence resulting in a high and squeaky sound which got a good laugh on every occasion.

I was thrilled when my lost luggage turned up by special courier that evening. I had already started making preparations for if it had been lost forever, rather than the airline just being a bit disorganised.

On arriving in my hotel room there was a large package waiting for me; it contained all kinds of useful things, including chocolate! It was from my ship "big sister," Sarah from England (all of us were assigned a more experienced ship crew member as a big brother or sister to help ease the transition.) After I had moved on board, it didn't take me long to figure out that mentioning western things that I missed in my newsletters resulted in them arriving a few months later in the ship mailroom. I was a little shocked (and grateful!) when one faithful couple took it upon themselves to send a big box including around fifteen large bars of Galaxy chocolate; the postage alone had cost twenty pounds!

I posted a Facebook message recognising the gift resulting in some interesting comments from fellow crew members including "Oh, you have chocolate…." which I translated as "I want some."

I was pleased to share it, though, realising that eating that quantity by myself might not have had a happy conclusion.

The hotel food was good with a buffet for all three meals. We had been allocated twin rooms and I was pleased that I would again be sharing with Mia as we had already got to know each other a little during the conference. During PST, we also became prayer partners and managed to meet once a week for prayer for more or less the duration of our two-year commitment. It was an unexpected blessing as we were very different characters from two entirely different cultures, China and England.

On that topic, my police diversity training obviously hadn't made enough of an impact as at one point during PST I asked Mia to translate something that Wonhee was saying. Wonhee looked confused because he hadn't understood my request, but Mia looked incredulous and I knew that she had understood as her English was more advanced. Just as I was wondering the reason for her astonished look, she said "Natalie, I am from China and Wonhee is from South Korea," at which point we all burst out laughing at my stupidity.

I know that ignorance is no excuse and that probably I shouldn't be admitting to that conversation. At that time, in my mind, Asians all looked fairly similar to each other so I just assumed they were from the same country and spoke the same language or that they would understand each other's languages. Throw in a total disinterest in Geography at school and that type of conversation was the inevitable result. I'm sure there are Asians who think that all Europeans look the same on first acquaintance as well...

Our room, which was quite high up, had a view overlooking the beach below. All around us were skyscrapers and looking around I felt quite insignificant in a foreign country living with strangers. We were allowed to swim in the sea, where unfortunately two of our number were stung by jellyfish, resulting in the rest of us becoming quite wary. Dany from France provided the entertainment for everyone and was frequently seen walking around on his hands, taking part in dare devil stunts or on one occasion opening his mouth and displaying a medium sized lizard sitting on his tongue. I didn't wait around to see if he actually ate the poor lizard as the stunt was a little too disgusting for my English sensibilities.

We were divided into small "fellowship" groups where we were encouraged to share our testimonies and other details about our lives. I found it hard to adjust to the openness at first but as that kind of sharing was common-place throughout my time with OM I was forced to get used to it. We spent most of our time at PST doing classroom based things and listening to lectures about ship rules and procedures. One rule was made very clear from the outset - yes, the ship was already in Penang but no, we were not allowed to visit it until we officially moved on board. The reason given was that those already living on board would be saying goodbye to the friends they had made; as we had arrived, another batch were leaving. They wouldn't want the interruption of having to welcome excited and energetic new people at that time of sadness and separation. I wondered why they kept repeating the instruction not to go to the ship ahead of our scheduled visit. I assumed it had been clear enough the first time and more naively perhaps, that everyone would be keen to obey the rules.

Another reiterated but widely overlooked rule was that concerning romantic relationships. The general rule was that we were not allowed to develop a romantic relationship within our first year on the ship. For some countries (South Korea and South Africa) it was two years; this was extended to spending time alone with a member of the opposite gender. There were exclusions if people were working together and obviously for those who were already married. There were also allowances for those who arrived on the ship already in a romantic relationship. But for the rest, the end of the year became a definite target as people lined up outside the Personnel Office to request 'Special Permission (SP)' which, if granted after the necessary people in home countries had been consulted, resulted in a small announcement being placed on the staff noticeboard. The notice stated that so and so couple had been granted special permission to spend time alone with each other with a view to determining whether or not to pursue a relationship. PST Penang had a relatively high number of matches both within itself and with people from other PSTs. Many later married, including one couple who had developed an affinity for each other during the initial training and who I'm sure were frequently in trouble with Personnel for flouting the rules.

As it turned out, it was very necessary to keep reiterating the rules, as some people in every group spent most of their time trying to find any and every which way to bend or break them. In relation to the SP rule, potential couples persuaded an unsuspecting friend to go out with them for the day and then abandoned their helpful friend somewhere or moved them into another group so they could spend time alone with the object of their desire. I had temporarily forgotten that I was in a group the average age of which was around twenty-one, so I shouldn't have been that surprised. I was turning thirty when I joined and having been in a disciplined police service for ten years was more inclined to obey the rules, provided I understood the reasons for them. Others were not quite so compliant.

At times the first question out of people's mouths when arriving in a new port or country was "Where's the mall and cinema?" and not "Where are the people and ministry?" There were also people who had clearly joined the ship ministry because they wanted to travel the world and others who probably weren't Christians at all. I found that difficult to understand due to the rigorous checks and interviews I had to undergo before being accepted for the ship but I'm sure recruitment practices in different countries varied widely.

During PST we took part in safety training in a local swimming pool and some fire-fighting. The latter I drastically failed as I wasn't feeling well on the day and didn't really fancy it. It reminded me somewhat of Public Order Training in the police where bricks were hurled at us as we hid behind shields.

The pool day was great fun as we jumped from a height whilst wearing life preservers and body suits. Then we had to sit inside twenty-five-person enclosed life rafts in the middle of the pool. The rafts were sealed all the way around and had a roof. It was a bit like being inside a tent but on the water. I began to feel panicky when taking part in the scenario which astonished me as I've never been prone to anxiety. I wondered if it was a throwback to my youth when we used to go caving as a family; I recall heading head first down a tunnel just big enough to fit me and when I decided I wanted to go back and get out I couldn't as there was another person hot on my tail.

Anyway, in the raft I began feeling claustrophobic and desperate for normal air as it got hotter inside with all the people. I surmised that even in the safety of the swimming pool, if everyone suddenly decided they needed to get out at the same time the raft might sink with us all trapped inside. The entry (and exit) point was just big enough for one person. I had to stick my head out of the small air vent in the roof in the end and couldn't remain inside for very long. That didn't bode well for me if we needed to use the raft for real.

During another exercise, we had to climb up the raft whilst it was at a forty-five-degree angle using a rope and balance in the right way to cause the raft to fall flat onto the water. Watching others do it I thought it would be fairly easy as I was relatively strong and a good swimmer, although some people were struggling, but I was partnered with Mia who couldn't swim. We managed to climb up the raft which was much more difficult than it looked, but we became entangled in the rope. Eventually, at the point when I was totally exhausted and had to let go, the raft fell and Mia got trapped underneath. She was recovered by instructors after a short while having nearly drowned herself. Of course, we were then made to repeat the entire scenario to ensure our safety on the ship. The second time thankfully we were successful, although I think the experience put Mia off swimming for life!

The most anxious moment during the three weeks training was probably when we were given our job allocations for our two-year commitment on Logos Hope. We had been interviewed and asked for our preference about which department we would like to work in whilst serving on board, but it was made clear to us that, whilst the leaders would consider our requests, ultimately we would be placed where the ship needed us to work. I chose not to express a preference in my interview, wanting to be flexible and believing that God would put me where he wanted me. The main options were a) working in the engine room, b) working on deck, c) working in the kitchen, d) working in the Book-Fair, e) working as a cleaner. My purpose in going to the ship had been to evangelise so I really wanted a role that allowed me to do that as often as possible. The best option was probably to work in the Book-Fair as the staff would have direct contact with the visitors to the ship.

We simultaneously tore open our small envelopes containing the big news. There was a chorus of shouts of delight, groans and in some cases tears as the allocations were read and shared. I, on the other hand, was bemused as I didn't see anything I recognised. My paper just said "Catering in the International Café." I had no idea what that meant. It appeared that I was the only person in our group of seventy plus with those words written on their paper. I asked a leader about my allocation. I was informed that I would be part of a small team of five or six people who would be working in the café on the deck that was open for public visitors. It was also where many of the evangelistic conversations took place when the ship wasn't too busy. When the new information sunk in, I was elated by the prospect that I might have even greater opportunities in that role than if I had been given a job in the Book-Fair. I was told that people were not normally allocated jobs in the café straight out of training and that it was a sought after position.

The general principle at that time was that we had to accept where God had placed us and do the best job we could do rather than complaining or trying to move departments. That sounds very spiritual and sensible and I thought it was a good principle at first and was determined to accept where I was placed, but later I saw the negative aspects of the policy. It left many people conflicted - they weren't happy in their roles either because their skills and training weren't being utilised or because they had a passion for something else, but they felt that if they complained they were questioning God.

So, they remained demotivated and discouraged as they fought an internal battle, sometimes for their entire commitment as they weren't offered another role in a different department.

I think the leadership team were just fed up with so many people complaining or wanting to change roles and they were trying to minimise that, but failing to recognise that mistakes could be made in job allocation wasn't really a great solution. One extreme example was a man who came on board for a few months and was working in the Galley (kitchen). On chatting to him I discovered he was a trained mechanic. The leaders were desperately appealing for mechanics to work in the engine room at that time. I asked him if he had told them about his training and he said he had mentioned it in his interview, but that it must have been overlooked. He believed therefore that God must've placed him in the Galley for a reason and he wasn't willing to re-highlight his skills and training or to question the decision that had been made, preferring to make the best of it in the Galley.

There were several comedy moments during PST - the first when Mia excitedly rushed up to me one day to tell me that Wonhee had previously been in some sort of serious accident during which he had had a heart, lung AND eye transplant (yes you read that correctly.) Apparently, he didn't want to talk about the circumstances of the accident. Although I hadn't paid that much attention in science at school, I knew that the statement had to have somehow been lost in translation, but Mia was adamant. So, I decided to ask Wonhee himself. In what turned into a VERY confusing conversation, I eventually established that he had registered himself on an organ donor list, in case of an accident, which was somewhat different from having a transplant.

The second comedy moment began when Jheanelle from Jamaica saw me looking at the board for the "Fun talent night." I had been thinking how much I detested that type of thing and how much of a waste of time it was. But she commented that she "hoped she would see me taking part" and for some reason my mind registered that as a challenge. I decided on the spot to fight against every natural instinct and take part. I found my friend Fiona, persuaded her to join me, and together we practised narrating and acting out an actual incident that had taken place during my police career where I had mistaken a drunken homeless man for a dead body. Most of our audience, not being aware that I had been a police officer, believed it was a scene of fiction, but they laughed anyway and were astonished when they discovered that it was true.

At the end of a very long three weeks, the day that we had all been waiting for finally arrived. We had completed our basic training and were ready to move to our new home on board Logos Hope. The ship had been waiting for us for a while and I discovered that most of the trainees had been preparing for their journeys for many years. I was one of the only people who had been accepted at the very last minute, so in some ways was the least prepared. Our collective excitement had been building for a month and we definitely felt ready for the next stage.

CHAPTER FOUR

Logos Hope

Our first visit to Logos Hope took place a few days before we were due to move on board. We were invited to join in with parts of the regular programme, the departing crew having left so we wouldn't be crashing any farewell parties. Arriving at the ship, I was immediately struck by how impressively huge it looked from the outside. We were told that there was a total of nine decks and that we would have access to most areas once officially living on board. The existing crew members were excited to meet their new colleagues. They had prepared a tunnel of their different countries' flags for us to run through whilst they held them in place (and got a good look at us!)

We exited the tunnel onto one of the gangways leading up and into the ship and then found ourselves in a very large and dark room with high ceilings, hundreds of chairs arranged in rows, and a stage with enormous curtains at the front. It was called the "Hope Theatre" and was on deck three where most of the big events were held. We sat through an induction meeting and were then taken on tours in small groups around the ship. I realised quickly that I would easily get lost probably for quite some time as the interior also seemed huge.

During the brief orientation, I was introduced to my new boss, Priska from Switzerland. I was a bit disconcerted by her opening question, "Why on earth did you come here?" She had read my background information and couldn't understand why someone would leave a stable job and career in the police to join the ship. I said the only thing I could think of, "I believe God called me," hoping it didn't sound like a cliché. She showed me around the I-cafe and explained a little about what I would need to do. She also told me that I would need to "close" my hair, indicating with her hands that she meant tie my hair up. I resisted the urge to laugh as I was going to have to get used to the varying English levels and resultant mistakes. In time, I became convinced that some people had arranged for others to sit the mandatory online English tests on their behalf in order to get accepted to the ship in the first place. Not very ethical but it looked to be the only explanation as some didn't speak a word of English.

I was also introduced to my first cabin mate, Ruth from the USA, who was also the ship librarian. One advantage to being slightly older than the majority of my group was that I was allocated a two-person cabin on deck five instead of a four-person cabin on one of the lower decks. It was given as a privilege recognising that we were likely to have lived independently prior to the ship and might require that extra bit of personal space. I was very grateful for the concession, more so when six months down the line I began hearing horror stories from those in cabins with a greater number of people when they had fallen out with each other. Our cabin was big and Ruth had managed to collect additional items of furniture as she had already been on the ship for a number of years. I took the top bunk which fortunately suited me as Ruth was already comfortable on the bottom. On seeing my cabin, I began to wonder what all the warnings of austerity had been about, as everything was great as far as I was concerned. That's one advantage of lowered expectations.

However, I was a bit irritated to learn that legally we would be forced to submit to weekly cabin inspections which would be marked on a sliding scale with one being "exceptionally clean and tidy" and five being "a potential health hazard requiring re-inspection." After collecting six ones they could be exchanged for a voucher equivalent to one euro in value, which may seem like a ridiculously small target, but as I was living on my twenty euros a month pocket money, every little helped.

I was informed by some incredulous fellow crew members that I was one of the only people on board attempting to live on that amount. I was surprised because, on joining the ship, I had virtually been told that I wasn't allowed to take any additional money with me and that everyone would be living on their pocket money. I had been quite happy to sign up to the limitation thinking it would be good for me, would help to prepare me for future ministry and it would be a challenge. But from the outset, I saw that people were not living solely on their pocket money, evidenced by lavish credit card spending by people from certain countries.

Ruth and I proudly displayed our series of ones in a prominent place in our cabin, until one day, towards the end of my time on the ship, due to a miscommunication about the inspection date, we received a five. On returning to find that judgement pronounced on our ridiculously untidy cabin by some leaders of the ship (unfortunately including my "ship dad"), I burst out laughing and added the five to our collection of results, thinking that it had to happen at least once during my time on board. Probably not the attitude of repentance that was expected but my rebellious nature may have needed an outlet.

People had gone to great lengths to make all the newbies feel welcome with encouraging notes and Bible verses posted on cabin doors. Amongst the selection was a note from my ship "parents," Rodney and Irene Hui from Singapore, which read:

"We are delighted to be your 'parents' in the next two years. We look forward to some great family and fun times together. We have the luxury of enjoying our family life on the go, in different ports and countries. This is cool indeed! We will get to know one another in time to come. For now, welcome to the Hui family!"

I was to learn that I had probably been placed in one of the most well organised and generous families on board, in addition to being the loudest. Some others with less active and often less interested families were envious as they observed our excited and energetic meetings in the dining room every Tuesday evening at "Ship Family Night."

Our family for the duration consisted of "Uncle" Rodney and "Auntie" Irene, Brian from Northern Ireland, Matt from England, Lydia from Germany, Frank from Taiwan, Jenny from Korea/America, Eumpa from South Korea, Shamy from Mexico, Raphael from Switzerland, Silas from Germany and Dany from France. I knew Brian and Matt from OM orientation in England and the others from spending a bit of time together in our fellowship group during PST as that was subsequently turned into our ship family. The meetings often degenerated, largely due to the behaviour of some of the guys. They discovered that I didn't like a big fuss being made on my birthday due to not wanting to be reminded that I was getting older.

So, they insisted on singing happy birthday to me at inappropriate interludes throughout the year; on one such occasion, much to my embarrassment, a lot of other families caught the spirit and joined in enthusiastically, being of course completely unaware that it was not actually my birthday at all.

The idea of being placed into a pre-determined family didn't sit comfortably with me at first (being British and liking my own space) and I resisted the closeness, but over time I realised that it was a great idea and I enjoyed being part of it. Our ship parents were very interested in the things we were doing and they became helpful mentors during the two years.

There was also a note from my big sister Sarah on my cabin door - she had already won me over by sending me the chocolate in PST. "I am so glad that you are here at last! I am looking forward to getting to know you … I think this scripture sums up living in the Logos Hope community well … 1 Corinthians 12 vs 12-31, we are one body made up of many parts, each and every one is important and dependent upon the other."

CHAPTER FIVE

Open for Business

Shortly after our first visit to the ship, the PST ended and we were finally allowed to move permanently on board in Penang. A typical week for most people involved working in their assigned departments between eight and ten hours a day, five days of the week, with one Connect or Evangelism day and one day off. Breakfast, lunch and dinner were served buffet style in the main dining room on deck six. There were two lines - one for crew, which could get very long at busy periods sometimes stretching fifty metres or so along the corridor, and one for families which was sometimes also utilised by Book-Fair shift members if it was really busy on deck four.

After work we were free to use our time as we wanted. There was a notice board with sign-up sheets for various activities. One of my first voluntary sign ups, when I was zealous and enthusiastic, was to lead a devotion for the school children who were living on board with their parents, most of whom were serving as leaders. As part of the devotion, I told them about my English friends and family using photos and asked them to pray for each person, which they were keen to do. It went well, apart from a slight faux pas when I was talking about my unmarried friend who has a baby.

The kids perked up and started asking some pretty awkward questions such as, "Why does your friend have a baby if she doesn't have a husband?" One of the other kids helpfully suggested that maybe it was because someone had given it to her as they didn't want it anymore. I looked around helplessly at that point only to witness some of the regular teachers sniggering at the back of the class as I tried to get myself out of the hole. I was slightly relieved to find that I obviously hadn't said anything irredeemable as I found a colourful thank you note on my cabin door:

"Thank you so much! We really appreciated your input and enjoyed having you as our guest speaker. On behalf of the school we would like to thank you for taking the time to invest in the children's lives. Thank you so much for all your hard work. Blessings."- the Logos Hope School.

I had been assigned to work in the I-café on deck four which was the public or visitors' deck. The deck had a circular one-way system which started and ended at the gangways which led up and down from the quayside. On entering deck four from the entrance gangway, there was an Information Desk. Next to that was a sample cabin, for visitors to get a rough idea how we lived on board. Then there was a larger than life-sized wooden red lifeboat with benches for seating. Visitors sat in the lifeboat to watch a short introductory video on a screen prior to entering the Book-Fair. The Book-Fair itself took up half of the deck in a semi-circle.

At the Book-Fair exit was the 'Journey of Life' which relayed a contemporary version of the prodigal or lost son story from the Bible using colourful pictures with some audio. We were trained to walk visitors through, telling the story as we did so or recounting elements of our own lives as they fit into the story. I'm not sure how many people actually listened to the story itself, although I know that some did and I even heard that there were some conversions as a result. I had wanted to use the walkway as an evangelism tool more frequently but it was hard to maintain people's focus notably when there were big groups. Due to the language barriers people often walked off as we were explaining the story or started talking over us or just make it obvious that they weren't listening and were impatient to go and drink coffee or eat popcorn in the I-café. But it was worth continuing for those who wanted to listen.

I often saw younger people in the Journey of Life posing next to one or other of the colourful illustrations as their friends laughed and took pictures. I noted that often the images captured were of the scene where the prodigal son was very lost in the world, and was lying beaten and injured in an alley surrounded by empty bottles of alcohol, or the scene where he was being lured by a scantily clad woman. They attracted the most interest and probably not for the right reasons.

In Asia and specifically in the Philippines where we spent most of our time, it appeared to me that culturally the people tended to live for the moment and were seeking the next entertaining experience. They didn't usually read a lot because their peers teased them for being 'bookish.' So, their levels of concentration were relatively low and they could flit from one thing to another. They also didn't take life that seriously most of the time and tried to make light of things. Their motto was 'It's more fun in the Philippines.' So, it could be particularly challenging to engage them on serious topics - Christianity, heaven, hell etc.

The I-café was positioned after the journey of life exhibit and then there was another simulation called the 'Life Experience' teaching people about the dangers of unprotected sex and AIDS. I wasn't too sure about the idea as I felt it might be too graphic for some teenagers and I would rather have had a clear Gospel presentation in that space, but it was a popular area with the visitors. Those entering donned headphones and were talked through a scenario of unprotected sex after a drunken night out and the resultant HIV scare. At the end participants were given a piece of paper telling them whether or not they were HIV positive within the pretend scenario. Hundreds of visitors left little yellow post it notes on the outside wall of the Life Experience stating how much they had learned and enjoyed that section.

The I-café was where visitors spent time after purchasing books, although some chose to spend all day on board sitting in the I-café and watching the assortment of activities taking place. Some crew performed drama and skits, whilst others sang and played instruments or used visual aids for Gospel and other presentations. It wasn't uncommon for people to hover in the I-café hoping that a kindly crew member would take pity on them and offer them a tour of the ship, which could happen on days when there were fewer visitors. Of course, there were others who were not quite as subtle - one woman, having spoken to me for a few minutes about her ministry, promptly asked me whether she could have dinner on board. I hadn't even had time to get to know her enough to determine whether she was just curious about the ship and wanting to avoid the queue for a ship tour, actually poor and hungry and in need of free food or just greedy and chancing her arm.

The ship mascot "El Capitano" wandered around in the I-cafe on most days. He consisted of a blue material body suit with a disproportionately large plastic head. The entire ensemble had no doubt seen better days or, judging by the partially exposed limbs of the lankier crew, maybe it was that one size very definitely didn't fit all. Crew members dressed up and interacted with visitors much to their delight. It was virtually impossible to identify who was wearing the suit at any given time. Some therefore used the anonymity as an opportunity to become crazy people when undertaking the role. They jumped, fell over, danced, played sport, made ice-cream and popcorn (badly) and did all manner of other things. Looking on we attempted to guess who the culprit was based on the behaviour of the mascot. It was not uncommon to see someone dressed in half of the kit running around frantically trying to find the other half before the ship opened for visitors. I even witnessed the mascot removing his head in an unguarded moment whilst the ship was full of visitors seriously shocking some of the smaller children who had believed he was real. Having promised myself (and others) that I would never take part in the ridiculousness, I did eventually succumb and became El Capitano for a few hours on one of my last days on board. I was amazed that some more regular participants had survived--wearing the suit felt like I was being cooked in a microwave.

During quieter periods, the I-café was the best place for evangelism as crew members routinely joined visitors at the tables whilst they drank their coffee and chatted with them in a relaxed atmosphere. But the atmosphere tended also to result in strangers occasionally feeling that the environment was safe enough to disclose things that they probably would not feel comfortable talking about in any other place. One woman informed me in a hushed and somewhat conspiratorial tone about the underground churches in her country that had a large Muslim population. She went on to say that in that same country the government was deliberately arranging marriages between Muslims and Christians in an attempt to ensure the Christians were converted to Islam. She whispered it to me as if, had it been the case, I could set about changing it!

The most difficult customers to observe were the women who were obviously in love with absent Western men and often had had children by them. The men left their "wives" and children for months or sometimes years at a time to return to their home countries. There was always a convenient reason why their spouses couldn't go with them. It was clear to me that most (if not all) of the men were living double lives of polygamy and that in the most part their Asian girlfriends or wives were oblivious to the fact. It troubled me greatly to see the heartache that the separation was causing the women who were often left pining and with no clear date for a re-visit. The selfishness of the men as they happily lived their carefree Western lives with their real families, occasionally sending a small amount of money to their Asian mistresses and feeling good about themselves for doing so, beggars belief. Sadly, it was common place and the gullibility and loyalty of the women made it even more painful to observe. It also made our role as Gospel witnesses more difficult as often the women saw the Western men as 'Christians' just because they had been born in the West, regardless of their behaviour.

Joining the Logos Hope as a crew member you became something of an instant celebrity, especially if you were from Europe or America and the ship was in Asia. Most Asians we met were dreaming of visiting Western countries and had completely unrealistic expectations of life in the West. Spending time in the I-café connecting with people resulted in photos constantly being taken and posted on social media sites. It was not uncommon to be chatting with a fellow crew member and suddenly to become aware that a group of foreign men had arranged themselves surreptitiously around and about in order to pose for a series of photos, even going as far as to lean in towards us or place a hand on a shoulder or arm. The fact that we were relative strangers and they had no clue who we were didn't seem to bother them as they could easily lie to their friends about us as they had photographic evidence of their encounter. It wouldn't have surprised me to find that whilst on Logos Hope I had unwittingly become the imaginary girlfriend of several Asian men, or that my image was shortly afterwards being cropped and photo-shopped before being daringly displayed as their Facebook profile picture with them standing proudly by my side.

The constant photo snapping was okay at first but after a while it did get a bit tiring - smiling constantly for cameras and posing with people we didn't know as if they were our friends. It was all part of being a crew member on Logos Hope and we just had to get on with it.

However, I did manage to avoid most of the cultural displays and presentations - crew members dressed up in their country's national costumes or practised their national dances for special events. Being from Britain I wasn't sure what I would've worn or sung in any event, probably jeans and a t-shirt singing "God save the Queen." Just as well that I managed successfully to absent myself on most occasions.

I struggled with some of the expectations placed upon me as a crew member and found that it could be difficult to get past the superficiality of some of our contacts to discussions of greater spiritual import. I even found that some people who had been following the ship ministry for years didn't realise it was a Christian organisation. They just thought we were doing 'good' work because we were 'kind' people. Conversing with people who had formed that opinion could be discouraging, but I could either give up in dismay or I could resolve to attempt to enlighten them and to ensure that everyone I interacted with heard the Gospel whilst they were on board. I reflected that it was inevitable that some people would come away with the wrong impression regardless of what was said to them due to the necessity of the Holy Spirit to open people's eyes and hearts to the truth.

CHAPTER SIX

International Café Mayhem!

I began my time in the I-café enthusiastically, always looking for opportunities to sit with people and share my testimony or the Gospel with them. They gave the impression that they were listening with interest; although I didn't always know the right words at the outset, I trusted that God would give them to me. My I-cafe co-workers sometimes became frustrated with me because they didn't always understand my desire to share the Gospel above all else. They sometimes got annoyed with me for failing to help them with the practical work as I was absorbed in conversation. I tried to resolve the problem by offering to swap places so that they could chat with the visitors, but most didn't take up the suggestion as they didn't see it as their gift.

Then there were the crazily busy ports with no chance to talk to anyone as we rushed around trying to serve ten thousand or more people a day, dealing with queues stretching from one end of the ship to the other. I recall having to fill one hundred and thirty-two bags of popcorn for one large student order; it became so complicated due to the machine being slow that we decided to take payment and issue receipts for later collection. That didn't really work as shortly after implementing the practice we noticed that we were issuing more bags of popcorn than had been paid for. I struggled to work out how that was happening as our procedure had looked to be foolproof, but the mystery was solved when on examining some of the receipts being presented, I discovered that a large number had been issued for books in the Book-Fair and not for any food items. I was the nominated person (probably due to being the only one willing) to approach the groups of students and ask them whether they had actually paid for the popcorn that they were cheerfully munching. On demand, one such group handed over money for an additional four bags of popcorn, obviously having felt the weight of conscience by that point. Fortunately, such incidents were a rarity.

One of our regular I-café duties was making chocolate and vanilla ice-cream (the most popular menu item) via a large machine that frequently broke down, normally during the busiest periods. Re-filling the machine involved carrying a very large and heavy bucket filled with liquid ice-cream, balancing on a chair and tipping the liquid into the top of the machine. There were many mishaps resulting in liquid sloshing all over the place as amused visitors watched from a distance, but it didn't seem to put them off as ice-cream remained our fastest selling item.

One such disaster involved a Korean girl, Lydia. She was a nice girl, from a relatively wealthy family, but she could be a bit absent-minded - failing to turn up for work in the middle of the day on occasion due to having been asleep. She planned to study "Fashion" after the ship which had always struck me as an odd ambition for someone then serving as a missionary. I had been speechless when she had first told me, wondering if it was a joke but quickly realising that she was extremely serious as she carefully related her plans.

Lydia, having already had one ice-cream related accident during the shift, had again mixed the powder and climbed up onto the chair with the bucket. Then without further ado she had tipped the entire contents, probably several gallons worth of mixture over the side and front of the ice-cream machine and onto the floor, completely missing her target by quite some distance. I and Dee, from South Africa, who were probably the two most outspoken members of the team, happened to be on the cash registers at the time. We had, up until that point, been serving customers at top speed in a vain attempt to reduce the never-ending queues. On hearing the sloshing liquid and the ice-cream machine beginning its furious beeping protest, we turned around in unison. The poor machine was by then also flashing numerous orange lights.

But the thing that topped the scene was Lydia. She was still standing on the chair, but was now holding an empty bucket and with a dopey expression on her face as if frozen in time. She looked at the two of us helplessly waiting for our reaction. She was probably expecting some sharp words as it was the last thing any of us needed with the visitor mayhem, and in light of her prior incident. But the ridiculousness of the situation and Lydia's defencelessness appealed to our better nature and on glancing sideways at each other Dee and I both burst into fits of uncontrollable laughter, much to the astonishment of the visitors who probably wondered if the whole thing had been staged for their benefit.

Continuing the tales of Lydia, I decided that our team needed a laugh during a particularly dull training day. I had easily persuaded her during a customer service exercise to tell a fake customer "Sorry, we don't sell those here, you must've bought it from somewhere else." They had been attempting to return an item unfit for human consumption. The unexpected response from Lydia, who I'm sure didn't have a clue what was going on, caused much confusion and temporarily brought the entire exercise to a standstill.

On another occasion, a group of us were playing cards. Things were going along smoothly until Lydia solemnly informed all of us that she couldn't take her turn as she only had "space bar." There was a silence and then a chorus of "What!??" from all those present. On delving further and looking at her cards we eventually established that she only had spades. Apparently, having thus far not been corrected, she had always believed the suit was called spacebar.

The joys of living in an international community, it was definitely far more entertaining for those with English as their first language. Later when trying to learn Tagalog (Filipino) I thought back to those times and wondered if I should've had more patience. But teasing was commonplace on the ship and most people didn't mind - plus people often teased me for my English accent or did impressions of me.

When Lydia's time on board concluded her farewell note to me read "Dear Natalie V, hello my friend, Thankyou so much for your love and taking care of me when I was sick. I hope you'll enjoy your new job and take care of your health. Be strong. God bless you next coming 1 year." So, I guess my jokes at her expense were taken in the spirit in which they were meant.

Then there was the daily burning of the popcorn, the resultant fire alarm and occasional evacuations of the entire public deck stemming from that. The machine didn't beep to alert us when the popcorn had been cooked so setting the whole vessel on fire was a distinct possibility. Other lighter moments involved a 'plastic glove as water balloon fight' when we were left to our own devices with minimal supervision one day. Eva, from Germany, begged us not to "bomb" her as she failed to hide behind a counter pending the inevitable soaking and then screamed as it occurred. On another occasion the battle involved ice-cream - after water was flicked in my face I had dragged one girl underneath the dispenser and pulled the lever dispensing ice-cream all over her. A Singaporean co-worker who had been observing and seemed to have been stunned into shocked silence then thought better of it and enthusiastically joined in. He ended up caught in the cross fire, with an entire cone laced through his normally spotless black hair.

Some visitors didn't appear willing to bear with our inadequacies and complaints did occur. One man who, having been handed two plastic cups containing cheap (and gross) powdered juice, actually expended energy by bothering to complain that one cup was slightly more full than the other. Temporarily forgetting the rule that "the customer is always right" which didn't seem to apply in Asia in any event, I looked from the cups to the man as incredulity spread across my face and I commented that I couldn't see any difference. I really couldn't. I then spent a considerable period attempting to rebalance the juice levels to satisfy the customer who had by that point made it clear that he was not leaving until our mistake had been rectified to his satisfaction.

Of course, our supervisors dutifully told us off for any and all things that fell into the "unacceptable customer service" or "having too much fun when should be working" bracket, when they heard about it. But, on the whole, the visitors looked as if they enjoyed witnessing some of our livelier battles. They commented about the fun we were obviously having whilst doing relatively menial work. I believe they saw our light-heartedness as evidence of a joyful spirit as we served God together.

After one frantically busy day, when I was particularly exhausted, I was encouraged by a postcard I was given by a student visiting the ship. It read "Hey Natalie, (we wore name badges) Just wanna let you know that you're doing a great job @ the I-cafeteria. Even though the crowds of students today were rather overwhelming, you did an amazing job! Keep it up...Though others may not see your efforts, it is ultimately God who sees it & he will bless you 4 serving him. God bless. Smile! Love Elise."

I noted that she timed the note 3:57pm Malaysian time. Very precise. I needed to remember her main message - that I was serving God and not men.

CHAPTER SEVEN

Hindrance or Help?

In the I-café the times requiring the most patience occurred when our fellow crew members, who usually worked in the Galley (kitchen), Pantry (washing up team) or Mess (engine kitchen), came down to make up our depleted numbers. Often, they had been assigned to their usual departments in the first place due to their limited English and/or a desire to prevent them being public-facing. I'm sure the Galley supervision also had to exercise patience with us as, whenever I was assigned to the Galley, I nearly always ended up having a huge water fight as the hoses in the large washing up area were far too tempting and there was always someone on hand to spar with me. One day a few of us ended up soaking ourselves to the skin and laughing hilariously like mad people over a sustained period, before heading back down to the I-café only to find our boss sitting waiting for us having come on duty unexpectedly. The expression on her face was priceless, incomprehensibly bemused, as she excused us to go and change before our dripping clothes made any further mess on the floor or startled any further visitors to the ship. We raucously raced off to do her bidding feeling a bit foolish, as her tone had no doubt intended.

Frank, who had by that point sorted out his Visa issues, made a reappearance as his usual place of work was the Pantry or the Mess. He joined us more regularly than some of the others due to his limited English getting him in hot water in other locations, particularly in the Mess. The engineers and other key personnel hungrily awaited their food having completed a good morning's work, and then suppressed collective groans on seeing that poor Frank was on duty to serve them. The problem was that he was pretty slow with his work and didn't understand the importance that some attached to their stomachs being satisfied. He didn't always have the food ready on time and it had been known for him to end up getting shouted at. I could envisage what had happened, as the hard-working engineers began by patiently asking him questions regarding the whereabouts of their sustenance, but the resultant blankness of incomprehension began to irritate, chafe and eventually cause outbursts of temper. It was really the wrong place for him to be working and, after some tearful negotiations, that fact was finally acknowledged and he was transferred.

Frank and I engaged in some highly entertaining discussions in the I-café, as I tried to teach him basic English. One day he asked me whether I had ever tried turkey ice-cream. Immediately images of live turkeys squawking as they churned around in blenders came to mind. I responded "No, disgusting." I couldn't figure out what on earth he was talking about until we went into it in some detail and I concluded that he must've meant Turkish ice-cream.

I was looking over his shoulder when he was writing some type of self-assessment and saw that he had written that his duties in the Pantry included "washing all of the cubs." I pointed out that a cub was in fact a baby bear and was unlikely to be an item in need of hand-washing in the Pantry or anywhere else. He also wrote "I'm sorry that the croissants do not have any feeling" which obviously should have read "filling."

When the resultant laughter had died down, Frank asked me seriously whether I had accepted a business contact card from an estate agent that I had been talking to in the I-café because I wanted to buy a house from him! I explained that I had been trying to share my faith to which Frank nodded knowingly before responding "Aaah yes, you want to buy a house in two years!"

Frank knew how to laugh at himself though. His stories were endlessly repeated around the ship until in time they became so completely lost in translation that no one understood what he was talking about or why he found it so funny.

The I-cafe was also where I first met Nick from Georgia who was to become a team-mate and one of my good friends as we worked with street children in the Philippines together. At that time though, Nick's English was also limited but his work ethic was not. He was obviously used to dealing with hordes of unruly people demanding things, maybe due to his cultural background. He stood at the cash desk surrounded by madness taking numerous orders and then repeating them back loudly in people's faces for confirmation, using his fingers (also extended into or very near their faces) to count the items off. He always worked hard despite his unorthodox methods so I suggested he lowered his voice a little so that the customers didn't think he was shouting at them, and then left him to it.

Really over time, working in the I-café was a case of being forced to laugh or having to cry as the ports became busier and busier and the queues longer and longer. The work was stressful and the need to maintain a perpetual smile impossible for someone like me who tended only to smile when the occasion called for it. I also became unwell with an ongoing thyroid problem which affected my mood and my ability to be around other people all the time. Explaining my health problem also became tiresome as people didn't understand and often asked me the same questions repeatedly in order to try and do so—"So, what was it you have again?"

Our team was difficult at times with the mixture (and clash) of different cultures and personalities. I somehow managed to offend a Korean sister for life by offering an innocent gesture of help during one busy period. She had dropped some ice cream on the floor behind me as I was serving customers behind the till. I was aware that she had crouched on the floor to mop up the spill. Not thinking anything of it and trying to be as helpful as I could in the circumstances, I grabbed a handful of napkins from the counter next to me, turned and threw them in her general direction, probably with a "here you go" and turned my attention back to my customer. Big mistake!

It was the second time that I was to get in trouble for casually throwing things around. She later explained that, according to her culture, I had committed an unforgiveable act and treated her in a derogatory manner - throwing the napkins at her as if she were a "dog on the floor." I was mortified and apologised profusely. But sadly, I really think she continued to believe that my careless actions represented my honest opinion of her. I tried to make amends and felt sorry for her in the end as she shared her personal difficulties on board and explained that being single at thirty in her culture meant that she would be under a great deal of pressure from her family on her return if she hadn't met anyone whilst on the ship. I was glad I wasn't under that type of pressure in addition to everything else.

Our working relationship did improve in time and I was forced to smother a laugh when my usually very serious sister, having chilled out a little since our prior encounter, asked a young guy from Switzerland whether he deliberately showed off his underwear by allowing the waistband to be visible at the top of his trousers. She observed that she knew that "some guys did that." The (by then visibly embarrassed) guy mumbled something unintelligible in response and probably decided to be more careful in future. At that point I made myself scarce.

I thought it might further help our working relationship if I volunteered to allow that same sister to cut my, by then very long and out of control, hair - she was acting as the designated ship hairdresser at the time. I asked to have just a few centimetres off the end and showed her with my fingers roughly where to cut it. But after brushing it out completely dry which turned my whole head into a crazy frizz ball (I never brush it dry) she then took away half of the length. Not only that but I had been forced to endure the humiliating episode in the staff lounge in front of many casual observers some of whom could see my embarrassment as I sat there looking like a Gruffalo. I couldn't complain really but I did secretly wonder whether it had been payback time for the earlier episode. If so it more than compensated in my book as it took me a year to grow my hair back to that length again.

My Korean sister wrote me a note on leaving: "Natalie, Hey I am grateful I worked with you in the I-café for a year. I learned a lot from you somehow. God taught me many things. I would bless u that He pours our fruits of spirit which are love, peace and joy. I pray that you have AMAZING time the rest of on-board. Thank you for your kindness and patience for me."

As with the earlier note from Lydia, I was grateful to receive the note realising that permanent damage hadn't been done.

Eventually smiling day in and day out and remaining cheerful twenty-four-seven became intolerable. Customers began asking me "Why don't you smile?" and I had to stop myself responding in ways that definitely would not represent Jesus to them.

Fortunately, I had by then been given opportunities to assist Trevor, the food Store-Keeper, whenever I needed a break and in due course that became a permanent placement as the stores needed re-organising and Trevor needed more of a hand.

CHAPTER EIGHT

Store-Keepers Living in Freezers

Trevor from Canada was an unusual but likeable character who took his job as Store-Keeper very seriously. I got on well with him and enjoyed teasing him by encouraging him to take 'risks' by not asking our manager before making any and every insignificant decision. Often after I had spent the morning persuading him that we could take a decision ourselves and had then left for the day, on returning for a forgotten item I would find Trevor on the phone clearing the supposedly independently taken decision with our manager thinking he wouldn't be discovered. He just couldn't do it and always caved fearing the rebuke of our manager much more than I did.

One quieter day when Trevor was absent, I decided to do some spring cleaning in his desk area and moved everything around. On his return, I explained what I had done and he acted as if he were slightly disconcerted as he was a man of routines. But I was highly amused that from that day forward he not only left things exactly as I had arranged them, but also began showing me that he was keeping his work area tidy and adapting to the additions I had been adding to his duties, all in the name of efficiency of course. He was very patient with me.

One of the advantages to being Store-Keeper was that as we were constantly circulating around the ship we often ended up in the right place at the right time to eat cakes and snacks that had been prepared for special occasions. I'm sure that's one of the main reasons that Trevor had willingly volunteered to be Store-Keeper and had kept the position for so long. I was just as bad though as one day I demonstrated to him how he could eat the additional icing from the used bakery cake sheets with no one being any the wiser. As I was speaking, Trevor was already at the sink and washing his hands in preparation for joining me. Sadly, after that moment, I always had to race him to get there otherwise the icing would all be gone. I never understood where he put it all as he was relatively slim.

Trevor also had a habit of sleeping during breaks in his work day but he didn't do what most crew did. He just lay down on his back on the floor wherever he happened to be working and fell asleep. I frequently arrived for work to see a pair of legs sticking out from some aisle or other with the other half of Trevor's body attached to them. Sometimes, I gathered other staff for a good laugh at his expense before waking him up. He didn't seem to mind working with me despite the mockery.

Once we ended up trapped together in a broken-down lift sat on top of a huge pile of cardboard boxes that we had been shifting from one place to another. As the minutes ticked past Trevor began fidgeting awkwardly and looking over at me (on the other side of the lift) uncomfortably. He started a conversation about SP and the fact that we didn't have it and therefore shouldn't be alone in the lift together. I pointed out that it wasn't intentional, that we were working and that we could not have foreseen that the lift would break. Also, that there was nothing romantic between us and was never likely to be, a fact I knew we were agreed upon. Trevor continued talking about it almost on compulsion as if he felt he had to fill the silence that had arisen due to the topic he had chosen. The discussion became more and more awkward the longer we were left in the lift so that by the time someone helpfully released us via an overhead panel I could be heard to say to them "Thank goodness you've got me out of there."

The freezers are worthy of their own chapter as they could easily have resulted in nightmares due to my very slight claustrophobia that I mentioned earlier. There were several freezers in the depths of the ship far away from any and all human life forms. One was a walk-in, although it was rare that you could actually do that as the food was often arranged in such a way that it was more of a sliding across the top of the frozen items to get to the thing you needed. That was pre-eminently the case when the containers had just arrived and the freezers were full. One slightly intense guy had told me that he sometimes went in the freezers to cool off, so I was always a bit wary on approaching any of the doors in case I opened it to find him in there, which would have been a bit weird.

It was the smaller freezers that really made me nervous though and I often thought about getting stuck inside as the door slammed shut and I slowly and painfully froze to death surrounded by pork chops and chicken casserole. There didn't seem to be much in place to stop that happening and it was possible to develop cold numbness whilst working in the freezers day in and day out despite the coats, hats and gloves that were worn. That aspect of the work didn't seem to bother Trevor who, when he was around, gallantly volunteered to deal with the freezer work but it definitely bothered me. Maybe also my dislike of all things cold played a part in that. It was worse as well when a box or item broke open in one of the freezers as the clean-up was obviously much more complicated. I found it amusing that courageous individual fruit and vegetables had broken loose of their containers and were living in isolation amongst the boxes and packets from which they had originated. Obviously clearing them up or using them wasn't a priority when striving to feed four hundred people three meals a day so they just stayed there strewn around, probably forevermore.

The plastic strips that hung at the entrance to the freezers to keep the cold air in when the doors were open were always annoying and one day ended up coated in BBQ sauce having been accidentally dipped in it as we were unloading a container. Of course, subsequently I got covered in the stuff which smelt so bad it made me gag resulting in a hasty departure for a change of clothes. There was also the day when I opened a large sack of oats before screaming and jumping back as it was literally alive with bugs. We were then forced to check all the others and finding that others were similarly crawling we laboriously had to sift all of the oats in order to remove the bugs prior to serving them for consumption by the ship's company. It wasn't as straightforward as just sending them back to the manufacturer as they had been shipped from different continents.

I enjoyed the physical aspect of the work as I felt it kept me fit and healthy although sometimes exhausted - lifting twenty-five kg at times. I also liked the freedom and independence, the chance to keep my own hours and to walk around the ship doing my work. The biggest responsibility for the Store-Keeper was 'Container Day' when the very large food containers arrived from several countries and all the food for the next three or more months had somehow to be squashed into the already overflowing freezers and store rooms. There were often lengthy delays in the planned arrivals of those items as customs officials waited for bribes which were not going to be forthcoming from a Christian ministry. On one such day I got covered in fish sauce when a bottle broke all over me and then coated in flour as a bag of it burst when someone I was directing crashed a pallet into a wall. I had been shouting for him to stop to no avail as he couldn't hear me. I concluded my catalogue of errors by pushing a heavily laden trolley through a doorway too quickly and crashing into the Videographer who was at the time filming someone else. As Store-Keeper I was meant to be keeping order!

It was not the first time I had lost control of my trolley which had a life of its own (as trolleys often do.) After mocking one male crew member (who lost a whole trolley load of soft drink cans across the floor of the I-café one day resulting in an explosion of Sprite having crashed into a post due to not paying attention) embarrassingly I committed the exact same error in exactly the same manner myself the following day. And of course, the object of my prior scorn happened to be looking on at the time and although rushing to help couldn't resist commenting that he was "very happy." When I crashed into a second post only a few seconds later upending the whole lot back to the floor, having just re-loaded everything, I think people did start to wonder about me. What they didn't know was that after I had gone back down to the store room in order to hide my red face, I had immediately stepped into a cockroach trap. Learning to laugh at yourself was a must that, if I hadn't adequately learned during my time in the police, I definitely learned during my early days on the ship.

CHAPTER NINE

Malaysia Ministry

My biggest highlight during my time on the ship was the weekly Connect (C) or Evangelism (E) days. I heard that they were called E days until someone pointed out that it might seem as if we were trying to convert people. The name was changed to the more politically acceptable C days. Yes, it happens everywhere. We were placed in small teams of between four and six people and were allocated pre-arranged ministry either on-shore or on-board. One person was assigned Team Leader and the team met in advance to pray and plan their programme.

A lot of my memorable ministry experiences were as a result of C days. I realised early on that C days were what you made of them. It was easy to turn an uninspiring 'teaching English' session into an opportunity for sharing a testimony or the Gospel, even when that hadn't been part of the initial request. We were sometimes warned not to share openly due to the countries we were visiting and their proselytising laws and we respected that.

We had been told the tragic story of the two grenades that had been thrown into the middle of an international concert hosted by the crew of Doulos (a previous OM ship.) It had resulted in the deaths of two crew members. Abu Sayyaf later claimed responsibility stating that they had carried out the attack due to the threat that the ship represented for Islam and also because some comments perceived to be anti-Islamic had been made by another crew member in a public setting. Attempting to share the Gospel whilst on the ship was the only time that I can ever remember attempting to get as close to a danger line as possible without actually crossing it. Most of the time I tended to steer myself and others away from those lines, but when there were souls at stake the urgency was obviously greater.

Malaysia was one of the 'difficult' countries, but it was legal to share with and encourage people who were already professing Christians. For one of my first C days in Malaysia I visited a juvenile home. Our team had planned to separate the sixty-strong group into three smaller groups by age. But on arrival things were somewhat different from what we had anticipated. We were unable to separate the group as we only had one room, half of the children were due to arrive halfway through, we were given two hours instead of the one that we had prepared for and the genders were not allowed to be mixed for cultural reasons. We regrouped and made some hasty amendments to areas of our programme.

Our team each held up the country flags of another crew member and the children were asked to guess which flag actually belonged to each crew member. We realised by the lack of response and blank faces that the activity was far too advanced for the group of children. The children didn't seem to know any country's name, let alone what their flags looked like. But we persevered. What else could we do?

Simplifying the games, we played a form of "Simon Says" using a ship Captain's hat for 'Simon' or 'Captain.' Some of the children were so small that the hat completely engulfed their heads as they shyly took on the important role of 'Captain.' We had similar problems when we decided to play a more athletic game involving ship lifejackets. The jackets were far too big so the game had to be delayed whilst the older children patiently stopped to help the younger ones. They didn't seem to mind any of our mistakes though and were very thankful for and excited about our visit.

Towards the end of our programme we asked the children if they had any questions. Total silence. I suggested they might want to know what we each did on the ship i.e. which departments we worked in. They eagerly agreed that that was what they had wanted to know by nodding their heads in unison. I silently patted myself on the back for having what I had thought was a light bulb moment. However, having spent more extensive periods of time in Asia, I now know that even the adults tend just to go along with whatever is suggested by a foreigner. We probably could've asked them if they wanted us to steal all of their belongings and they still would've nodded and smiled, fearing the shame of the potential conflict had they protested.

As things were drawing to a final close, I used the 'Wordless Book' (see appendix 4) to explain the Gospel message of salvation to the children. It was a tool I used frequently on the ship. I made one big mistake during the presentation. In seeking to explain the concept of sin I had asked the children if they had ever done anything wrong, expecting immediate acknowledgement of the fact. But we were in Asia, a shame culture. So, some of the children said "no", the implication being that they were perfect. I was flummoxed but forced to recover myself quickly. Instead I asked them to put up their hands if they had ever told a lie. Fortunately for me, that time all hands went up. I had already realised that the only other relevant sin in my mind was 'stealing,' which could've started a confession session with serious consequences for the children after we had left! Lesson learned - assume nothing.

At the end of our presentation we had the chance to be shown around and to chat privately to the Pastor leading the ministry. We were a little shocked to learn that the children were forced to get up at 4:30am every day for prayer. Then they had to copy one chapter from the Bible per day and were fasting for one day a week. He enthusiastically informed us that all of the children were Christians, a fact I was surprised to learn due to some of the responses I had received during the Gospel presentation. He then informed us that his car had been donated to him by a Chinese Buddhist and his Church building by someone else. He had his eye on a larger building that he believed God wanted him to purchase and he took us on a tour of the building before taking us to KFC for a meal.

I had felt that things were not quite right at the home; there may have been a touch of fear evident in the children, a lack of warmth from the Pastor or maybe it was just an element of legalism. I had heard the children calling each other by biblical names: Jeremiah, Peter, Bartholomew etc. Naively, I had been amazed, wondering how in a non-Christian country like Malaysia all of those children with biblical names had ended up living in the same orphanage. Of course, the Pastor had renamed them on their arrival. I thought that was great.

There was also a very old man present for our gathering. I noticed him not only due to his age but because, despite having no teeth, he was grinning happily throughout our visit. I was informed that his name was 'Abraham' and wrongly assumed he was a relative of the Pastor, but apparently the Pastor had witnessed him stumbling along the side of the road a few months previously. He couldn't speak, had little clothing and was very hungry so the Pastor had taken him home. The family had established that his wife had died and his children were unconcerned for his welfare; they had given him a permanent home. The story touched my heart and provided a true example of Christ-like behaviour towards someone in need. It was really a joy to see the dear old man standing smiling amongst the children for the mandatory photo session.

I decided that a person who demonstrates a kindness like that without regard for his own convenience or for the financial implications must sincerely be attempting to serve God even if discipline at the home wasn't always implemented in the wisest manner. I learned a valuable lesson about not making a judgement based on first impressions.

CHAPTER TEN

Sometimes It's Wrong!

The C Day assignments were exciting due to the variety of activities and team selection. It reminded me of my police work - never knowing the exact nature of the next call to come in. I had a strange experience though whilst we were still in Malaysia. Our team had been asked to conduct visits to some poor families and to an old people's home. Our brief was that we would be accompanying a local Christian charity who conducted regular visits in order to provide food, clothing and toys. The charity was, in the main, staffed by local Pastors; well, at least the persons accompanying us carried the label.

The first apartment was high up in a dilapidated block, the corridors stank and people peered curiously at us on our approach, obviously not used to visitors. Inside the apartment, we found a Grandma, an Uncle - who had just been released from prison having served a sentence for drug related offences and, judging by his emaciated state, looked like it wouldn't be long before he was back inside, a three-year-old boy and a six-month old baby. There was no electricity, no furniture, no carpets and no possessions. The family had half a linen mat on the ground serving as a dirty bed, presumably for all of them. The three-year-old had a visible skin condition all over one of his legs that resulted in him constantly scratching; he was lying half on and half off the dirty mat and slept for the duration of our visit. He was very thin, but I was more bothered that his 'Grandma' couldn't remember his name when we asked for it.

It was not uncommon for children to get passed around amongst friends or neighbours if their parents had vices. 'Grandma' was more a title given due to age rather than anything else. Sadly, it was often evident that the temporary guardians were not biological relatives in the lack of affection displayed towards the children who were emotionally as well as physically neglected. It was sometimes difficult as the children immediately formed close bonds with us sensing a love and concern that they craved, only for us to abandon them after a few hours of visitation.

After we had spent what felt like a very short time with the family and given our meagre gifts of food, clothing and toys the Pastor said a quick 'God bless you' before leaving. He informed us that they were a Hindu family and it was therefore illegal to share the Gospel with them. I felt very emotional on leaving their dwelling; I had been shocked by the poverty and neglect. In England, the children would have been removed long before by social services and we would at least have been able to offer hope in Jesus to the whole family should we have stumbled upon them in that condition. We had met their immediate material need but what good was that for their immortal souls? I wondered what the purpose of our visit was. I had to hope and pray that the Pastor would take other opportunities to witness to them.

The second house, which was detached and in a more rural location, at least had a few furnishings and material items - there was a small TV in the corner, two small dirty sofas and slightly more clothing. The small amount of monthly rental was collected from Grandma's pension - the second "Grandma" appeared to be a real one and demonstrated more care for the children. On our arrival, she was alone with a four-year-old girl and a two-year-old boy.

During our visit, however, the mother, carrying a five-month old baby, suddenly burst into the house in a state of excitement. She began rambling as she told her story to Grandma. A Pastor rapidly translated for us, our eyes widening in horror as the facts became known. The baby had become jaundiced so the father, deciding that the family couldn't afford treatment and not knowing what else to do, had, without consulting the mother, sold him! On discovering the baby missing and learning what had happened the mother had gone straight to the local police which had somehow resulted in the baby being recovered and being reunited with its mother - the father had been arrested. The story was relayed in a matter of fact manner as if trafficking in babies was a regular occurrence in those communities. Grandma and mother were professing Christians; there was evidence of religious faith on the walls of the house in the form of pictures of Jesus and a Bible verse.

One of the Pastors who had accompanied us for the visit then decided that we should all gather round and pray for healing for the little girl. Her mother had informed us that she had been ill for a long time and the Pastors had subsequently spent a while visually examining her to try to determine the cause of her illness. I felt a little uncomfortable encircling the child as I thought we, as foreigners, might scare such a small child if we cornered her. But I didn't yet really understand the culture; the Pastors knew the family and had conducted regular visits. I also wanted to submit to our local leaders and I knew that it was biblical to pray for healing, so I kept quiet but remained at the back of the group gathering for prayer.

Shockingly, the prayer session swiftly descended into chaotic chanting as one of the Pastors began to bind evil spirits and was trying to cast demons out of the child in the name of Jesus. Everyone (apart from me) prayed aloud resulting in what seemed like some kind of competition to be heard amidst the cacophony of voices. I prayed silently but sincerely for the girl and, at one point on opening my eyes briefly, caught a glimpse of the terror on the poor child's face. No wonder, you might think, shoved into the middle of an unruly bunch of people chanting and swaying. I wondered afterwards whether that type of behaviour by strangers in the child's home would be enough to put her off Christianity and all types of religion forever. It might at least cause her to fear them and those who claimed to represent them. Although one of the Pastors had informed us that the whole area was under the influence of Satan, he had not provided any evidence of that apart from his general feeling of spiritual oppression. He had also failed to provide any proof to us or to anyone else that that particular child was possessed by a demon. She was exhibiting no obvious signs; indeed she was whimpering due to the pain of her illness as one might expect a child of that age to do.

That, as I mentioned, was one of my most bizarre experiences whilst serving with Logos Hope. I hoped and prayed that it wasn't a sign of things to come. Our team, once alone in the van and on the way back to the ship, ended up having a heated debate about what had transpired. I was repeatedly informed by those assembled that what had occurred "wasn't wrong, it was just different." I was to hear the phrase time and time again over the next months and years. After hearing it for the four hundredth time one day, I eventually snapped "Sometimes, it's wrong!" at the poor soul who had spouted the post-modern mantra that was being used by the Christian church to justify anything and everything. But at that stage of my journey, I had only heard it a couple of times and it hadn't begun to grate on my nerves, though the logic of such a statement was, to my mind, immediately suspect.

On further discussion, I learned that the type of charismatic practice that we had witnessed, although strangely out of place in my world, was not unusual for most of the others. Only one girl from France mentioned that she had been similarly disturbed. I queried the evidence of demon possession or the need for such loud and raucous 'deliverance prayer.' I vowed not to put myself in such a position again, next time I would leave the house regardless of the consequence in terms of broken relationships. At least we had been able to give the household some needed supplies in the process of causing much spiritual confusion.

Our final visit was to an old people's home, although I think we all felt a bit exhausted by that time and the debate in the van certainly hadn't helped the team bonding process. I recall an elderly blind lady who, though frail in body, was alert in mind and asked a lot of intelligent questions about the ship. I felt sad that she was languishing amongst those with dementia and sure that she was grateful for some relatively normal conversation. Once again though our Christian lips were sealed due to the law of the land, although I was encouraged to discover that some of the staff were Christians. There was hope. In that type of environment, it would have been ideal to have ship fliers containing the Gospel as we were allowed to advertise the ship, but they hadn't materialised.

At the conclusion of that ministry day, my mind was working overtime attempting to process all that had happened and the implications for the rest of my time on Logos Hope. However, it must've all become too much for me as, lapsing back to simpler matters, we ate a Chinese meal together and I wrote concisely in my journal "Don't have soup again as it's always too hot."

CHAPTER ELEVEN

Evangelicals or Catholics?

A large proportion of the Asian population in most of the countries we visited were Roman Catholics. I was pleased that OM's policy for service on board Logos Hope was that they would only accept those with a personal relationship with Jesus who were not in any way adding works to the evidence of their faith. That therefore excluded most who were attending a Catholic church. That was helpful when ministering to Catholics as we were able to make a clear distinction between a Catholic and a Christian knowing that we had the support of our organisation. Often the people didn't realise that there was a difference, believing that they had been born into their faith. Unfortunately, fellow crew members didn't always realise the important distinction either.

So, it was that, after a slight collision with another ship on our arrival in Kuching, Malaysia, which predictably grabbed the headlines, we were assigned to take part in a Catholic church youth event for one of our C days. We were tasked with preparing a programme to share our ship experiences and how they had impacted our faith with sixty to eighty teens and some University students. I shared my salvation testimony in conjunction with the Parable of the Lost Son. I joked with the students that as I was technically still a police officer (I was just on a career break) they should all be on their best behaviour. That produced a laugh apart from the odd student here and there who looked genuinely terrified. I explained that one of the great things about living in a Christian community was that if we had arguments or problems we could seek forgiveness in a way that wasn't always possible in a non-Christian group as we had a genuine love and care for each other due to our unity of faith. One of the other crew members shared how he had been called to the ship and the others in our team shared their ship experiences.

But the extremely evangelistic speeches had to be set in the context of a prayer to Mary, a crucifix on the wall and a suggestion by the MC that we should consider bringing rosary beads to a subsequent prayer event, which was a little disconcerting to say the least. I was a bit surprised that we had ended up in the situation as I thought the programme's content would have been checked in advance by the Line-Up Team, who had prepared the ministry for us prior to the ship's arrival. But it appeared that Asians had a tendency to change details, times, personnel and everything else at the very last minute and they didn't always communicate effectively with those with whom they were partnering, even in ministry.

After the programme, I was approached by Andrew, a twenty-year-old university student studying Zoology. I was fascinated by his subject choice having thought that only Europeans created degree courses in obscure subjects. I wanted to ask him about that but refrained as I could see that he wanted to talk about matters more relevant to his soul. He told me that my testimony had touched his heart and asked me a question that no one had ever asked before. He said "How can I avoid the temptations you fell into when you were younger?"

What a great question! Andrew was struggling as a lone Christian in the midst of a vast number of Muslims at school and none of his family members were saved. Having established that he was actually 'born again' despite being in a Catholic church, I encouraged him, offered some practical advice and then arranged follow up contact for him with one of the guys from the ship. He emailed me some time later to tell me that he had been baptised and having remembered my advice not to date or become involved in a relationship with a non-believer he had found himself a Christian girlfriend.

After one event in Malaysia we had been taken to a local restaurant for dinner. The Malaysians (and Asians in general) were very hospitable and eating out together was a large part of their culture. I wasn't feeling well due to having suffered my first bout of food poisoning in the preceding days.

I had woken in my cabin feeling queasy and managed with some difficulty to get out of bed to go to work. I struggled to shower and dress knowing that I would at least have to make it to work if only to tell my supervisor that I was in fact unfit for work. I was also pleased that she would likely see that I was telling the truth when, on looking in the mirror, I saw that I had turned a strange shade of grey. I stumbled along the corridor towards my destination feeling worse and worse as I progressed. I arrived in the I-café where fortunately my supervisor was waiting and told her that I was about to be sick, the motion having brought me to the edge. I then ran for the Clinic which was some distance away, as she shouted after me that I would need a 'sick note' to be excused from work. Really!?

That was a practice I resented on the ship as it reduced me to child status. Even in the police we just had to phone in sick and only had to produce a 'sick note' after seven days of absence. Rules like that provoked my rebellious nature which mostly I kept in check. The rule had no doubt been designed for those who had come to the ship straight from school or college and who, having had no proper experience of the disciplines of work, came up with a variety of creative reasons for absence. But it applied equally to us all as was necessary when living communally.

I arrived at the door of the Clinic gasping, before running straight to the nearest cubicle, no doubt surprising the receptionist who had been waiting patiently for my request. I was relieved to see that I had chosen wisely and ... you don't need to hear the rest. Needless to say, I was granted the precious 'sick note' and after returning precariously to see my boss again, finally made it back to bed, just about in one piece but feeling totally exhausted.

Sitting in the Malaysian café with our kind hosts, but feeling the uncomfortable aftermath of the past few days, I didn't take the necessary time properly to digest the contents of the menu. I was more concerned by the fact that it was common practice in Malaysia to eat with one hand and to use the other for a much less sanitary procedure. I was disturbed by that knowledge every time I saw someone leaving to go to the rest room and even more so on their return to their table to eat. I'm sure the practice was not as widespread as I feared but it definitely distracted me. I was therefore mortified when, fifteen minutes after placing my order with a flippant wave of my hand towards the first thing I had seen on the menu, I was handed, by a smiling lady, who was probably also the cook, a large bowl containing two solitary chicken's feet, complete with leg stems.

I smiled politely at the woman who, waiting patiently, appeared disappointed not to receive a more enthusiastic response. I stared at the bowl for a few seconds not really believing what I was seeing. I subsequently failed to observe best cultural practice by, at the first possible moment following the cook's absence, informing one of our hosts that I hadn't realised what the menu item translated to and that I couldn't possibly eat the delicate morsels in front of me. Honestly, just looking at them made me queasy and I wanted to gag, although I didn't tell him that and managed to restrain myself. I couldn't believe that out of all the possible items available which, looking around the open plan restaurant, looked to be much more appetising and normal, I had ended up with the legs of a chicken and that there wasn't even a sauce or any decoration to accompany them. They looked like two twigs. Telling myself that might have made them easier to stomach and if it weren't for my recent illness I may well have given it a go but my heightened sensitivity made it impossible.

My fellow Logos Hopers looked on, appalled by my offensive outright rejection of the local cuisine, but I really didn't care and comforted myself with the thought that any one of them could have been in the same position and that they would no doubt prefer me to take that course of action than the likely alternative result if I were to attempt to eat the legs. On reflection, I should've offered to share my dish with all present referencing my recent food poisoning as a reason not to partake!

CHAPTER TWELVE

Hopelessness

Probably my most distressing ministry day was to a government children's hospital in Malaysia. I dreaded the visit as it had always been one of my most difficult tasks when in the police - visiting the local children's hospital, usually to deal with inconsolable family members diligently watching over their sick children night and day and praying for recovery. The fact that the police were involved usually meant that something untoward had happened to the child which made their circumstances doubly upsetting and it wasn't easy to maintain the necessary professional detachment in that environment.

During our ship devotion earlier that morning the visiting speaker had shared openly how his daughter had survived a hanging. (He said she had been raised from the dead; I wasn't convinced of that but believed that an extraordinary event may have taken place.) The story had put me on edge and our visit was also around the anniversary date of my own brother's death in a car accident nearly a decade before. I didn't really want to go to the hospital and considered asking for a reassignment or cancelling my ministry day for the week. In the end, I made myself join the team after praying that God would change my heart and attitude. One of the reasons for my initial hesitancy was that we had been told that the children were Muslims so we would be unable to share the Gospel with them. I dreaded seeing children who were terminally ill and being unable legally to offer them true hope.

On arrival at the hospital we crowded into the lift and stood silently waiting. We were all apprehensive although some more than others. We walked along a white corridor towards a series of rooms. The corridor was spacious, airy and light streamed in from the windows. At least the atmosphere wasn't dreary as staff bustled around. I had been afraid that poverty would have made the whole experience unbearable and the children might be languishing forgotten in a run-down shack or that they might be begging us for things that we couldn't give them as they struggled for breath. Actually, that was far from the case and my overactive imagination hadn't helped me at all.

We made our base in a day room, the walls of which were lined with colourful pictures obviously having been drawn by the children. There were books and toys strewn around and chairs and tables in useful places. There were several children already in the room; some had relatives visiting. We learned that some had invited friends or relatives especially for our visit. The children played quietly and seemingly contentedly. The only discernible difference between a healthy group of children and those not so fortunate was that there was no noise. It was as if the children had accepted their various prognoses and were patiently waiting for their time to come. It was terribly sad.

Here I met Booga, a ten-year-old Malaysian girl from a Buddhist family; she was draped in an over-sized green hospital gown and had a towel around her neck. When I had first arrived, I had observed her as she came shuffling out of a nearby ward and we exchanged smiles. Then she slowly manoeuvred her tired body into an adjacent ward before returning for our programme. She looked really ill and sadly dejected. Via the Pastor, I established that she had advanced kidney disease. With her faithful mother by her side, she expressed a love of drawing. We had some children's books to distribute, so I wrote a short note to Booja in one of them with a contact email, realising that she probably wouldn't have access to that type of technology. I felt helpless in the extreme and desperate to help the young girl without hope or meaning in this life. After spending some time with Booja and learning more about her life in the hospital and her diagnosis, I handed her the book stating simply 'God bless you' which was as far as I could go. I prayed that the Pastor who was involved in longer term work with the children would have a better opportunity to share at some point.

I also met Jude, another ten-year-old, who, wheelchair bound, had joined us during our programme. His head had been shaved and there were visible scars that were difficult not to look at. There were also lumps on his body, the result of recent operations. He had been diagnosed with bone cancer and was scheduled for an operation the following day. By all accounts, his case was more hopeful than poor Booja's. His family were Catholic so the Pastor was at least able to pray with him. We then sang "Jesus loves me this I know" to him and his younger sister who was looking on. This was in the presence of the other children, but without a clear explanation I could only hope that God would have mercy and use the name of Jesus to touch their hearts before it was too late.

The visit was truly heart-breaking and I struggled to control my emotions throughout. I was reassured that others in our team were also visibly moved. We discussed our emotions after the visit and resolved not to think about it too much as there was nothing that we could do apart from to pray. Putting out of my mind what I had seen was easier said than done. I frequently thought about that visit and those two children after that day. I wondered if they were still alive and whether the Pastor had returned and managed to offer them hope in Jesus. Realistically I knew that it was unlikely due to the laws of the land. The Pastor was intent on abiding by the law believing that he would lose his access to the hospital and therefore the opportunities with other patients should he overstep his bounds.

In the end, I had to come to a place where I believed that if God wanted those children to come to know Him that He would make a way. But how hard to watch children suffering and not be able to share true hope with them if their families were Muslim or Buddhist. It was definitely worse having seen the love and care of the parents who sincerely believed that they were doing the best for their children by sticking rigidly to the faith that they had been taught and teaching their children to do the same. They believed, as we all do, that their faith was the true faith but sadly some other religions forbade even considering or looking into other faiths on punishment of eternal damnation. The freedom to investigate and learn the truth was not even a possibility for the families who were part of a religious and cultural hierarchy teaching that it was more important to honour an elder and accept what had been taught to you than to know if what you had been taught was true. Some even went as far as to prefer not to know if their faith might be on shaky ground as they didn't want to face the terrible consequence of having to change what they believed. It was easier to toe the party line and carry on as normal even if there were doubts. Some might face estrangement, banishment, torture or even death in so called 'honour killings.' We really are privileged in the West still to experience relative freedom of conscience and expression, although that is gradually being eroded.

I faced an internal battle many times whilst on the ship but the hospital visit was probably the time when I felt the most helpless and hopeless and it stayed with me.

CHAPTER THIRTEEN

Taming the Tongue

It was after a few months of my Logos Hope journey that I had begun to journal actively. I wrote "I am inspired to start journaling after starting to read *How I fell in love with Africa* (authored by the daughter of my ship dad, Marianne Hui.) I realised as I was reading that I am also capable of writing a book about my mission experiences one day and I don't want to regret not having the material to do so."

That was where a lot of my experiences were recorded and it brought back a lot of memories on review, although I stopped journaling about halfway through my journey as my emotions were overwhelmed by the ministry I later became involved in and writing reams of never-ending waffle about it felt unacceptably unproductive.

In our second or third month, we were advised by the ship leaders that we should seek to become more involved in ship life by signing up for additional duties and roles. I guess the timing of the announcement was meant to allow us to settle in a bit before putting pressure on us, but they needed people to participate more actively in order for the ship to function properly. Logos Hope was really what you made it in many ways as it was possible to retreat to a cabin after working each day and do little else. Some decided to do that, probably either due to health issues or because they couldn't deal with the culture shock and felt excluded. I felt that there needed to be more awareness of the individual crew members and how they were doing emotionally and spiritually. There was a voluntary mentorship scheme but it felt like a drastic event had to take place in order to get recommended for it. My ship family would have quickly picked up on it if I were depressed or ill for long periods but others didn't have the same type of family. It was possible for someone to slip under the radar in the busyness of activity and ministry.

I was ready and willing to get stuck in and began by taking a driving test to enable me to drive the Logos Hope vans when required. On hearing that I had passed, one of my friends at home in England mistakenly thought that I was at the helm of the ship! I would probably have been clearer in my newsletter had I considered that it was even a possibility that someone might make that mistake.

During my first trip to the airport to pick someone up I was accompanied by a whole crowd of crew who either wanted to meet the person we were collecting or who were just excited to accompany us for the drive for novelty value. The shipping agent, required by law to join us, casually informed me within a few minutes of conversation that he couldn't believe I had been a police officer as I looked more like a model! As I was recovering from the shock of having been spoken to so directly about such a personal matter, he added, whilst we were stuck in traffic, that the reason all of the male drivers surrounding us were looking at me was because I was a "good looking foreign woman." I looked around and sure enough many drivers were openly gawping and making no attempt to hide it. I was embarrassed and felt the colour making its way across my face.

I learned to take compliments, if that was what it was and not a bad pick-up line, like those with a pinch of salt as any foreign white woman in Asia was similarly described regardless of their comparative beauty. But initially it had definitely been a bit too much for my reserved British disposition and I had been more inclined to cut the speaker down with a biting reply than to muster a gracious response.

My next acts of civic duty were to join the ship Gospel Choir singing the Alto part, learning how to share my testimony using a sketch-board and accepting the role of Andrew (the disciple) in a group which acted out the entire book of Mark in front of live audiences. The rehearsals often degenerated into hilarity which placed me in a spiritual quandary as obviously I found the mistakes and comedy moments funny, but wasn't sure if I should be laughing as it related to the Bible. I decided in the end that it was okay as long as it didn't involve the more serious aspects of the Gospel. Mostly, it was the way that mistakes were incorporated into the drama as people tried to keep things going; so often the audience remained in the dark about what was meant to have happened.

During rehearsals when there wasn't the need for a smooth uninterrupted performance things sometimes got a bit out of control. Someone accidentally shoved me whilst we were sitting in a fishing boat so I dramatically keeled over and subsequently fell overboard; the other disciples then concocted an elaborate plan to 'rescue' me from the terrors of the carpet sea, completely abandoning the Biblical storyline in the process. During our first live performance with a two hundred strong audience we were pretending to collect bread from the crowd for the feeding of the five thousand, but one person actually handed us some potato chips which we were forced to incorporate. When 'Jesus' appeared one lady reached out and touched him then began telling all her friends in a loud whisper "I touched Jesus."

I guess it must've been pretty realistic. The guy representing Jesus also forgot his lines at one point and because he was looking at me I assumed it was my line and blurted out "Who then can be saved?" about four scenes too early. As you might imagine, that caused great confusion. When there were no small children in the audience one day, 'Jesus' was forced to use an adult representative which brought laughter as, not having much of a choice, he chose a six-foot male, very non-child-like crew member and sat him on his lap.

Perhaps more significantly I volunteered to lead a small, girls only, six-week study group. We could choose a topic, post it on a board in our staff lounge and then those who wanted to study the topic signed up underneath our name. Honestly, it was more a test of popularity as many people just signed up to the groups being led by their friends or the designated leaders on board rather than some random crew members. I decided to lead a group dealing with James chapter 3 in conjunction with the book *Taming the Tongue*, which I had borrowed from the ship library and recently read. It listed all of the possible ways we could sin through our speech and then suggested ways to combat each individual sin. Mia loyally signed up for my group along with two other girls, one of whom switched to another group at the last minute. Most of the crew had signed up to groups dealing with lust issues inspired by the 'Every Man's and Every Woman's Battle' books. I had read both of them, wasn't that impressed and wanted to focus on another area.

As part of our study we examined some Bible characters and how they had responded to provocation and dealt with sins of the tongue. We looked at Elijah and the youths, David and Shimei, David and Goliath, and of course Jesus and Paul (Acts 5.) We set ourselves the practical task of monitoring our speech for a day and were horrified when we re-grouped and realised how often we sin in that area; it was hard not to be discouraged and one of the girls said that it felt impossible. I thought about the fact that we were just dealing with our speech and not even touching on our thought lives. We talked through our experiences and by the end were all thinking that it would be better if we remained silent for the majority of our interactions with others!

By the conclusion of the study, we had worked through the paralysis of conviction and had all benefitted spiritually from that challenging area of the Bible. I had enjoyed preparing the studies and learned that the size of our group had actually been beneficial in the end as we were more willing to be open and honest with each other due to just being a small group of girls. One of the girls had made steps to break a long-standing silence with her step-mother and the other left a note on my cabin door thanking me for the studies and saying that she was "learning so much more because it's intentional," although notes of encouragement were banded around a lot on Logos Hope, I did appreciate it as I knew she was sincere.

I also signed up to be a mentor for people who wanted to talk through issues or be discipled. I was amused during the early sessions of our training when Viktor (Hungary), who was known for being outspoken, told us during our discussion about 'feedback' that he had asked forgiveness from a girl whom he had offended. She had accepted the feedback and then he had said that there was some feedback that he would also like to give her and asked her whether she was willing to receive it. Her answer a flat and decisive "no." As that had no doubt been the reason for Viktor's initial apology he became a tad downcast as we failed to contain our laughter.

I joined a group seeking to memorise the whole book of James in six weeks. I spent hours going over and over chapters of the book during my daily devotion times and finally managed to learn it and repeat it verbatim. We then began a group to learn 1 Timothy; I was leading the group and at our initial meeting explained how our previous group had learned James and what a blessing it had proved to be. Maybe I should've kept my mouth shut or not been so enthusiastic about James. One girl who had attended our initial Timothy meeting emailed me shortly after to advise that she had been so inspired by my comments on learning James, that she had decided to learn that book instead and would no longer be participating in the Timothy group! I was a bit stumped but decided it was a mixed blessing as she would at least still be memorising Scripture.

The Timothy group failed drastically in the end as people dropped out one by one due to other commitments. One guy even admitted that he hadn't made the meeting as he had been playing UNO; I didn't know whether to be grateful for his honesty or appalled by his lack of personal discipline. Honestly, I was also struggling as I was still trying to retain James which involved faithfully repeating it regularly in addition to the new material. I don't know how some of the missionaries of previous generations managed to do it but I think our minds have probably become lazy due to lack of use. Still, learning James was definitely worthwhile and I can still recall verses that God brings to mind at relevant times and in certain circumstances.

I signed up to be a 'buddy' for one of the port volunteers. In each port we visited, local people came to help us on board. A buddy was assigned to show them around and teach them the ropes as it were, a similar idea to the 'big brother' and 'big sister' for new crew members. I became a buddy to Amy who was very enthusiastic about her service on board. She invited me and Fiona to tour the area on our day off. I'm sure that some crew only signed up for that type of duty in order to have a host to take them around. Due to their overwhelming hospitality, most of the locals probably wouldn't have minded even if they had known that as they were keen to have the company and a foreigner to show off to their friends and neighbours. Some would even admit that we were doing them the service by accompanying them which was when things got really weird and we felt a bit like celebrities. Amy wasn't like that though and I'm sure she genuinely enjoyed showing us a bit of her country.

We accompanied Amy to a 'space show' where we sat in a large auditorium and watched a very lame display of the solar system using an assortment of colours projected onto the ceiling around us; even Amy was embarrassed by the poor quality of the display. Then we clambered into a fishing boat and were rowed by a local man across to a special house that made 'local food.' The food was all brightly coloured and square shaped. It looked more like children's toys or Lego blocks than food but we sampled some and, despite being of a rubbery texture, it had an interesting not unpleasant taste.

Next, we discovered a glass lift that reminded me of the *Charlie and the Great Glass Elevator* book by Roald Dahl, as it looked as if it went on forever. We thought it would take us to a vantage point to look out over the area and excitedly filed in. We shot up at a high rate of knots and I began to feel a bit ill as the lift felt totally exposed and we could literally see everything through the glass. I understood then why lifts were usually solid rather than see-through. When we reached the top floor, we stepped out into a mess of building work and rubbish. Looking around in confusion it wasn't long before a worried and official-looking man came rushing towards us to inform us that the lift was out of service due to being broken. There had been signs to that effect, which we had obviously missed. He didn't stop us retreating back into the lift, but in hindsight we thought that perhaps we should've taken the stairs. We collectively held our breath on the way down wondering if the bottom might suddenly fall out or the roof cave in. Exploring with Amy had been fun but it was good to land safely and to head back to the ship still in one piece.

CHAPTER FOURTEEN

We Come Begging .....Swimming

There was a definite need for humour due to some of the sad situations we found ourselves in as we ministered to poor and sick people in countries with no Gospel light. Several things stand out from my earlier days on-board - the first whilst we were still in Malaysia. I had gone to a beach with my friend Joan from Fiji on a day off, hoping to swim. It might sound strange that living on a ship surrounded by water we would even want to swim but it was a strong desire for most crew members. The problem was that we were not allowed to swim in the vicinity of the ship and that mostly the areas where we docked were either close to sewage pipes or polluted for other reasons. There were a few occasions when Joan and I abandoned reason and swam at night near the ship, but far enough away not to break the rules, or at least not to be seen by those keeping watch. We couldn't see the pollution but we knew the water was full of rubbish. We were desperate. Ideally, we were looking for a more pleasant experience and many of our days off were spent searching for places to swim.

Disappointingly, on arrival at that particular beach a local informed us that there were jellyfish in the water. We could also see that the beach was quite rocky with little sand. I thought the man meant large jellyfish that would be easily avoidable on sight. I knew that some had been stung during our PST; they were the fortunate ones. Nick from Singapore, who was serving on board as part of the STEP (Short-term Exposure Programme) for three months, was bitten by a stonefish which, by all accounts, could've been a lot more serious, although he did end up on crutches. He commented defiantly on Facebook in response to the possibility that he may have been killed by said fish, "Please, it would take more than a stupid stonefish to kill me!"

But as I couldn't see any jellyfish large or otherwise, on approaching the sea I braved it anyway; Joan sensibly remained safely on shore. Cautiously I waded my way through the shallow water heading for swimming depth, but then felt something gently brush my leg. Shrieking and looking down I saw that there were hundreds of very small pink jellyfish all around me. I was surrounded and trapped, thinking I couldn't move as I might tread on or walk into one causing it to sting me. Eventually I managed to follow the lead of a local man who had also entered the water and was heading back towards the beach. I felt somewhat foolish but was glad not to have been attacked.

A few weeks down the line, thinking that all the local beaches would be the same as the first, we had given up on the idea of trying to find a nice spot to relax and catch up on some reading. But rumours on the ship persisted that there were some really nice sandy beaches with clear blue sea fairly nearby. So, hopefully we gathered details of two of the locations and, in order to make sure that we went to the right place, we booked a taxi to get us there. Unfortunately, the taxi driver informed us that the named beach was, you guessed it, unsuitable for swimming due to the jellyfish. He suggested taking us to another location. We agreed thinking that a local would know best and happily paying the extra money to get there. It was only on arrival that we realised that we were at the exact same beach as before having just entered from a different direction.

Not wanting to admit defeat but also not wanting to pay another exorbitant taxi fee we decided to walk around the area to see if we could find another beach. So, we set off along the main road in our beach-wear, causing many locals to stop and stare both in confusion, as they knew there were no beaches where we were headed, and probably in surprise that we were wearing our beach-wear on the highway as it was a moderately conservative place. We failed to detect the meaning of the expressions on the faces of the locals as we route-marched confidently away from the only beach in the area.

After an hour of walking in the hot sun feeling pretty miserable we saw a large hotel from the road. On entering the driveway, we could also see a small pool of water (when I say small I mean it, it was probably four metres square and very shallow.) We thought that at last we would be able at least to dip ourselves in the water and by that point we were willing to pay whatever it cost. But the staff, clearly not sensing our desperation, and not being willing to abandon the rule book even if they had, callously informed us that it was only available for hotel guests and anyway it was not within regular swimming hours.

Finally, realising that our water search was fruitless, we found a children's playground. Driven slightly mad by the heat and futility of the day's events, I abandoned all attempts at decorum and jumped on the back of some type of animal on a child's roundabout. Joan began pushing the roundabout at a comfortable speed. But suddenly a local middle-aged man appeared as if from nowhere and came enthusiastically running towards us with a big grin on his face. Behaving as if I were a small child in need of a bit of entertainment, he began pushing the thing so vigorously that I feared I would fall off or go flying. I hung on for dear life, not knowing whether I was more embarrassed or panic stricken. I'm sure an expression of fear was by then contorting my features, as Joan laughed uproariously from the side-lines. Finally, realising that the man was not going to stop pushing the thing for all he was worth and that I couldn't communicate sensibly with him, I managed to jump off as it was still in motion. Joan and I, giggling, then walked away from the crazy Malaysian man who, uninvited, had decided to 'add' to our fun.

CHAPTER FIFTEEN

Bright Lights, Exciting Sounds and Shopping Malls

On first arrival in Singapore I was totally shocked, we had docked practically on top of a large shopping mall. The colourful lights reflecting off the water were pretty impressive but that was the only redeeming feature as far as I was concerned. I detested shopping and it felt like the Singaporeans didn't really want us there - some were quite cold and indifferent and few visited the ship. Essentially, the people didn't need us or our message of hope and it felt as if they resented the intrusion or maybe the reminder that there was a different Way. It was possible that material prosperity had bred religious apathy.

It was ironic that the ship leadership had determined in advance of our visit to Singapore that we had to make the outside of the ship as beautiful as possible in order to attract visitors (and because we would be in the centre of the city and very visible.) The crew working on deck spent weeks painting the ship and chipping away at the rust, but when it looked like time was running out and we were preparing for departure, they were instructed simply to paint over the rust. Some crew believed that it was superficial, a case of Christians trying to conform to worldly standards in order to make their message acceptable, but others said that it was a case of trying not to give unnecessary offence and attempting to fit in to the local culture. I could see both sides but I did smother a laugh when one outspoken crew member stood up in a prayer meeting and used a spiritual analogy - putting plasters on spiritual struggles and failing to deal directly with God, in order indirectly to complain about painting over the rust!

One highlight in Singapore was a visit to Rodney and Irene's house (our ship parents.) To get there we travelled on a train-like vehicle that was on rails high off the ground. It was wider than a train and the windows were floor to ceiling, so we could see everything around. I wrote that it travels "without a driver on a track like a rollercoaster" but on reflection, I don't think that is actually legal or true. After we alighted, Dany, the by then acknowledged craziest member of our family, took the opportunity to scare us all half to death by completing acrobatics on his hands on a bridge structure over a very large drop (maybe fifty metres) with a canal running beneath.

We later watched *Just for laughs,* a reality TV comedy series where unsuspecting people are set up in a range of creative scenarios, for a slice of Western normality. For some reason the sight of a person dressed as a gorilla attempting to scare an old couple by jumping out at them stuck in my mind. Probably because the couple didn't jump at all or even look frightened; they stared at the creature as if to say "What on earth are you doing?" or "Are you crazy?" The by then thoroughly embarrassed gorilla slunk back into the undergrowth muttering to itself. Priceless.

But by far the most entertaining moment and definitely in the running for "best moment on board," occurred during an I-café team bonding day in Singapore. Prior to that we had done a number of other things to foster closeness including racing toy cars attached to cotton and a game involving hitting each other with a rolled-up newspaper. Our leaders had decided that it was time for some air so we ventured outside to some grassy areas not far from the ship. After playing sport for a while I was pretty hot and decided to look for some water (no, not to swim) just to splash on my face.

After a short fruitless search, I was on the verge of giving up when I saw an old man crouching and leaning nearer to the ground. He was washing his face with water although I couldn't yet see the source. I waited discreetly until he had finished and then on approach, discovered a very small tap hidden in some undergrowth next to some neatly planted flowerbeds. Joyously I called the others over and began turning the tap to what I thought was on. I kept turning it as nothing was happening but that was obviously a mistake and before long the entire tap had come off in my hand. Whether my action was over-exuberant or whether the tap was loose, I don't really know, but the resulting furious gush of water heading in a stream high into the air made me think that an essential pipe must've exploded.

By that point some of my co-workers had joined me and were looking on, wondering what on earth I would do next and starting to worry. I began to try to stem the flow using my hands but that was clearly going to be impossible as the water pressure was too intense. My team leader started panicking and asking what would happen if we couldn't turn it off and saying that she didn't want to get into trouble. I had visions of us all being hauled up in front of the ship's company and having to give an explanation as to why Logos Hope had been asked to leave Singapore prematurely as we hung our collective heads in shame. After all we were all meant to be on our best behaviour in that particular country and the fiasco definitely didn't fall into that category.

The water was spreading across the ground and merging into a deep puddle and there was no sign that the gushing was about to cease. Then as if to add insult to injury, a man with a radio came running over, sized up the situation with a worried look on his face and then went running off again whilst jabbering into his radio - presumably he was calling for help. In the meantime, knowing that I had to take some action, I persevered in trying to replace the broken tap and with a bit of reluctant help from one of the others. Eventually I managed to force it back onto the pipe and turn it slightly to lock it back on, in the process getting absolutely and totally drenched. We all sighed with relief at that point and then, having averted the crisis, looked at each other and promptly burst out laughing!

CHAPTER SIXTEEN

It's More Fun in The Philippines!

Most people remember our voyage from Singapore to Cebu in the Philippines as it wasn't plain sailing. I really felt for the many people lying in different spots around the ship in the full throes of seasickness. And I seriously pitied those who felt seasick the minute they set foot on the ship even when she was docked, as was the case for a few select individuals. The problem was that most people hadn't sailed or been on big boats or ships prior to coming to Logos Hope and there was no way to tell in advance how the rocking motion would affect them. Seasickness was one of those things that you either had or you didn't. I was one of the lucky ones who didn't seem to suffer at all. But I did find it impossible to sleep as I was thrown around in my bed (literally) and things fell with a loud clatter off the wall or the desk. Even trickier was trying to walk along the corridors in a straight line and finding yourself suddenly rotating and heading into a wall or taking off and losing contact with the carpet, before being deposited elsewhere or crashing into others who had bravely ventured out of their cabins.

During smoother voyages, after the mandatory safety and lifeboat drills where someone was always asleep despite the numerous pre-warnings, we were usually given at least one day off from our usual work requirements. Some people ate their meals sitting on chairs outside on the decks as we glided through the water. You might think that on a ship with four hundred people it would be difficult to find time alone especially during sailings when everyone was on board. In actual fact, a lot of people stayed in their cabins, taking the time to rest and recuperate. Parts of the deck were virtually empty when venturing outside; it was easy to sit and chat with a friend without being disturbed or overheard.

When there was a possibility of pirate attacks all of the outside deck lights had to be switched off. At those times, when opening a door leading out onto the deck it could be literally pitch black outside. A few of us reverted to child-like behaviour as we felt our way along the railings, found somewhere to sit and then chatted alone in the dark as the journey progressed. When it was really warm, as it was most of the time in South-East Asia, we could lie back on an elevated area at the front of the ship and feel ourselves being carried along by the waves almost as if the ship wasn't there and we were flying. There were also opportunities to see dolphins racing along near the front of the ship at times.

During a calmer part of the six-day voyage to Cebu we took part in a poverty simulation, presumably to prepare us for our first real experience of a third world country. We were divided into groups and had to spend part of the day sitting on white sheets that had been spread as coverings on the floor. Our group was tasked with making paper bags with glue for several hours, whilst other groups that were supposedly slightly richer were allowed to do more exciting things, like using masking tape. I felt that we should have at least been creating things that could be useful but I guess that was one of the points that they wanted to make - the work was mundane and the people who were living like that didn't have a choice as they needed to put food on the table each day.

I felt sorry for Silas as it was his birthday and Ship Family Night, but the poverty simulation was meant to be ongoing for the day and into the evening. Usually a birthday would be loudly celebrated with much banging on the table and singing. On that day, it seemed somewhat inappropriate for us to celebrate with our usual enthusiasm. Therefore, a downcast looking Silas was solemnly presented with a cake made from bread, jam and raisins, which looked bizarre. I gave him mint smelling bubbles that I had found on a giveaway table in the ship lobby earlier that day. He gave the impression that he was pleased although a little perplexed. Silas himself was the topic of many of our discussions that day and on other days as well, as he had decided not to shave for a year and was by then sporting a rather large bushy beard which made him look twice as old as he actually was.

On arrival in Cebu we had our usual community briefing grandly entitled 'Port Orientation.' The point, of course, was for locals and people who had previously spent time in the country or port to tell us how to behave and dress and what the ship policies were for the port. It was also where we heard the loudest cheers and groans as we were told "You must go two by two" and "no shorts" etc. I recall that at some Filipino ports we even had a "three by three" policy meaning that there had to be at least three people in any group that left the ship and that one of them had to be a man.

It created an interesting dilemma one evening as one of my I-café friends Eva was leaving the ship in the not too distant future. She wanted to have a private chat with me before doing so. We had wandered from the ship temporarily forgetting the policy and then decided to return on remembering it halfway to a park that we had headed for. As we were turning back we suddenly saw a male crew member whom we sort-of knew; he was walking along with around four street boys. We asked him who they were and he looked confused as if realising for the first time that the boys were with him and said that they must've just followed him. The man helpfully agreed to accompany us to the park so we could have our chat but in practice it didn't really work as he had nothing to do other than to wait for us. He amused himself by hiding behind the trees and benches or walking past us whistling or suddenly popping out when we hadn't been aware that he was nearby. Needless to say, in the end Eva and I ended up in hysterics due to his conspicuous body-guard-like behaviour and decided to go back to the ship to talk in private.

It was decided by the leadership that in order adequately to orientate us to the Philippines, volunteer crew members would eat the local delicacy balut on the stage in front of all of us. Balut is chiefly a chick that has grown inside its egg (obviously) but without hatching. Filipinos eat it straight from the shell. Those selling eggs in the street marked the shells as to whether they were plain eggs or whether it was balut, so that ignorant visitors didn't get a nasty shock. Young Leo and several others foolishly went up on the stage and attempted to stomach the crunchy animals, but they had over-estimated their Western body's abilities to keep such a thing down and, before long, most of them were gagging and rushing back-stage to much hilarity in the audience.

After witnessing that I refused to taste balut for at least another two years despite living and working in the Philippines and being constantly offered it, I eventually succumbed when Pastor Jeremy Walker from England visited my church in Manila and immediately agreed to the challenge that was presented to him. Being a resident missionary, I couldn't have a foreigner outdoing me so I also took up the challenge and ate a whole one; it was actually not bad and tasted like......chicken.

CHAPTER SEVENTEEN

Introducing the Street Children

Having been thoroughly orientated to Cebu and knowing what to expect, at least in terms of buying and eating eggs, I set out on my first ministry day with keen expectation. We had been assigned to play with the local street children who congregated in a nearby park. The idea was that we would take some balls, Frisbees and *Sesame Street* style monster puppets (I don't know why we had them on the ship) to play with them. We didn't expect that they would speak any English so our Gospel work would be limited but maybe we could build relationships with them and arrange for a Filipino to share with them during the course of the ship's visit.

We had had a lengthy discussion during our team planning meeting as to whether or not we should buy them food. They were obviously going to be hungry but feeding them for a day and then disappearing again might detract from our purpose in being there, create expectation in relation to rich foreigners, cause them to neglect their usual methods of obtaining food and create dependence on us. My views in that area have vacillated over the years and I do think that if there is longer term work going on and the children are hungry, it can be difficult to get them to pay attention or even listen to you at all if they are not fed, but any feeding should be of secondary consideration. It should always be in conjunction with sharing the Gospel, which should take priority. With short-term work, as on Logos Hope, feeding them for a day would probably make things worse - we decided not to feed them.

As soon as we walked out of the main gate leading away from the ship we were bombarded by shabbily dressed young children; they clung to us and wanted us to play with them. We led them back to the safety of the park, along a main road with vehicles charging everywhere. We played games and swung some children around whilst the others climbed all over us. The numbers of children, who were aged between five and twelve years old, constantly increased as more and more appeared as if by magic. We learned that some of them did go to school and others were from an orphanage nearby, some hadn't eaten and ALL of them were thirsty. We had brought our own water and gave the remnants to the kids but I did feel a tad guilty after we had encouraged them to run around with us. But were then unable to give them water due to not having enough for ourselves.

When we were all far too hot and exhausted to continue, we collapsed on the ground only to find the children crawling all over us and throwing their arms around our necks. We tried then to share with them a little about Jesus but the language barrier was significant. The kids just wanted contact and someone to pay attention to them. The realisation made me sad but also glad that we could at least give them some fun and that other crew members would no doubt return subsequently and continue the games. The ship cameraman with us took over three hundred photos. Sometimes I found that difficult as it felt like people watching might think that we were only playing with the children to raise money for our ministry by sending the photos abroad to our supporters. I preferred not to take photos of those living in poverty, although the children were more than happy to pose for them. Sadly, there were fake ministries that used those types of photos to raise money from sensitive souls abroad although I think awareness has increased in recent years after documentaries showing where the money was actually going.

Then it began to rain (rain in the Philippines is not like normal rain and can be torrential or turn into typhoons) so we took shelter in a large stone circular building within the park. The children followed us asking all the things that children do in their broken English, "What is your name? How old are you? Where are you from?" They were more pleased with themselves for daring to try speaking in English than interested in the answers. They repeated the same questions over and over oblivious to the fact that we had already answered them.

After a while I was approached by a security guard who asked me my age. He looked shocked when I answered truthfully and asked me why I wasn't married before informing me that I should be married because then I would have someone to talk to. His next comment made me decide that it was time to think about heading back to the ship despite the inclement weather: "I'm thirty-four, that's only four years older than you."

I hastily advised the man that I was a Christian and therefore believed that God would send a man when the timing was right, before my rapid departure with numerous children hanging from my arms and legs. That was my first real introduction to street children although there would be a lot more of that to come.

CHAPTER EIGHTEEN

Desperately Seeking

Whilst we were still in Cebu in the Philippines, I was mooching around the I-café one day feeling irritable and not really wanting to talk to anyone but realising that I should at least make the effort. After a while I began to realise that it was often when I felt like that and was unprepared, at least emotionally, that I had the best opportunities, rather than the planned evangelistic endeavours. God's ways are higher than our ways. On renouncing my slothfulness, I saw two girls sitting at separate tables and quickly prayed that God would lead me to the right one.

Making a decision, I sat down opposite a girl who looked to be in her twenties as she made a big mess of a croissant and tried to cover it up in embarrassment. Being a foreigner, my sitting down had immediately doubled her humiliation. Phoebe, in her twenties, was a trainee nurse whose family were immersed in a form of Roman Catholicism which involved them having an altar in their home and worshipping a statue of the baby Jesus.

There was a widespread superstitious belief that Cebu was protected from typhoons and other disasters by the 'Santa Nino' statues. I found it strange that not only did many people bring their baby Jesus statues to the ship for their visits but, on leaving, many also left them behind. It was odd that a possession of such spiritual import to a people group could be casually misplaced in such large quantities, especially as they believed it was necessary to carry it at all times to ward off the danger. I don't think that if a group of Christians had attended an event there would have been a large number of Bibles left behind; Christians don't even attach superstitious significance to the Bible. We had to come up with a suitable way to dispose of the idols without offending the local population who would inevitably find them if we chucked them in the nearest garbage disposal. I can't be definitive about what was eventually decided in the leadership's "What shall we do with the large number of abandoned foreign deities we have accumulated?" meeting, although I would have liked to have been a fly on the wall!

There was a minor earthquake (6.9) during our visit to Cebu. The terrified people ran out of their houses clutching the statues. They honestly believed that the reason their homes hadn't fallen and killed them outright was because of them. It was really very sad. I had been in my cabin at the time of the quake; I'd felt things shaking and noticed a rattling noise for around thirty seconds but had assumed crew members were fiddling around in the engine room. I was shocked to learn that there had been an earthquake and on hearing about the chaos for those who had been off the ship and in the community when it had occurred.

Phoebe related that she had become dissatisfied with her life and religion over the years. On that day, she had been walking past the ship with a friend and had asked the friend if she would mind if she went on board; she hadn't known anything about the ship. She had been feeling unhappy and looking for something but she didn't know what it was.

Phoebe's family required strict obedience in all areas of life. She had three older married brothers and her mother appeared to be trying to live her failed dreams through Phoebe, thus putting her under a lot of pressure. Phoebe had wanted to study Business Administration and had worked hard towards her goal. She had achieved good marks and was ranked highly amongst her peers. She had thought that her hard work might convince her parents to let her pursue her dream job, but her mum wanted her to be a Nurse and had insisted on it. She had become a Nurse but disliked her work and was unhappy.

We discussed her parents' faith and she admitted that she only followed it because of her upbringing. I suggested she should find the truth for herself and shared my testimony with her. Phoebe said that she occasionally read the Bible but that it was a family Bible and she didn't have her own. I was able to give her a Bible and on receipt of it she became emotional and told me that it was more precious to her because it had been given as a gift than if she had bought it herself.

We talked further about Jesus and I explained that he had come to set us free from the burdens we were carrying and that nothing we could ever do would be good enough to meet God's holy standard. Phoebe admitted she knew that was what she had been trying to do but that although she was outwardly obedient to her parents she was stubborn in her heart. She told me that her brother had been a drug addict who injected drugs but that he had been clean for at least a year after becoming a Christian at rehab. Her friend was also a Christian. They had told her the same things that I was saying. She told me that she could see that I was happy and had peace within and she wanted that freedom as well. I was glad that she could see beyond the bad mood I had been in prior to meeting her. Her comments reminded me that our Christian walk is always being observed whether we realise it or not.

I told her how to become a Christian, advising that she should think about her decision and pray about it asking God for forgiveness of her sin. We prayed together and before Phoebe left the ship I gave her an audio device containing sermons that she could listen to in the following days. She said that she would be meeting her Christian friend that evening and that they would discuss what had happened whilst she was on the ship. I was really so very encouraged by our conversation that day and even more so on receiving an email later down the line advising me that she was reading her new Bible every day.

I don't know whether Phoebe took that final step of faith, but I had given her the tools to do so and if God was drawing her to Himself then I knew that she would one day be saved. As Christians, we can only plant seeds ensuring we explain the Gospel clearly and pray for people; it is God who gives the increase and causes growth. There may be many links in a chain before someone becomes a Christian and they need to count the cost and understand what they are doing when they make that decision.

CHAPTER NINETEEN

Children, Children Everywhere

The Philippines will definitely be remembered for the smiling faces of the numerous street children who were everywhere we went. On one of our ministry days we were collected by our host in a pick-up truck. There were six of us and the only place to sit was in the back which was completely open to the elements. We packed in like sardines with several people balancing precariously on the edge for the one-hour journey. That was a pretty standard practice in Asia as the road rules (where they were in existence) were fairly relaxed. To demonstrate that, think of any type of normal Western vehicle and consider the maximum number of passengers that would be allowed according to the law, which is normally based on safety. Now treble or quadruple that number and you have the situation in Asia; we're talking people stuffed into any and all areas: floor spaces, roofs, you name it.

After our programme, we clambered back into the pick-up. We continued singing and playing the guitar for the hundreds of street children who followed the pick-up's slow progress along the dusty narrow roads near to their houses. It really felt like we were in a movie as the kids enthusiastically followed us for quite a distance. I was reminded how much our visit had meant to them as they had little else in their lives. I hoped they would also remember the Gospel message we had left with them.

On another ministry day, we took part in a feeding programme for street children. We spent hours pulling green leaves off stalks in the hot sun; they were minute, maybe a quarter of an inch in diameter. The leaders from the charity we had partnered with told us that we had to take the stalks off the leaves or the children would pick them out of their food and throw them away in disgust. They said it was important for them to have greens in their diet. Whilst I agreed with the principle I couldn't see how that amount of tiny leaves could make much difference to anyone's health. I suppose I was also thinking that if the children were really that hungry they would eat the whole plant - stalks and all. But I accepted what they told me and got on with the job.

During the programme, I shared the Gospel, using the Wordless Book, to around one hundred children and was astonished to find that they already knew what all of the colours represented. It was clear that they had seen it before. I didn't know whether to be encouraged that they had remembered it from the prior occasion, or slightly annoyed that someone had stolen my thunder and I had nothing original to show them. At least they wanted to hear the message again and didn't groan as kids in England may well have done when sitting through a repeated message. I just hoped that the children understood the Gospel meaning and hadn't just learned the colours to impress a previous team or whoever it was who had originally shared with them.

The food that we had prepared earlier in the day: rice, small pieces of chicken, soup, small green leaves, and potato was dished out to the dirty, unkempt children with ragged clothes. They lined up not so patiently outside our vehicles with their bowls and spoons, some of which had been creatively fashioned from other household items. Some of the kids found their way onto the roof of our van. Those of us who weren't directly involved in the food distribution wandered around trying to talk to the children or help them get organised in the very long queue, which was not an easy task.

I ended up carrying around a small boy aged about three, who had no trousers on, for a while. I kept trying to put him back down but he kept reaching out to me to be picked up again. Eventually, when I was called upon to do something else, I gave him to another male crew member who had just finished talking to the large group of adults who were looking on. The adults laughed on seeing the surprised expression on his face when he was unceremoniously landed with the small partially clothed child as I walked off to address the other matter.

The adults themselves were a sorry sight. Many wore dirty clothes with holes, their hair greasy and in poor condition. They were missing a lot of teeth but grinned at every opportunity. Some of the men were drunk and others were sleeping half-naked on old items of furniture in the middle of the street, surrounded by the children. It was chaos - the adults having no control or authority over any of the children. I'm sure that many of the children were not living with their own families and had experienced serious losses to drugs, drink and a range of health problems. That was a community in serious crisis - they had banded together for solidarity, but the communal needs were great and poverty was threatening to overwhelm them all. Where would their help and hope come from?

At the conclusion of the day I wrote in my journal:

"I was overwhelmed by the hopelessness in the Philippines in general. Men just lying in the street or on beds - lazy or unemployed? Is there a desire to work? The poverty was terrible to see and the lack of material goods and basic living conditions dreadful. Yesterday I saw children picking through a rubbish dump with bags. I know the only solution is Jesus but the need is so great. It makes me sick to think of all of the things we have in the West and even on the ship and all of it so unnecessary. I don't know if I will be able to return to England after two years of this."

CHAPTER TWENTY

Stop the Wedding!

I met Caroline with her mum and aunt in Cebu in the Philippines. I was just chatting to them in the I-café about the ship and sharing my testimony. Caroline was very enthusiastic about the ship ministry and asked me several times how she too could join. I had begun to explain the process but it had proved difficult because her aunt constantly interjected in the conversation. The aunt wanted to inform me that Caroline was backslidden. There were obvious parallels with my past life that I had been describing to them as part of my testimony. I felt sorry for Caroline and could see that her well-intentioned aunt, obviously wanting to help her, was inadvertently pushing her further away from God. She was highlighting her flaws and judging her in front of me, a stranger, causing her to feel ashamed.

I didn't really want to interfere in the family dynamics but I did want to try to help Caroline. To combat the problem of her outspoken aunt I decided to ask Caroline if she wanted to accompany me elsewhere on the ship for a more private chat. She quickly agreed, so the two of us headed to the crew dining room. She admitted that she had been in a relationship and living with a non-believer, but she said that the relationship had recently ended. She related that she had been a worship leader and very active in her church but had become disillusioned and fallen into sin.

Caroline said that she had been crying out to God every day to try to put things right. She told me about her 'big plans' to serve Him in the future almost as if to make up for her mistakes. I understood her thought process - inherent in human nature if we don't guard against it. But I knew that I needed to tell her that she couldn't earn God's favour. I cautiously advised Caroline that her plans would surely fail if she didn't begin with God as her firm foundation. I suggested that she went back to the basics of her faith--confessing sin, repentance, reading the Bible, praying and finding a local church. On further discussion, she broke down. Seeing and feeling her pain and knowing what she was going through due to my own background I couldn't hold back so both of us ended up in tears. I looked around to see if we were being observed but everyone was preoccupied. I recalled the meaninglessness and emptiness of life without God and was desperate for Caroline really to hear the truth and be set free, but I knew that she had to make her own decision when the time was right. It appeared as if she really wanted to change and to re-commit her life to God. We hugged, prayed together and agreed to stay in touch before returning to face the other members of her family.

I accepted an invitation from Caroline's family to take me out to dinner, not realising at the time that I needed to take another crew member with me due to the policy for that port area. I guess I should've been paying more attention in the orientations. I rarely knew the official rules and relied on word of mouth a lot of the time. Caroline's relatives picked me up in a rather flashy four by four which surprised me as I hadn't realised they had money. I learned that her Filipino aunt, although a frequent visitor to the Philippines, actually lived in the USA having married an American. Caroline wasn't with them when they arrived; she had gone to school for some kind of review. I was thankful when she turned up. I hadn't been one hundred percent sure whether, in Filipino culture, it would have been acceptable for her just to leave me with her relatives for the evening. The four of us went to a shopping mall nearby to eat dinner. We passed un-fazed through the heavily guarded security checkpoint at the entrance. I still wasn't quite used to seeing large guns in the holsters of all of the numerous security guards dotted about. Most English police officers are unarmed so security guards definitely don't carry guns!

We settled on a Chinese restaurant, were seated and had received the menus. Caroline suddenly decided that she wanted to eat English food instead, having already asked a fair few questions of the staff who were waiting patiently for us to order. I was embarrassed and wondered if the display was somehow for my benefit to demonstrate an independent Western spirit. I hoped that was not the case and was concerned that our sudden switch would no doubt have left the Chinese staff perturbed and wondering what they had done wrong.

Having departed the 'unsuitable' Chinese restaurant and found a restaurant that served English food and suited Caroline, we again sat down and began perusing the menus. I wondered whether there would be further switching drama and waited apprehensively. Thankfully once was enough so we settled and placed our order. Our food arrived and we got stuck in; Caroline and I chatted as we ate.

During our meal, I suddenly became aware that Caroline's mum had disappeared. I hadn't noticed earlier due to being absorbed in conversation. At first I thought she must've been paying a visit to the restroom, but half an hour later, when she still hadn't returned, I asked Caroline with an appropriate level of concern whether she knew where her mother was and whether she was okay. Caroline hadn't been as worried as I had been probably being used to her mother's disappearing acts. She called her mum on her phone in order to respond to my question. On hearing the explanation, I stopped myself from loudly exclaiming, 'what!?' Her mother had gone grocery shopping without telling any of us - in the middle of our meal, leaving her food half eaten! I decided it must be a Filipino thing. She reappeared after some time looking slightly embarrassed, no doubt because of the stir that her absence had created.

As we continued eating, Caroline's aunt mentioned her desire to drop everything, including her numerous university degrees (as she just "loved studying"), her life in America, and presumably her husband, in order to join the ship as a crew member herself. I was a bit confused believing that an individual needed clear leading from God to become a missionary. I also feared that Logos Hope wasn't necessarily the best place for all those keen Filipinos. There was a lot of evangelistic opportunity in the Philippines (and in the USA where the Aunt already resided) and they had families who needed them at home. On the other hand I didn't want to discourage her zealous spirit.

I needn't have worried as, just as suddenly as the life changing decision had been verbalised, the conversation was dramatically switched to whether or not I wanted to go swimming with them the following day and how it could all be arranged. I informed them that regrettably I would be working. I wondered whether they too didn't have some form of work as they were remarkably free to ferry me around wherever I wished at the drop of a hat. "Most bizarre dinner experience ever" concluded, I returned to the ship, only feeling a little guilty about having inadvertently broken the accompaniment rule for the port of Cebu. I comforted myself that it was a genuine oversight and that I had at least been with other people, which was the safety reason for the restriction.

Fast forward a few years to 2014 when I was in the Philippines working as an independent missionary in Manila. I found myself invited to, and subsequently attending, Caroline's wedding as she married a Christian man in Cebu. Unfortunately, on arriving at the destination airport, I was informed that the wedding was about to be possibly, maybe, kind-of postponed! Apparently, the parents of the groom had suddenly changed their minds about the prospective union and had subsequently withdrawn their consent and financial support. But, the bride (Caroline) was adamant that she wanted to go ahead with the ceremony regardless.

Then followed a ludicrous request that would only ever be made in the Philippines. I, as the only foreigner invited to the wedding and therefore seen as somewhat of a 'Special Guest,' was asked by some of the family members of the Bride to communicate to her that maybe it was a good idea to postpone her wedding until the necessary permission could properly be obtained. The suggestion was that they would turn the wedding into an engagement party. At first I refused, my loyalties resting firmly with Caroline, who had of course invited me to the wedding in the first place. But seeing the mournful faces of the family members and realising the predicament they were in, eventually I relented and agreed to do my best. Theirs was a culture that shied away from any and all confrontation. I realised that I was perhaps the only person present able to have that conversation with Caroline, but I wasn't excited at the prospect. I felt a bit like I had landed in "bizarro" world for the day.

I whispered softly to the person standing next to me that I would like to speak to Caroline. She was by then adorned in her wedding gown having spent the best part of the day in preparation for the big event which, as far as she was concerned, was definitely going ahead as scheduled. My request was passed along and at length Caroline emerged and we ended up having one of the most awkward discussions of my life. It all took place just outside the make-up room and hopefully away from prying eyes and ears. I gave my best cold feet speech believing that she would in fact regret her next steps if she didn't heed my well-intentioned advice. I suppose I was looking at things from the perspective of being in her shoes. I wouldn't have wanted to marry someone whose family had withdrawn consent and who had refused to attend my wedding. But on the other hand, it sounded as if the reasons they had given may have been partly to do with the different classes of the couple and that they had another suitor in mind for their son. They had also waited until the very last minute to withdraw their support, which was clearly unfair and had created an impossible situation whichever way one looked at it.

Realistically I knew that Caroline wasn't going to cancel her wedding on the day and that I was just humiliating myself on behalf of her family. One of the main instigators of my involvement unexpectedly joined us during our conversation. I appealed for her support only for her to deny that she had made the request of me in the first place. I was indignant. She conveniently blamed the situation on another non-present family member. I had been abandoned and seemed to be fighting a battle on behalf of some unidentified persons. By that point I was emotionally exhausted and slightly bewildered by the entire fiasco. Caroline patiently waited for me to say my piece, calmly refuted all the points I had made, told me she was still going to get married and went back into the preparation room.

I went downstairs with Caroline's relatives who seemed to have accepted the inevitable - the wedding was going ahead. They acted as if nothing had happened and if I hadn't been party to the discussions I wouldn't have suspected anything was amiss; their behaviour was impeccable. The whole event became unbearably tense and difficult for me knowing what had gone before. It wasn't just some trifling decision - I had tried to talk a bride out of marrying her groom on her wedding day! Watching the ceremony, standing and smiling in the photographs, being called upon to give a speech during the reception, all the while knowing that I had just a few hours earlier been part of a failed plot to disrupt the entire occasion, was incredibly awkward. I was relieved when some of the groom's relatives had traipsed in just as the ceremony had been about to start. At least his entire family hadn't boycotted the day.

I left the wedding party early not wanting to string out the uncomfortable saga. I felt somewhat shell-shocked by what had occurred and hoped that my friendship with Caroline had not been damaged irreparably. She got in contact with me on social media a few months later and didn't mention the unmentionable. I will never forget what happened that day. My only consolation was that if, by some uncanny stroke of bad luck, I was ever asked to stop another wedding I could say in good conscience,

"You know what, do it yourself."

CHAPTER TWENTY-ONE

Emotionless Police

There was an emotional farewell to the large group of crew members who had reached the end of their two-year commitment. We then welcomed a slightly less substantial new batch of recruits in Cebu before preparing to sail to the capital Manila. I became a 'big sister' to Cat from England who, on being shown around, commented that my cabin was small. It was probably one of the largest cabins on board and she, being younger than I, was going to have to share with three other people rather than just one. I hastily pointed out that Ruth and I had a lot of clutter in our cabin in a somewhat clumsy attempt to reassure her.

I survived the PST Cebu welcome party during which I witnessed the most disgusting thing I had seen since my police days in the 'Toothpaste drama.' In a nutshell, a group of people inadvertently using the same cup of toothpaste water until one unlucky person at the end drinks the whole glass. I also saw it enacted for the public during one of our on-board events and wondered why it had been included as there was no spiritual benefit that I could see. At least with some of the other dramas they had a moral purpose. But generally, if I asked questions about that, I received comments like "Well it wasn't my idea" or "It was just a bit of fun." I decided that maybe I needed to lighten up a bit.

We had formed close relationships with the local volunteers who had been on board in Cebu. They lined the quayside with banners chanting our names and singing as we sailed away. As we entered or left any port as many crew members as possible were encouraged to gather on the different decks with their own countries' flags. It created quite a publicity spectacle as the big ship that was familiar to so many people arrived or departed with hundreds of people excitedly waving a multitude of different coloured and sized flags. The outward appearance of unity in the midst of such incredible diversity of cultures was difficult for non-believers to comprehend. How could a volunteer crew of so many nations not only work side by side in such a close environment but also keep the ship functioning with few professionally trained staff?

The Cebu street kids threw caution to the wind and in their excitement jumped into the water surrounding the ship. I heard one of the leaders remark with a touch of indignation "But I told them not to do that." Street children don't generally listen to instructions from adults when they are issued politely with no reward attached in the expectation of obedience.

We arrived safely in Manila after a very short time at sea; I was asked by our on-board Events team if I would be a guest speaker for a group of approximately two hundred Filipino Christian police officers. I knew they were probably mostly Catholic by background as that was the majority religion in the Philippines. I agreed with some trepidation. I wanted to challenge myself to speak publicly when necessary as I had never really conquered my fear in front of large audiences. Events asked me to share a relevant story about my police work in England.

I prayed about what to share with the officers. I decided on one humorous story and one story with a spiritual lesson relating to honesty because there was rampant police corruption in parts of Asia. Somebody else was teaching a Bible message. I related the true story that I had also shared in PST of the time when I mistook a sleeping tramp, who had been upside down sleeping in a narrow dirty staircase, for a dead body. I was a bit disconcerted when on concluding my story, which people usually found highly amusing, there was no reaction whatsoever. I looked around the room nervously whilst wondering if my speech had been presented with the setting on mute. I mean there was no face twitching, no smirking and no noise. Deathly silence with all eyes on me. I considered whether they had actually understood the story but it was too late to go over it and, as we all know, it's never funny when someone starts explaining their jokes.

With nothing to do but to move on, I became a bit shaky as I told my second story, thinking that the first had been an unmitigated disaster. I explained how I had lost my interest in money and material things by making a decision at work to do what I thought was right as a Christian even though some other colleagues were doing something different. I had decided not to use my police badge to obtain free train travel to and from work and instead to pay for my ticket each day. The decision had obviously cost me financially but it had also released my heart's grip on material things and I had held them loosely since making the decision. It had also given me an opportunity to witness practically to my astounded colleagues about my faith, showing them that I was willing to apply my beliefs to every area of my life.

I concluded the second story by reminding them that "If I really believe that God is there then I will act with integrity and honesty all the time, even if it means I will lose financially or materially as a result. I can rely on God to provide my needs." I explained that my situation had also reminded me of the verse found in 1 Samuel 2 vs 30 "Those that honour Me, I will honour."

I waited apprehensively although I was by then a little better prepared than previously. Again, no reaction. I wanted to say "Come on people, not even a small smile or nod for encouragement? I'm not expecting a standing ovation here."

I left the stage feeling like an utter failure but decided to watch the next person in line as he took the microphone, just to see what happened. I was expecting the contrast to be painful as they clapped and cheered him on. I was obviously relieved when there was no visible reaction to his performance either. But I wondered then whether the room was really full of people as it appeared to be or whether for some reason known only to the Events team we had been presenting to a large number of robots.

I returned to work in the I-café, having taken time off to take part in the event. I felt disappointed as I had put a fair bit of thought and prayer into my presentation and the passivity had made me very nervous. After a while some of the police came into the I-café and I saw that they were laughing and joking with each other. Witnessing that just made me feel worse as I realised that they were capable of showing emotion but had chosen to suppress it for my performance. Maybe it was all an exercise in humility.

My discouragement was short lived as I was swiftly approached by one of the leaders of OM Philippines who had organised the event. He had been looking for me in order to thank me for speaking at the event. He said that he could tell that my testimony had impacted the police. He thanked me for being open about my mistake and also for sharing my decision to act with integrity. He believed the stories would affect those present due to the parallels in their culture. The police tended to cover up their mistakes and many were taking bribes. I gratefully responded that I was relieved to hear what he said because I had noticed that there had been no visible reaction to the passionate and enthusiastic relating of my stories. He reassured me by stating that Filipino police are trained to be 'emotionless' and just to reflect on the things they are hearing passively without expressing a response. "How strange" I thought,

"Phew" I said.

CHAPTER TWENTY-TWO

Only in the Philippines

I received a red heart with the words 'Happy Balentine' on February 14th 2012. (Filipinos pronounce their v's as b's.) A group of us then arranged to go ice skating at a local rink as it was our day off. The idea had originated with Frank who, during a Ship Family Night, had asked Jenny, another of our number, if she would go with him. The question had unfortunately been posed like some kind of date and so Jenny had responded in the negative. In actual fact, there was already a group going and Frank was just being friendly. Jenny looked totally confused when Frank commented that she had broken his heart by her refusal. Continuing the 'love' theme Silas from Germany then asked Eumpa from South Korea how to ask someone in Korean "Will you marry me?" Eumpa flushed with embarrassment and after umming and ahhing for a while said "It's kind of difficult!" Eumpa also told Brian that he had a small head and that she "didn't like it." Brian took it in his stride and joked that he could try removing it or covering it up. Those were the type of bizarre discussions that took place at Ship Family Night as the cultures intermingled and we all learned to laugh at ourselves and not to take offence easily.

Frank's English had definitely improved remarkably by that stage, although he still went around saying to people "Thank you for your hard working." On the occasions when he didn't understand relatively simple conversations I exclaimed seriously and with a trace of urgency "Frank, what's happened to your English?" which inevitably resulted in him looking firstly like a deer caught in the headlights and then as if he were being harassed, before saying "Sorry, sorry," with a bewildered expression on his face.

At the skating rink, things were going well as I whizzed around, gaining in confidence with every stride. Until Frank who, unbeknown to me had been skating behind me, suddenly shouted my name. The resultant jump of shock and automatic swivelling of my head to see who it was, was beyond my abilities whilst keeping my balance. I fell flat on my face on the ice with a resounding bang echoing around the rink, prompting a few concerned skating coaches to come rushing over to try to help me up. My pride was dented more than anything else, although I was winded by the impact and discovered serious bruises later on. I was extremely grateful when Frank came to my rescue apologising profusely in his heavily accented English. Taking full responsibility, he repeated over and over "I'm so sorry my sister." I let him carry on for a while, in the hope that people would at least know that I wasn't a complete klutz as my accident had been caused by someone else.

A group of five of us also decided to try to go swimming - different country new possibilities and maybe no jelly or stonefish. We walked to a big building in the city centre that had a sign outside advertising activities including swimming, a bird show and a sea lion show. The staff politely informed us that we would only be able to swim between the animal shows as they needed the pool for the animals. No, it wasn't a joke, they were definitely serious. I had visions of the animals climbing out of the water and exchanging greetings with us as we got in like a scene from a Disney movie. Intrigued, we purchased tickets for the next available people swimming slot noting that our tickets were labelled 'Swimming and Fun.'

The pool was a strip of water stretching through the centre of the giant open roofed stadium from one end of the building to the other. It must've been over fifty metres in length but was very narrow, probably around just two or three metres wide. Relieved to see that the animals had vacated prior to our entrance, we noticed immediately that there were at least a hundred Filipinos sitting in the stands of the auditorium. As we entered the water and began larking around with each other we quickly became the centre of attention. White people swimming for the entertainment of the locals, or that must've been how it appeared. Some of them moved nearer to the edge of the water or stood up in order to take photos of us. Knowing that we would never see those people again and finding their fascination with us hilarious, a few of us began to dance and pose in the water. After a while we realised that the people would never tire of our antics and may well stay there all day. I felt like we were part of an exhibit in a zoo. We tested the nearby Jacuzzi which proved colder than the pool itself. Having enjoyed our unusual swimming experience, we headed back to the ship.

Back on board we were telling our swimming story to a couple of guys who had just returned to the ship having spent the day searching unsuccessfully for a slum to visit. My outrage grew as their tale progressed and I couldn't wait to ask them the question, "What on earth were you doing trying to visit a slum in the first place? We were specifically told in orientation NOT to visit or go near any of the slum areas!" One of the guys breathed defiance as he commented that he hadn't been at the orientation, as if that justified the obviously deliberate rule breaking.

Those were the types of conversation that made me realise what a difficult job the leadership had keeping law and order on-board and why the rules were continually re-emphasised. Although the rules were sometimes frustrating there was generally a reason for them; Manila was not as safe as Cebu. Another crew member had already discovered that having been robbed of a necklace at knifepoint soon after our arrival. I only knew the details as she had approached me after the event to ask for self-defence techniques having chased the robbers up the road. Fortunately, they had continued running away and she had failed to catch them. I told her how foolish she had been - chasing several knife wielding robbers in a foreign country whilst she was alone. Refusing to offer her advice, I asked instead whether her jewellery was worth losing her life for as that could easily have been what ended up happening.

CHAPTER TWENTY-THREE

Smokey Mountain

I had received my first real dose of poverty in Cebu whilst playing with and ministering to the street children. But I was about to realise that it could get worse, a lot worse. We had been warned about 'Smokey Mountain,' a huge rubbish dump where people made their home. In fact, as mentioned already, we had been refused permission to visit the location or anywhere like it without a local guide who knew what they were doing. It could be dangerous and foreigners might become targets for robbery or even end up being taken as hostages for ransom demands.

It's probably human nature automatically to want to go somewhere that you are not allowed. But in that case I really wasn't sure, I knew that I might see things that could not be erased from my mind. I knew that from working in the police and absolutely refusing to view any images of child pornography as it wasn't part of my role. Some officers wanted us to view them as a training exercise to get us used to the work. But I refused repeatedly on the basis that I didn't want to see anything that might end up churning around in my thoughts, unless it was mandatory.

I wasn't sure about going to 'Smokey Mountain' as a tourist in order to "have the experience", when there were no plans for us to carry out ministry there. Surely, we would feel desperately helpless and was it right for us to traipse into the homes and lives of the people there just to have a look at their situation? They were people, not artefacts in a museum or paintings in an art gallery. Having had the concerns and discussed them with a few people, I joined the group on the basis that I personally was by that point thinking of returning to the Philippines for future ministry. I definitely knew that I wanted to work with those in poverty in the future, possibly living amongst them, so I decided that I needed to get a real idea about what it would be like. I was still slightly afraid of what I might see.

We were escorted by a local guide who led us at first to the original 'Smokey Mountain' which hadn't received 'fresh' rubbish for ten years. We climbed up a steep embankment to reach the dwellings and saw slight evidence of life on reaching the top of the hill. Most of the people had moved on when the government discontinued dumping garbage at the location. The reason they lived there in the first place was to scavenge in the trash for food and other items to make a pitiful living. There were fifty-four families still living at the first location; they had been granted permission from the government to stay there. I thought it was crazy that anyone would need permission to stay somewhere like that but that was the reality of their situation. The government exercised tight control even in places where it looked as if they had abandoned the people to squalor, disease and a probable early death. The people's homes were made of wooden planks nailed together, sometimes with tin on the roofs. Inside they were filthy with mud and other dirt caked on the floor. Some had chickens and other small animals wandering around. People and animals alike were skeletal and desperately hungry. Hopelessness was written across their faces. The only advantage to living in that location as far as I could see was that the air was probably fresher than if the site had been on lower ground.

Shockingly, I had heard that whenever a foreign dignitary or other such important person, for example the Pope, was visiting the Philippines, the government rounded up all of the squatters and slum dwellers in the area in advance of the visit. They were placed temporarily in luxurious accommodation; their homes having been permanently destroyed so that they didn't blight the landscape for the special visit. However, after all the ceremony and pomp was over and the famous person had departed, the people were tossed back out onto the street. Their circumstances, though difficult before, had become totally diabolical. They had no food, shelter or clothing and no dignity with which to begin again, having been treated worse than animals. Their country's image on the world stage was the priority for the authorities and corruption was rife.

After meeting the first group of people, next we visited the illegal trash dumping area that was in use, 'Smokey Mountain' itself. We were not allowed to go into the area containing the mountains of rubbish, but we could see small children swarming all over the mounds looking for items to eat or sell. Many of the children had swollen stomachs due to malnutrition.

An old man agreed to show us the area where the people lived. We followed him along alleyways and down narrow pathways where there was sewage strewn around. There were thousands of people living there as evidenced by the wooden shack houses, most of which were slightly elevated from the ground on wooden stilts. The stilts were due to the site being virtually on top of a polluted water source. The smell was dreadful. We followed our guide through an area that was so dense with smoke that I started to cough and gasp for air. I covered my face with my T-shirt but still couldn't breathe and became desperate to get out of the smoke. I was horrified at that moment to see people including children living in the middle of the smoky area. Having moved through the worst of it, which was coming from some burning rubber nearby, the leader declared solemnly that there were a lot of respiratory and eye problems in that area. Hardly surprising. There were also flies everywhere and the condition of some of the animals was truly revolting.

Adults, including the very elderly who looked as if they could barely walk let alone carry sacks loaded with garbage, were diligently collecting rubbish items that would be saleable. I noted that almost everything from the original garbage disposal was being collected for reuse or sale and that the people were sorting the filthy rubbish with their bare hands. They were then dragging their bags to a water source for cleaning prior to sale. A huge bag of plastic recyclables might earn them five pesos (ten pence.)

I smiled cautiously and said hello to the people we passed, lightly touching the children to show warmth. Most responded positively by smiling in return, although some looked as if they were in a daze. Some of the children followed us along holding our hands. They asked for our names and then thanked us for speaking to them. The gratitude was humbling as we had done nothing worthy of thanks. The cheeriness of the majority of the people contrasted with their surroundings made our visit more bearable in an odd way but also more terrible on reflection. At times my original fears were realised and I felt like a rich Westerner gawping at the poverty. For that reason, I didn't want to take any photographs, but others in our number took many. Incredibly there was a church in the middle of the slum and it was full of people who were just sitting inside it as they had nowhere else to go and nothing else to do.

My most vivid memory is of an area of dirty water about four metres square. We came across it after walking for a long time along an extremely narrow ledge of wood next to the polluted river. There were shack houses next to us all the way along and we were walking within feet of the people's homes. We could see right into the dwellings, which I found very awkward as it felt like we were definitely invading what little privacy they might have been expecting. There were adults just lying inside staring into space or some were probably high on cheap substances. But the small area of water was a different story. Although it was full of rubbish and clearly polluted, there were numerous happy smiling children of all ages swimming around in the middle. They shouted to us joyfully as we stood and watched them. There were even dogs swimming about. We balanced on wooden planks that we had walked along to reach them. I wondered whether they were even aware of the dangers of disease. But most slum dwellers just lived for one day at a time. I suspected that life expectancy was short.

Reflecting afterwards, I knew that I wouldn't be able to forget what I had seen, nor should I. I found it difficult to spend money on anything for a while after the visit as it really put the trivial things that I valued into perspective. The most frustrating thing about our visit was being unable to offer the people hope. I'm sure there were longer term workers regularly visiting and there was obviously a church providing some light in a very dark place. I knew that it would really require dedicated workers to get in amongst the hopeless people, maybe even living there in order for the Gospel message to ring true.

On a deeper level and perhaps surprisingly, I found parallels with my earlier life as a police officer. I had left the police to become a missionary partly because I felt that I couldn't share the Gospel adequately in the police due to restrictions on free speech, although I could share with my colleagues. I had followed God's leading to the ship but was unable to share openly in our first country of Malaysia due to the law, which more particularly applied when sharing with

Muslims. In our second country of Singapore we were able to share openly but the people weren't listening. And, in our third country of the Philippines, we were unable to share due to the language barrier. I was beginning to realise that being on the ship wouldn't necessarily give me any more opportunities to share my faith than I had had in the police. It was a sobering moment.

I began to think instead about why God had led me to the ship. I thought about the friendships I had formed on-board and the connections I had had with some visitors. I was reminded that Christian ministry is about quality not quantity and that God wants us to follow the leading of His Holy Spirit when witnessing, not just to place ourselves where we are likely to succeed or see mass conversions. God is concerned with individuals and is looking for humble people whom He can use, not those who already have their own plans and purposes. Those were tough lessons that I continued to dwell on during my time on board and tried to apply them to my life and when making decisions.

CHAPTER TWENTY-FOUR

Faithful in Small Things

Looking back, our first months in the Philippines (before dry dock) was the time when I had a lot of ministry experiences that impacted and shaped me spiritually. I learned the practical importance of being faithful in small things and the necessity of keeping the focus of our ministry on sharing the Gospel.

They may sound like basic lessons, but on a ship with four hundred missionaries there could be an unhelpful tendency to want to compete for 'success' in terms of numbers of conversations or even numbers of conversions. The root is of course pride, but it was sometimes hard to resist in a community where we were encouraged to share our achievements in order to encourage, build up and inspire others. That was particularly evident during events like 'Port Praise' at the end of each port - a ship community meeting during which people took the stage to share their ministry stories. I wish I could say that we all listened appreciatively throughout, but there was sometimes the inevitable - I wish I had done or been involved in that. Then there were individuals who regularly stood up and proudly announced that a large number of people had been 'converted' during their recent visit to such and such a place, although, details of the mass conversions tended to be lacking on attempts to corroborate the stories afterwards. There was also a problem with follow-up practices which, if they existed, were often less than ideal.

One of my ongoing spiritual struggles on Logos Hope (and probably in life) was finding the right balance between help and hope ministries. I continue to feel strongly about the issue. I believe that it is one way that the enemy keeps us distracted - causing us to invest our time and money in helping people but often in the process forgetting about or side-lining their spiritual welfare. I made it my resolve to ensure that in any programme over which I had influence, assuming it was legal in that country, the Gospel would take centre stage. We can help a person practically but what of their soul?

Other people didn't always see things like that, their culture having taught them that "You can share God's love with a smile" and "Share the Gospel, use words if you have to." Some people used those phrases as justification for not going further or being more direct with the Gospel. The underlying reasons were wide ranging but I believe included: cowardice, fear of causing offence or losing a friendship, over-sensitivity to cultural etiquette and an inability to articulate their beliefs. In the worst cases, there were probably even those who wanted to obtain a shallow acceptance of the Gospel as their only goal was to add another soul to their list of conversions. The latter probably knew deep down that if they explained the Gospel in a clearer fashion asking a person to count the cost of following Jesus they might reject the idea. Sometimes it seemed to have become a lot about numbers and the individual person being ministered to had been lost. That, in turn, had led to a lack of compassion or true concern for a person's eternal welfare - hearing of a conversion, or in many cases multiple conversions, no longer made the heart of a believer jump for joy but instead became the norm and almost like 'old news.'

My personal reflection on the oft-quoted mantras led to an important question, "How can they know it's God's love if we don't also tell them?" A well-known speaker had helpfully already changed the second popular slogan to read "Share the Gospel, always use words." His point was that God has chosen the foolishness of preaching to bring people into His Kingdom. It is God's method - He will only bless and reward that which He has ordained.

On the more positive side, some crew members did make the effort to stay in touch with those they had ministered to and some churches eagerly received those who were sincerely seeking. People obviously did become Christians through the ministry of Logos Hope and details of their conversions were still a joy to hear. It was a blessing to have some leaders during my time on-board who were inclined to listen to suggestions for small improvements that could be made to ensure we were presenting the Gospel to people at any and every opportunity.

I used what I was learning personally to prepare to give a devotional talk one day for the staff of a Christian bookshop. Another crew member Matt, from England, was due to give the main message and I didn't know what he would be sharing. I was a little apprehensive, honestly, as Matt could be a bit of a joker and I didn't know whether he even had a serious side.

During a ship family event just prior to our joint ministry day we had arrived on an island for a relaxing day of swimming and snorkelling. On the island, there was a school that appeared to be in session but, on peeping through the doorway, we had discovered that the teacher was temporarily absent. Matt, seizing the opportunity, had confidently walked to the front of the class, apologised for being late and begun teaching the Filipino children. The children had immediately acknowledged him as their teacher, probably because of the respect they always gave to foreigners. They began paying close attention to everything he said. We were all in stitches outside the door. Fortunately, when the actual teacher returned, she saw the funny side. But on removing himself from the front of the class, having seen that their teacher was a pretty young lady, Matt had, by that point, gone a light shade of red. I wondered if his embarrassment had taught him a lesson, but I guessed that he would probably do the same thing if given the same opportunity again.

So you can see why I was slightly worried about working side by side with Matt in a ministry situation. I began by sharing what God had been teaching me through my ship experiences by using four main points

    1. That I couldn't do anything in my own strength; I had become very aware of that especially with my ongoing health issues.

    2. That I must be willing for God to use me.

    3. That if I was faithful in small things then that could lead to bigger things.

    4. That only God would know a lot of the things that I did for Him.

God was teaching and convicting me using verses like Colossians 3 vs 23-24

"Whatever you do, work heartily, as for the Lord and not for men, knowing that from the Lord you will receive the inheritance as your reward. You are serving the Lord Christ."

And Psalm 118 vs 8-9

"It is better to take refuge in the Lord than to trust in man. It is better to take refuge in the Lord than to trust in princes."

I was somewhat relieved to see that Matt did have a serious side as he shared from James chapter 3 with the question, "Who is steering the ship?" He was well-prepared and breathed sincerity as he espoused a challenging message. I was astonished by the tie-in with what I had said, although it shouldn't have been a surprise as we had prayed for team unity and a coherent message. I was encouraged that God had been at work and was leading that meeting. Afterwards we chatted with the staff who had been challenged by our presentation.

Before leaving the shop we obviously had to check out the books in their shop thoroughly to size up the local competition - Logos Hope being primarily a literature ministry. It was a serious consideration in some ports where book shops could lose all of their custom during our visit. Sometimes the ship gave donations of books to make up the losses for local Christian bookshops. There was even a shop that obtained permission to move their stock on-board in one port and began selling alongside us. We tried to do what we could to work in partnership with local ministries but it was difficult due to the temporary nature of our work in each place. We hoped that the businesses would be able to see the spiritual benefit and allow that to supersede the business concerns, but it was easy for us to say that. It was their livelihood and they were poor countries.

CHAPTER TWENTY-FIVE

Spiritual Sight

One C day I had a great opportunity to lead a team for eye-glass ministry in Manila in a women's prison. The ship had partnered with a group who supplied free reading glasses to those in deprived areas who needed them. Crew members were trained to test the eyesight of recipients using basic equipment. They used a series of lenses and then asked the person to read a Bible verse or the Bible itself through the lens to test their clarity of vision. The crew also attempted to get the people into discussion as they went through the testing process.

Many people were delighted with their glasses as they were finally able to read, sometimes having been unable to for years. We couldn't help everyone as some needed more urgent treatment or operations to remove cataracts. We referred those people to specialists, hospitals or eye clinics for follow-up treatment. But often they couldn't afford to pay for the treatment so they remained partially sighted or blind. That was the most difficult thing about the type of ministry - the hope as the person waited patiently for their diagnosis and the disappointment on learning that we were unable to help them personally. Sometimes they couldn't understand and thought that we were rejecting them as an individual as they saw all their friends receive glasses. We tried to make our explanations clear but they didn't always believe us.

We were a large team of eight (usually the teams were four or five.) The first thing we discovered having assembled on the quayside was that we were locked out of our van. We took turns twiddling a piece of wire in the door lock to try to jimmy it open. For some reason, everyone thought I would be skilled in that department having worked in the police. I explained that usually the UK police aren't going around breaking into things as I failed in my endeavour. Eventually one of the guys succeeded after switching to using a knife.

Our early morning woes had not yet been concluded. We were finally on the move, having piled into the back of the van, when the tail gate flew open and we nearly lost a member of our team out of the back door. We hastily rescued the person and someone held onto the broken door for the rest of the journey as the driver didn't seem inclined to stop to mend the vehicle or ensure the safety of his passengers for the duration.

On arrival at the prison, our Filipino driver, having spent an age manoeuvring into a parking space to allow us to alight, then promptly reversed into a tree. He joined us in having a good laugh about it but there were those of us who were scratching our heads and wondering why he had reversed the vehicle at all as he had already parked in a suitable spot. The amusing scene ended with two women dressed in prison garb appearing as if from nowhere, hacking away at the damaged tree, removing a large offending branch and disappearing again as quickly as they had arrived. We managed to put the strange occurrence out of our minds as we proceeded towards the prison entrance.

We were partnering with another organisation, Operation Blessing, for the ministry. There were some familiar faces as we had partnered with them quite regularly in the Philippines. But there was a big debate during the planning stage as they wanted to do things differently from our anticipated programme. They wanted to check the eyes of the women but to hold off giving them their glasses. Local church members would issue them in due course. I consulted my team about that and in the end, we made the difficult decision to reject the suggestion. We were concerned that it might appear that we were putting 'religious pressure' on the women or even offering bribes or incentives for them to receive a visit from the members of a local church. We wanted our gift to be a free gift without conditions. The situation had arisen because the church members who had wanted to be involved had not been able to accompany us on the day that had been chosen for the ministry due to other commitments.

However, I also wanted to ensure that the evangelistic zeal which may have been the reason for the suggestion wasn't lost in the rebuff. We reassured our partners that we also wanted the Gospel to be central and that time could and should be taken to chat with the women about Jesus. We made sure that every woman we spoke to was given a copy of John's Gospel (in the local language) and prayed with, in addition to having their eyes tested and receiving their glasses.

They were also offered additional counselling by the Operation Blessing team in a separate room. Initially they had insisted that all of the women partake whether they wanted to or not. But we received reports of groups of women sitting in silence in the room because they didn't want to be there or had nothing to say. Women also complained to us asking whether they couldn't just get their glasses and go, rather than waiting in the long queue for counselling which they didn't want and didn't need. The women doing the counselling were also feeling pressurised to get through everyone by the end of the day and were rushing those who really needed assistance. It reminded me of what can happen in a Doctor's surgery in England when they have just ten minute slots but someone needs an hour and someone else thirty seconds. After some healthy debate, the arrangement was amended to everyone's satisfaction. We had worked through it - flexibility was the key.

We tested over two hundred women, most of whom received free reading glasses. One woman was overjoyed that she could finally read her Bible after such a long time. I was humbled that that had been her main objective in getting the glasses. If only everyone had been looking at life through that lens.

Our team worked well together; everyone got involved and showed a genuine love and concern for the women. Unfortunately, our visit was again overshadowed by internal politics as, towards the end of the day, I was summoned to meet with a senior prison official. I was asked to explain why we were only planning to hand out two hundred pairs of glasses. Apparently, our Line Up team (that had arranged the visit) had promised one thousand! I pointed out that there were just under two thousand prisoners at the jail and that it was unlikely that half of those would even *need* reading glasses. It didn't seem to register as a legitimate reason. I had already observed that sometimes the more we gave people the more they seemed to expect. I was surprised that the official didn't seem to be at all embarrassed to be having a conversation like that with me in a shame culture where conflict is generally avoided. Even in England, where people are more used to demanding their rights, I can't imagine a situation like that occurring. We were a Christian charity giving freely to the prisoners.

The official continued to insist that we arrange a further visit in order to fulfil the promise that I personally had no knowledge of. I explained that I couldn't make that decision and that my team members had work commitments on the ship. I asked them to speak directly to our Line Up team about the situation. At one point the meeting atmosphere became so tense I thought they were going to keep me hostage until I agreed to return on subsequent days. Our partners from Operation Blessing then decided to compromise and started giving out our leftover frames to the remaining women who had yet to receive glasses so that they could purchase their own lenses. I didn't want to make a big fuss after what had already transpired but I had to put a stop to that practice as well knowing that other teams might need the frames for ministry at other locations later in the week.

I was grateful to have had a supportive team for the eye-glass ministry. Being team leader with all of those decisions and problems had been quite stressful. Maybe the enemy had been trying to stop us presenting the Gospel to the women by causing internal divisions. But we knew that our struggle was not against flesh and blood. Afterwards, when we had returned to the ship, we debriefed and discussed the response of the women. It had really been a great day of ministry despite the wrangling. We were encouraged by the prospect of how God might use all the conversations that had been had, prayers that were offered and all of the Gospels that had been safely deposited in the prison with the ladies, perhaps for years to come.

CHAPTER TWENTY-SIX

Subic Dry Dock

'Subic Dry Dock' became a seemingly never ending nightmare for most people as it continued day after day, week after week and month after month. It had been intended to last for two and a half months and it was carefully explained to us at the outset what the plan was and how long each stage would take. A combination of factors meant that we ended up in dry dock for a total of nine months during which time some key personnel left the project, sometimes citing "irreconcilable differences" in working practices. I wasn't sure whether the differences related to the working practices of different crew members (who, don't forget, consisted of sixty-five nationalities in the first place) or the local Filipino dry dock workers vs the Engine leadership team, which consisted largely of men from Holland and Germany. It was probably a recipe for disaster as you would be hard pressed to find countries with cultural and working practices more different from each other.

Despite all that, to which we remained largely oblivious at the time, all was not lost from my perspective as I ended up taking part in some of the most memorable ministry on shore for much of the period. Maybe I'm getting a bit ahead of myself here because the ministry I refer to - working with street children addicted to a solvent called 'rugby,' has been extensively documented in my previous book *They're Rugby Boys, Don't You Know*? (For those who have read the book already, I'm not planning to re-hash the details here but there may be a slight overlap in content for the sake of those who haven't.)

When the ship first went into dry-dock for repairs I was initially kept amused by the various signs that had been erected, probably to abide by the numerous Health and Safety rules for the dry dock period. With a community of mostly non-English speakers required to speak (and sign) in English there were some amusing ones.

"Please let this door always close" was probably my favourite, as if the door had a personality and will of its own that we humans might be in danger of frustrating. But the award for "most indecipherable" definitely goes to the Swiss Chef's sign on the Bakery Storeroom freezer:

"This freezer is only for the bakery, galley and Store-Keepers. All other "staff" we bring in the dining room for everybody!!! They will be excited. Please check the door is colse." On looking at it carefully for quite some time I decided that he meant that only certain staff were allowed to go into and remove 'stuff' from the freezer and not that there were people living in the freezer and that the ship's community would be excited when they were brought out to the dining room to be eaten. There was also a printed message on the cockroach bait stating "Roach bait - do not eat" as if that might be a temptation for someone.

Work-wise during dry dock I was first tasked with cleaning the store-rooms and baggage locker (where the crew suitcases and extra dry food were kept.) I quickly became completely covered in thick black dust as a result. I was so dirty that, on seeing me, the ship's Captain asked if there had been an explosion on board. I remarked that I was surprised that he hadn't heard about it already. I informed another crew member, who looked to be similarly shocked by my appearance, that I had been sweeping chimneys. I was amused when they didn't bat an eyelid seeming to accept the explanation even though we were living on a ship. I joked with someone that Trevor was leaving me all the hard and dirty work. Co-Store-Keeper Trevor, who had been present during my comment, and had laughed along, later took me to one side and revealed his sensitivity by asking me whether I really believed he would do that. I hastily apologised for my blunt British humour and decided to be more careful in future.

I hadn't been that motivated to take on the cleaning tasks knowing that people were still working and welding. I protested that we should wait until the dry dock had concluded and then clean everything. But my protests fell on deaf ears. I wondered if at that time it had been more a case of trying to keep people busy as there were too many crew and not enough jobs.

Trevor eventually confronted me accusing me of planting the words "is this really necessary?" in the minds of some of our younger team leaders who had subsequently gone and checked that very thing with the managers higher up. I was amused that Trevor, knowing me quite well by that point, had observed that the thought must have originated with me and that he had had the nerve to challenge me about it.

In the store-room I managed to drop a full box of small jam punnets into a gaping hole in the floor. Apparently, it was the entrance to one of the large and relatively empty fresh water tanks which had been left open that day probably due to being cleaned. I watched helplessly as the box, having slipped out of my hands as I was re-arranging food items, disappeared from view. After a few seconds of panic, I decided not to worry about it as someone working in the tank would surely find and retrieve it at a future juncture.

I walked into the store-room a few days later to find a group of senior ship personnel gathered around the soggy and mangled punnets and trying to decide what to do about them. The men wore very grave expressions. At first I was bemused wondering why the solemn faces, they couldn't be worried about the waste of a few punnets of jam could they? I was reluctant to admit my involvement in case I had committed a cardinal sin of some sort, or it had caused a problem with the mechanics of the ship. Although I didn't see, even with my extremely basic technical knowledge, how that would have been a possibility. The decision was made for me in the end when one of the men, still wearing that same serious expression, informed me that they thought the local Filipino dry dock workers had stolen the jam and had hidden the punnets in the fresh water tank for collection at a later date!

Of course, I couldn't stay silent at that point and, despite my embarrassment on owning up to being the culprit, was glad they saw the funny side. A few days later I asked one of the crew whether they had found any further jam punnets and he casually replied "Why, did you throw any more down there?" which quickly shut me up.

My semi-claustrophobia became more of a problem during the dry dock as I tried and failed to take part in several jobs in the nether-regions of the ship. We were expected to join in wherever help was required which sometimes resulted in some bizarre dynamics, like the day the engineers and deck workers (majority men) joined a line of people throwing unboxed tampons, sanitary pads and nappies along the line until they reached the storeroom.

I was assigned to the FLEX (flexible) team working in the engine room. That included wire brushing in a tank with a face mask, goggles, ear protectors, huge gloves and other safety equipment. The donning and use of the protective items was more rigorously monitored after one girl wire-brushed her face. It sounds careless but it was easy to do as the machines were pretty heavy and controlling them when tiring towards the end of a day wasn't straightforward. We were blessed that there were not more accidents of that nature and that none of the sustained injuries were major. I thought I was going to be ill when heading down into a confined space like that of a tank. I coped with the first one that I was assigned to because I was right next to the tank entrance and could see some light from above, but I struggled to breathe properly due to the heavy equipment. In the end my wire brush turned out to be faulty. I hadn't been making much headway anyway due to the rust being high up on the wall and my arms being too weak for any lengthy activity. So, I was relieved to be removed to lighter duties.

I had at times been praying for the strength to do the job thinking I was useless. Despite the prayer, I was still having to stop every few seconds. I was also scared of the equipment which didn't help. I went to my cabin every lunch time, removed all of my heavy work clothes and lay down exhausted. Afterwards, I figured that it must have been the close conditions combined with my thyroid issues that had made me so ineffective. I was able to do some of the work at times in less confined conditions where there was fresh air to breathe. I was amazed by the energy and stamina of a few of the smaller girls who worked tirelessly at their tasks day by day. I felt guilty that I was unable to do the work I was needed for and kept thinking that maybe I should offer to go back in the tanks. But most of the other tanks were at the end of narrow tunnels and the thought of it filled me with fear and apprehension.

Therefore, I was assigned tank watch duty. I had to watch others disappear into the black hole of a tank entrance that they could just squeeze into. The worst one I recall had its entrance underneath a large, floor to ceiling boiler or electrical unit which was extremely loud. The person had to climb into a black hole feet first. The hole measured about three feet in diameter. The person shimmied in and then on through another entrance that was also pitch black. I'm told there were overhead pipes inside the tunnel that they could use to pull themselves along as they lay on their backs in the darkness. There was a big, transparent, plastic tube attached to a machine containing oxygen inserted into the hole after the person. It was also noisy and nearly blocked the entire entrance so I couldn't see anything beyond the tunnel entrance. When the person wanted to come out they shook the tube and I had to move it so they could get out. They remained in the tanks for up to two hours at a time wire brushing, hammering, painting and doing other things. They reappeared covered in welding dust.

Honestly, watching them go in made me feel nauseous and anxious but definitely caused me to take my tank watch duty seriously. I prayed fervently for their safety and that they would come out again. I had heard horror stories (not from within the ship ministry) about people being trapped in tanks like those. Some had died from a lack of oxygen due to a miscommunication meaning they had been shut inside the tank, or when a sudden medical problem had developed whilst they were inside.

Most of the tanks were underneath the metal floor panels which had to be removed to access them. During dry dock, which felt a bit chaotic at times, there were too many tanks being worked in at any one time for warning signs to be placed. So, we learned to avoid disappearing into the deep black recesses of the gaping holes by being careful where we walked! Revolutionary. Although I avoided falling into one of the many unguarded holes, I did somehow manage to injure myself by getting my hand caught in a rotating metal fan bruising all of my fingers. But that was a relatively minor inconvenience.

In addition to tank watch, I was assigned 'fire watch' duty whilst people were welding. But it became a disappointingly pointless task from my perspective. When there actually was a fire it was expediently extinguished with a fire blanket before I could move a muscle. I guessed that allowing the fire to spread in order to make me feel slightly more useful by being able to put it out wasn't on the agenda.

I spent several days using a vice and knife to cut clothing into engine rags. Whilst I was diligently working, a large circular heavy steel thing about six inches in diameter flew off someone else's machine right next to me. It travelled past the back of my head and landed on the other side of the workshop in the vicinity of another five people. We all looked around, then stood for a minute in stunned silence, realising that any type of contact at that height could have killed one of us. We thanked God for his protection.

The other guys started jokingly carrying around large metal sheets as shields whenever they were near to the work space of the guy who had made the faux pas. He didn't seem bothered by their mockery or indeed by the incident itself. I, on the other hand, deciding that I needed my head for full-time mission work, casually moved myself away from the offending machine, and the inexperienced engineer.

CHAPTER TWENTY-SEVEN

Fitness Fanatics

One of the things that most people struggled with whilst living on board was keeping fit, notably during dry dock. The girls were warned that by the end of their Logos Hope service they would likely have gained weight. I ended up losing about two stone due to a combination of illness, stress and my stomach eventually rejecting the food offered. At that point I felt a bit like the Israelites in the desert when they rejected the 'manna' that God provided as I had never been a fussy eater. As with most exercise regimes, I had started off well with gym schedules and plans to join the competitive sports teams. But, on seeing that the gym was tiny (literally) and usually occupied by several male fitness fanatics working on their abs, my motivation had waned somewhat. One such reformed fanatic remarked in his final farewell speech to the ship's company that he had become convicted about the priority he had been placing on his exercise regime and had decided to read Christian books instead. He pointed out that "physical training is of some value but spiritual training is of eternal value."

I shared the views of the speaker and definitely preferred reading to any type of exercise but I knew that I should make the effort for the sake of my health. I joined a few basketball games but found that they consisted largely of male participants and I struggled to learn and apply the rules. I was used to playing netball where you can't run with or bounce the ball. I often found myself hesitating when in possession of the ball for that second too long as my brain reminded me "this is basketball." But there was really no time for whirring cogs and dallying. By the point I was ready to go, I had inevitably been tackled and the ball had been removed from my possession.

When I did get more involved in the game I found the guys were very polite and considerate, at times treating me like a delicate flower rather than a serious adversary. When one of them did manage to crash into me, knocking me off my feet and causing me to brace myself for the inevitable impact with the cold concrete surface, he somehow managed quick as a flash to manoeuvre himself into a seemingly impossible position, so that he could catch me in his arms just before impact, before placing me back on my feet. It had all happened before too many people had observed the slight red flush that had appeared on my face due to the romantic appearance of the scenario, but not before the other guys had started to tease him.

The game was eventually abandoned when the ball repeatedly bounced off into the nearby sea. After initially using a ship net to fish it out, the guys then 'borrowed' the Coastguard's boat in order to recover it for the second time. But on the third occasion our fun came to an end as they had run out of creative ideas for a rescue mission. Honestly, I think the guys had been enjoying recovering the ball more than the game itself.

Usually, Joan and I played basketball together on the quayside after noticing a lone hoop ready and waiting. We mostly shot hoops, placing the standing line farther and farther away from the post and lobbing the ball with less and less chance of accuracy. It was all very well until the ship was in a busier port and the area behind the net had become a carpark for the ship's visitors. The visitors watched apprehensively as we played our reckless game, only once or twice hitting parked vehicles and fortunately, more by luck than judgement, not causing any damage. Sadly, not all sporting events ended safely as we were reminded when we were informed that some of our crew had been playing basketball with some local youths. One of the lads had fallen, hit his head on the concrete and had to be rushed to hospital suffering concussion.

I also joined our PST Penang football team for a brief spell, managing to shock everyone by scoring a goal. But I quickly realised that it wasn't really my game so confined myself to watching from the sidelines for the big matches. The guys always took those things far too seriously and I was scared I might get run down or berated if I missed a shot!

I didn't have the exercise dilemma and whether or not to get seriously involved in ship sports teams for very long. Soon after entering dry dock I was informed I would be joining several teams that would be sent away from the ship for the remainder of the dry dock period.

CHAPTER TWENTY-EIGHT

Dasmarinas Challenge Team

I had been assigned to a Challenge Team which was to take place whilst we were still in Subic Dry Dock in the Philippines. We were placed in random groups (the leadership said they weren't random but I'm not so sure), assigned team leaders, and sent to a ministry destination for three weeks. My first such team was to be sent to a place called Dasmarinas City, Cavite which was near to Manila, the capital of the Philippines. Being part of a Challenge Team was generally looked forward to by crew members. It was meant to provide a lengthier break from ship life and was to be a time for a more intensive focus on ministry in a smaller team. It would be a bit like an extended C day.

My team members were Jheanelle from Jamaica, who was the team leader; Daniel from New Zealand as assistant leader; George from England; Nora from Hungary as medical rep; and Bethany from Ireland. I was asked to look after the finance for the team. After the thirty or so teams had been posted on a public noticeboard and in the weeks leading up to our departure, I was informed that 'everyone' was discussing our team. The main reason being that we had some strong personalities in the mix (including my own) and people were curious as to how we would get along with each other. From my perspective, Jheanelle and Nora were from my PST so I knew them a little. I had developed a distant friendship with Jheanelle but hadn't spent any real time with Nora. I didn't know Daniel, George or Bethany at all.

Our initial preparation meetings were stormy, to say the least, as Jheanelle laid the law down and explained what she expected from us. She also informed us of her personality and characteristics including the negative traits. I wondered whether she might have done better to allow people to form their own opinions rather than setting herself up for a fall, but maybe she had decided to lower our expectations so that we would be pleasantly surprised with the reality. It felt a bit like a teacher and pupil scenario but I knew it was probably because she was nervous so I decided to bear with her and give her my support. Others in the team found it more difficult to do that and sometimes turned up late or missed meetings altogether. I could see from the outset that it was not going to be plain sailing. We had Jheanelle - an organised, serious, disciplined, focused leader wanting to control every detail and for her team to be successful versus Nora and Bethany who were less of all those things, but more creative, spontaneous, charismatic, humorous and loud. I was somewhere in the middle but, personality wise, more towards Jheanelle's side. The two guys, Daniel and George, were the stabilising influence bringing balance to the team. It was going to be a long three weeks!

Setting off, we had to travel in a van and then a bus to reach our destination. Jheanelle became physically ill during the journey so we had to stop a few times. It wasn't a great start to our Challenge Team which I realised had been aptly named. I deliberately listened to loud Christian music on the bus to drown out the extremely violent and offensive horror movie that was playing on the big screen at the front. All the other passengers, apart from our small team, including young children, were transfixed by the movie. I struggled with the lackadaisical attitudes towards things on TV and watching movies throughout my time in the Philippines. Even in Christian circles it seemed to be culturally acceptable to watch anything and everything regardless of the content.

We finally reached our destination and were collected by Pastor Lem, the Senior Pastor at Blessed Church which would be home for our three-week visit. Pastor Danny was with him. The church actually had three Pastors which was maybe a little excessive for a less than one-hundred-person congregation, but was another cultural anomaly that I learned to accept. As soon as the Pastors turned up they started taking photos, of course. I don't know why I had thought it would be any different, we were still in the Philippines after all.

The Pastors treated us to dinner at a pizza place on the journey back to the church. I absentmindedly tallied that the equivalent meal would have cost six times more in England. A few hours later we arrived at the church only to be offered another meal. It was to prove a difficult balancing act for me throughout - how to keep the weight off without offending our hosts. Filipinos ate five times a day and seemed to have a much faster metabolism than Westerners and most definitely faster than me with an under-active thyroid. They ate rice morning, noon and night as well as large snacks in between. I knew that I just couldn't do that as it would double my weight in no time. In a way, I was glad to be able to blame my limited appetite on my health problem.

We were shown to our rooms which had obviously been renovated for our visit. Sometime after we were shown a video of all the work that had been done in preparation for our arrival, including the fitting of Western toilets. I was shocked to discover that the church had been saving money for months for our visit. The Pastors had instructed them that if they were serious about mission they needed to prove it by properly hosting us as foreign guests. They in turn advised us that we had done enough work on the ship and that they intended our visit to be a relaxing vacation. I found it difficult to get my head around this as I had gone on the team prepared and wanting to be involved in ministry. I knew that accepting and enjoying hospitality graciously was important, but I didn't want to be treated like royalty for three weeks or to be pampered. I definitely didn't want to watch the church spending their hard-earned money on us when some of the members struggled to put food on the table.

We were cautioned that there were a number of dogs living on the roof above our room and that they would be set loose at night. That was a bit strange because sometimes we could hear the dogs barking but we never actually saw them. The pictures in our minds of huge snarling creatures with sharp teeth, like the dog in *Turner and Hooch,* were probably not at all realistic. It's incredible what the mind can do when there is no accurate visual representation. To begin with we lived in fear of the animals suddenly pouncing on us and potentially mauling us to death every time we ventured downstairs or outside. We had been told horror stories about what happens when a person catches rabies. By the sound of it the initial injection that would be required at the hospital should someone be bitten by a rabid dog might be worse than the disease itself. I reassured myself that rabid dogs would likely be obviously rabid, foaming at the mouth or living in aggressive isolation. But the locals weren't so sure believing that any dogs could have the disease and that it wouldn't necessarily be evident. And, of course, we had never actually seen the dogs so rumours abounded.

On being shown to our Westernised rooms and after a brief rest we were called to eat again. The others laughed at me for putting a tea bag into a tiny cup that barely contained it as I was desperate for some English tea. The small cups looked like they belonged to a teddy bears picnic set; maybe they had done at one point. I had thought that was all that was available but then I saw the larger mugs and realised why the others had been laughing at me. After that our hosts decided to show us some of the local sights beginning by driving us to a park for a "nice country walk!"

We walked around the green park with huge stone animals littering the paths. They were illuminated by pretty lights. We took photos of each other pretending to be eaten by dinosaurs and other large mammals. We began walking across a small bridge which wobbled dangerously as we reached the centre. Fortunately, the instability caused me to hesitate as when I looked down I saw that there were whole planks missing from the bridge. They were large enough for a child or one of my legs to fall through which would've been extremely uncomfortable. I commented that it would definitely not be allowed in England and Bethany astutely observed that the whole bridge wouldn't. Then I saw that the electricity and phone cables were tangled above us in a mess of tree branches. On being asked the question, the Pastor soberly informed us that they couldn't cut the trees back as they were protected. Another clear case of misapplication of Western law. The life of a few old trees isn't going to be especially relevant when a bunch of people get burnt to a crisp after being electrocuted.

As we were crossing a road in the park, the Pastor acknowledged a man on a motorbike who had said "Exciting?" to me. I wasn't sure I had heard correctly and didn't know what he was talking about, so I said to the Pastor "What does that mean?" He looked confused and a bit surprised before calmly responding "Well that's an English word Natalie." The man had been referring to our experience of walking through the park and had wanted to know our observations. The others thought the exchange was hilarious and kept referring back to it whenever there were language problems.

During our walk, we became aware that we were being followed by two young men who were dressed as women. Nora and I got one of them into conversation as the other disappeared. We shared the Gospel with him. He admitted that he had become confused as he had thought he was gay but had been attracted to us as we had passed him by. He was homeless. Some of the church members who had accompanied us took over the conversation in Tagalog which eventually resulted in his wanting to become a Christian. There was a sincerity about him and he had broken down when talking about his life and many vices. After praying with him, our group got up as if to leave and began wandering away. I asked the Pastor what we were going to do to follow up the conversion so he asked the man if he could attend the church on Sunday. The problem really was that we had travelled a fair distance to reach the park and were not in the vicinity of the church. I wanted to do more for the homeless man but I recognised that he needed to make some efforts himself to prove that he was a serious seeker and also I couldn't impose on our hosts.

We had done all that was possible in the circumstances and were preparing to leave the park, but then one of our Logos Hope team members who had been quietly observing the last few minutes of conversation suddenly announced that they believed that God was telling them immediately to baptise the man with water. The person asked the Pastors for water in order to proceed. I felt really uncomfortable with the idea. The man had only just made a profession, had had no follow up or discipleship or time really to know what he was doing. If he had truly converted, he might want the opportunity to use his public baptism in the future as a witness to family and friends. I asked the person to reconsider but they felt that they would be being disobedient to God if they didn't go ahead with what they saw as a divine command.

On hearing that response, I couldn't say anything further as I might be arguing with God's direction, but I was shocked and wished that the person would wait; I didn't see why it needed to be done immediately. The person then spent a few minutes explaining what they were going to do and obtained consent from the man who appeared oblivious to what was going on. Then they poured a small bottle of water over his head and rubbed it in, announcing that they were baptising him. He looked totally confused and slightly fearful as we walked away having apparently "baptised" our first Challenge Team convert.

All that flashed through my mind was pity for him because he would be sleeping on the street with a wet T-shirt that night. That wasn't that much of a big deal in the circumstances as the weather was generally hot, but in my eyes it just added to the inappropriateness of the action. Even in a church when someone is baptised at least they have a towel and fresh dry clothes to change into. We headed back to the van and church after that. As I had expected, we never saw the man again.

The impromptu baptism caused a rift in our team as we held a meeting to discuss what had happened. None of us knew that the ship's policy was that team members should not be involved in baptising anyone or get baptised themselves without consultation with their home church. The policy was reflective of the fact that it was such an important and serious decision. On returning to the ship after our three-week commitment, I was discouraged to see that one of our hosts at the church had obviously emailed the incident to the ship leadership soon after it had happened. They had held it up as an example of the zealous and fruitful ministry that our Challenge Team had instigated and taken part in. We had only just arrived at their church and already we were baptising people! The leadership had posted that with a photo of the event, of course, on the noticeboard for the attention of the ship's crew highlighting the good work, despite their policy about baptism. I just shook my head and resolved to choose my battles.

CHAPTER TWENTY-NINE

Welcome to Blessed Church

During our first few nights at Blessed Church we were plagued by bugs, mostly ants and the odd cockroach as we were sleeping on mattresses on the floor. In the haziness of sleep, I squashed a bug squirming around on my face and then moved a black 'leaf' off my pillow. But even being half asleep I was startled when the leaf came to life and crawled along the floor. Then there were the lizards which made a weird noise all night but generally kept to themselves and remained clinging to the walls and ceilings which definitely suited me.

On our first full day, the church members threw a huge welcome party with banners, speeches, gifts and food. They even sang a song for us which made some of the girls cry. A blind man took to the stage to welcome us which made me cry. We were all a bit confused when a local man introduced himself as 'George Simpson' (the full name of one of our team) and began talking about details of his life. George himself looked shocked. The church had carried out research on us and proceeded to repeat their findings about each of our lives. Fortunately, we were already used to those types of very public disclosure having lived on the ship for a few months. Nothing we did or said remained private, it was like a large goldfish bowl.

The Filipinos then had us playing some pretty silly games including getting us to eat a really dry biscuit made of dough and then trying to whistle, which was virtually impossible. We were blindfolded and had to try to feed each other bananas. I was paired with George and kept stuffing more and more banana into his mouth because I couldn't see whether or not he was keeping up and swallowing it. By the time it was my turn I was bent over double crying with laughter and clutching my stomach. That resulted in George trying to feed the banana into my hair as he couldn't see that I was bent over laughing.

Judging by the raucous background laughter, I'm sure it was even more hilarious for all those looking on, which was no doubt what had been intended.

After the craziness, the focus was changed and the Pastor shared a message from Romans chapter 10 reminding us "how can they be saved if they haven't heard?" as a motivator for evangelism. Having been inspired initially, I found the main part of his message difficult as he was once again highlighting that we as 'missionaries' had 'beautiful feet' and that the church members needed to serve us during our stay. It felt as if we were being given a special status as missionaries when actually we were all new to mission work and were still very much in training. We were no better equipped to share the Gospel than anyone else. I wanted to assist the church with their programmes but not to take over and have them admire us as we would only be there for three weeks. I didn't feel it was helpful for the church members to see a Western version of Christianity as their target or to see us as role models for their church members.

On our second day, we were assigned to conduct eye glass ministry. I was asked to co-ordinate it having been the only one who had already done the training. I became increasingly exasperated during the day when I realised that some of the locals were pretending their prescription was wrong in order to obtain more fashionable glasses at a different strength. On the positive side, we gave out one hundred and fifty pairs of glasses and prayed for each person individually. Some people cried as we prayed for them as they had believed their lives were insignificant. They were humbled that foreigners, whom they saw as far above them, would spare the time to listen to their problems and demonstrate care for them. It was an important lesson for us to learn; it was easy to give glasses but what people really wanted and needed was our time and attention, to know that they mattered as individuals and that we wanted to share the Gospel with them because their lives were important to God. We had translators for each crew member so the language barrier was not as much of a problem as it had been at the prison when I had previously carried out eye glass ministry.

We faced another difficulty on discovering that one of the Pastors, unbeknownst to us, had promised to supply a certain number of pairs of glasses to another organisation. We didn't have enough left of the differing strengths required to fulfil the obligation. It seemed crazy to promise to send a specified number of pairs of glasses anywhere - how did the organisation know what strengths they needed without first testing the people's eyes? We should just agree to test a certain number of people in order to ascertain whether or not they actually needed glasses. It seemed to be another example of the local people just wanting freebies. I suspected that many of them would not even have worn the glasses should we have given them; they would just keep them as a souvenir from the foreigners who had visited and tell all their friends about them.

One evening we took part in an event to try to get to know some of the members of the church youth group. We watched the Christian movie *"Facing the Giants"* and discussed it in small groups. We were asked to share our testimonies in the small groups to encourage the youth to open up in return. But Filipinos are extremely shy, more so in the presence of foreigners, so it really was a disaster as the youth sat in awkward silence. It felt a bit like being at school and waiting for someone to answer the teacher's question. I don't know if forced sharing in groups like that is a good idea. Maybe friendships need to be developed in a more natural environment over time. Perhaps it wasn't a good idea for us to be encouraging the youth to open up about their problems and faith struggles when we would be leaving in a few weeks. Maybe it would have been better for them to talk to their youth leaders who knew them and who would be around to help them spiritually and practically with the issues they identified. But we were almost looked to as miracle workers capable of dramatically changing situations and people's lives. Somewhere along the way we were going to be a big fat disappointment and that weighed heavily on me.

The next day we were taken around the town by a female church member who insisted on paying for everything. In fact, we had to be careful about expressing an interest in anything throughout our stay, as it would likely end up being purchased for us whether or not the church could actually afford it. They saw it as their Christian duty, I think, and they had a special budget for us. We went to meet the local congressman for a 10am appointment. I found it strangely encouraging when he kept us waiting for an hour and a half, before turning up to spend only five minutes with us. At least there was someone who didn't consider us to be on a par with royalty. His wife was the local Mayor - they were clearly a powerful family with wide influence.

Next, we were invited to visit another church member's house for dinner. Afterwards I wrote, "The food was good but I feel terrible from eating all of the time. It is really difficult to refuse without offending people but I'm going to have to find a way or I will become ill." It continued to be a problem throughout our time at Blessed Church and we had all gained weight by the end of our Challenge Team. The Filipinos saw it as a good thing representing health and vitality as they remarked "You've got fat," a perfectly acceptable observation in their culture.

On the third day, we had been asked to get up for a birthday party for Daniel at 5 am. We refused and managed to persuade the church members to change it to 7:30 am but it was still early. Our team were all rubbing their eyes as about thirty very smiley Filipinos gathered around Daniel who had been forced to sit on a lone chair in the centre of the room. They were playing guitars and singing a song that they had written specially for him, the lyrics of which were all about his life. They were going through the motions of a very Filipino celebration including cake and yes, lots of food. We learned that some of the church members had stayed up until 2 am preparing the song which did move me slightly. Filipinos don't do things by halves.

We took part in some visitations with the Pastors in smaller groups during the day. I met a widow with five children who had been a Catholic but who had converted to Christianity through the Pastoral visitations. She maintained a statue of the baby Jesus and a crucifix in her home despite her conversion but I knew that those things sometimes took time to change. I was more concerned when she said that she rarely read her Bible, but was encouraged when the Pastor offered to arrange to conduct Bible studies with her. A few of us shared our experiences with the lady in an attempt to encourage her. We had a team discussion afterwards about finding the right balance between being direct and truthful without being unnecessarily judgmental or lacking compassion.

After the visit, we headed for what appeared on first sight to be an abandoned concrete building in the middle of nowhere; it wasn't even a building really as the walls were crumbling and the roof was virtually non-existent. Apparently, it was the location for a Sunday Bible study that had been started amongst a group of between ten and fifteen teenage boys. The boys had been inspired to clean up the building's interior and had even collected a few items of well-worn and obviously discarded furniture. On arrival, the Pastor asked the already congregated boys if they had prepared a welcome for us. We were expecting something dramatic as befitted their culture, but in response one of the boys with a sly smile quipped "welcome," causing me to hide my own smile. That was more my kind of welcome than the usual drama.

We crossed the road into the more civilised environment of an actual house. The boys accompanied us, increasing our party to around thirty people. There were introductions all round as we crammed into a lounge area which was nicely furnished. The church member hosts then made a big fuss of us, which of course included supplying copious amounts of food. Naively I complimented the richness of the peanut butter - I was presented with several jars of it a few days later.

I returned to the church ahead of the others due to being in desperate need of a rest. However, my relaxation had to wait because I was immediately bombarded by teenage girls from the church. They came to my room wanting to chat to me about all manner of things. The first question was of course what I wanted to eat. I knew that "Nothing" or "I've already eaten" or "I'm already full" would be an unacceptable answer. I tried to remember what we had eaten earlier in the day at the church so that at least they wouldn't have to go out and buy more food. I tentatively mentioned oranges thinking I could quickly change my mind if they indicated that they didn't have any left. But, they were already out of the door and heading cheerfully to the store to buy them before I could say anything else. I just had to let them get on with it really.

The girls chatted to me in the bedroom for quite a long time. They all wanted to be missionaries! I wondered whether their stated aspirations were an attempt to impress me or to follow in the footsteps of the Logos Hope team. I encouraged them to pursue their goals to work for God, and hoped they would be properly guided by the church leadership along the way.

One of the girls was a youth leader at Blessed Church but she admitted that she had been dating a non-believer until he had recently converted. I told her that I was glad that he had become a believer, but she followed the good news by mentioning that he wasn't really involved in a church because he was too shy. I realised that I needed to be cautious in being too forthright knowing that her Christian parents, who attended the church, were in favour of the match. I was learning that Filipino cultural practice sometimes over-rode God's instructions in the Bible. I was also going to hear the phrase "It's not wrong, it's just different," many more times.

CHAPTER THIRTY

Poisoned

On the fourth day of our Challenge Team, I became very ill. I will spare you too much detail but the stomach pains were unbearable. Jheanelle prayed for me in the middle of most of the nights that I remained ill as I was in a lot of pain. The next few days (and nights) were terrible as I struggled to stabilise my system and work out what had caused the problem in the first place. I decided in the end that it must've been some coconut juice that I had purchased from a street vendor. The strange thing was that as the days progressed I wasn't getting any better and at times I felt as if I were actually deteriorating. I was crying from the stomach pain at times and couldn't remember ever having felt as ill. I even thought at one point that I might die and wondered whether I was ready if that was what was going to happen.

It didn't help that the church members were mortified that one of their 'special missionary team' had fallen seriously ill on their watch. They were constantly badgering me - bringing food, drinks and everything they could possibly think of to try to restore my health and my spirit. Actually, I needed just to be left alone to recover as I was so weak that I couldn't smile for visitors and didn't want to end up snapping at them. One of the host's consistent suggestions was that I should drink Gatorade, a disgusting, brightly coloured, energy drink that serves as the proposed cure for any and all health problems in the Philippines. I tried it, well I had to as they kept bringing it to me by the gallon. It was a sickly-sweet mixture no doubt full of sugar and just made me feel worse. I knew that the main thing I needed to do was to drink a lot of water so I forced myself to do that. The helpful hosts brought the large blue plastic water container and placed it outside my bedroom door to facilitate easier access.

However, when my health didn't improve I began to wonder about the water as it was the only thing that I was really consuming. I asked the others in my team where they were getting their drinking water from. I learned that I was the only one using the source outside my bedroom door. It must be suspect. On prizing open the container, we discovered that it was swarming with ants that I had been merrily drinking for a few days. Immediately I switched and started drinking bottled water purchased from local stores, but by that point I was considering the possibility that I might not make it to the end of the Challenge Team and that I might need to return to the ship. The Church of course were not going to allow me to leave under any circumstances, worrying that it would reflect badly on them or that they had failed adequately to host us. In actual fact as you have probably gathered the opposite was true. We had been very well looked after and my opinion was that those things sometimes just happened and that that was life. The leaders began holding fairly charismatic prayer meetings for my healing.

Eventually I reluctantly went to the hospital for some tests because our hosts insisted on it. As soon as the nurse had read my information sheet and before any tests had been conducted she wanted to place me on an intravenous drip to rehydrate my body. Horrified at the thought and not sure it was necessary, I protested that it was surely far too early for that dramatic type of intervention. She wanted to give me medicine via a drip; bemused, I wondered what had happened to tablets. The nurse then decided that my thyroid medication was the likely cause but I had been taking the pills for years and my symptoms had no connection to my thyroid. Losing confidence by that point and concerned that I might end up in surgery for something unconnected to the actual problem, I tactfully suggested that maybe I had food poisoning which seemed the most likely solution to the medical dilemma.

Lying on the hospital bed wondering what the final bill would be, I was re-approached by the nurse, who had armed herself with two bottles of Gatorade. I resisted the temptation to cry as the well-intentioned nurse clearly believed that the thick sugary energy drink was the answer to all of my problems. I didn't have the heart to tell her that I had been drinking the stuff for a few days already. The taste and smell alone made me feel nauseous. The results from my tests finally came back and I was given a prescription that I didn't pay enough attention to before being discharged.

We then went to the pharmacy and collected the prescription. I insisted then on doing my own food shopping so that I could select food that I would be able to eat. By that point virtually all food or the thought or smell of food made me gag so I had to choose carefully. I abandoned my usual frugality as I spent emergency ship funds believing that it was life and death and that I had to force myself to eat. I had started feeling unwell not only due to whatever was plaguing me but also due to not being able to eat by that point. I recall buying Pringles and tinned tomatoes, amongst other odd items, as I knew I could eat them. That put an end to our hosts' attempts to force me to eat fried chicken which they kept bringing to my door.

On arriving back at the church and re-entering my room, I found that I had accidentally left a biscuit wrapper with some crumbs next to the edge of my bed. The whole area was swarming with ants who, having collected the delicious crumbs, were marching purposefully in a line along the nearest wall and off into the distance. The inconvenience in my already fragile state was too much to cope with. I burst into tears. Jheanelle dealt with the ants.

Nora, our medical person, who had so far been conspicuous in her absence in relation to my declining health, handed me some salt rehydration tablets that had come with the ship medical kit. I dissolved them in the water, took a swig and then, much to Jheanelle's horror, as there was no excuse for that type of behaviour, promptly spat the whole mouthful on the floor. It had tasted like poison and had burnt my throat as if it were acid with a strong chlorine-like taste. I apologised profusely to Jheanelle and then turned to stare at Nora, wondering what on earth was going on and whether she had tried to finish me off. My mental faculties obviously weren't up to much by that point. Everything I touched prolonged my sickness.

I started taking the prescription tablets obtained from the pharmacy but my stomach pains just got worse. I began experiencing acid reflux all the way up my oesophagus. I knew it must be the tablets as they were the only new thing that I had started taking. But I thought I should persevere with them as the hospital must know what they were doing; maybe it would get worse before it got better.

The gut wrenching pains that night though made me think twice and in the end I looked the tablets up on the internet. I was totally shocked to read that they were actually antibiotics for the treatment of a serious infection and that they should not be taken unless that infection had been confirmed. As far as I was aware I didn't have any type of infection and my test results had been normal. I stopped taking the tablets immediately. I read on and discovered that they should not be taken with thyroid tablets or sugary drinks (Gatorade.) The side effects were nausea, diarrhoea and...you guessed it acid reflux. My fears about going to hospital in the first place had been realised. My Filipino hosts were furious but I just wanted to forget about it and focus on getting better.

I had by that point contacted the ship leadership who were seriously considering removing me from the team back to the ship as it had been nearly seven days of sickness and I didn't seem to be improving, but the ship sick bay was already full. It made me pretty upset as I could feel that I was also placing a burden on our host church. I felt guilty even though I knew it wasn't my fault. I also felt useless not being able to join in any of the activities.

I woke one day with large bites on my leg and finger and on another occasion on my eye which had swollen shut. I had believed they were insect bites of some sort but had not considered that it might be due to cockroaches as the thought alone was disgusting. When the hosts said that they were in fact cockroach bites, I recalled an unpleasant 'dream' from the previous night. A black thing had been in my bed or on my skin. In my panic as I didn't know what it was, I had thrown my whole sleeping bag across the room. The thing, whatever it was, had then scuttled away into the distance with a clicking sound. I wished that it had remained as an unpleasant dream as it just added to my catalogue of woes.

From a spiritual perspective, I had obviously been asking myself some tough questions about what was going on and was struggling to maintain a positive attitude. Jheanelle looked after me constantly but confided in the end that even she didn't know what to do and that she was extremely worried about the whole situation. I started asking God what the purpose of my sickness was and had received no clear answers which just made me more frustrated. To top it off I could tell that there was friction within the team in my absence although they tried their best to keep it from me. I was glad not to have to get too involved due to being ill but I felt sorry for Jheanelle as the team leader and wished I could've been more of a help to her as she was being to me.

In general, conflict within a Christian team environment should in theory be easier to resolve but that relies on the assumption that everyone is seeking to obey God and therefore wanting peace and reconciliation. I was learning that that was not always the case and that sometimes people were willing to disregard Biblical instruction in order to do what they wanted to do. When there is no common faith foundation, sorting out disputes can become very difficult. Sometimes on the ship even the authority of the Bible was brought into question with comments like "Well the Bible is corrupted," or "The Bible isn't relevant today," or "I only believe the New Testament," or "The Bible shouldn't be taken literally." I was not expecting to face liberalism whilst serving with a large group of evangelical Christians. I should add that the attitudes and beliefs did not originate from the ship itself but accompanied those who had come from many different countries and church backgrounds.

Eventually, the ship leaders arranged a bed on the ship for my return as they accepted that it was serious and that I wasn't just making a fuss about nothing, but the rest of my Challenge Team said that they didn't want me to leave. The church leaders also informed me that they wouldn't let me leave even if I wanted to. So, under pressure to remain and not really wanting to give up if it could be avoided, I decided to give things one more day. It was a good decision as it turned out because it was the day when finally I began feeling better and was able to rejoin the team properly. I had been seriously ill for the best part of ten days though and I still didn't know the reason. I had to trust that God had a purpose and was teaching me a lesson.

CHAPTER THIRTY-ONE

Music, Motorbikes and Misunderstandings!

One of my lesser trials on the ship was the loud modern worship music. I definitely preferred hymns. I adjusted somewhat whilst on board and decided that I liked some of the lyrics for some of the contemporary songs, but I still missed the hymns and felt that some of the worship was repetitive. The focus was often on us as worshippers and our feelings, wants and desires rather than being about God. That type of worship was replicated across the Philippines in most of the churches we visited including Blessed Church - it had become the cultural Christian standard.

The youth church band practised loudly on Saturday nights in preparation for the Sunday service. It was sometimes so loud I couldn't hear myself think. The main church meeting was held in a courtyard with a stage that was open to the elements on all sides. It was therefore necessary for the worship singers to shout in order to be heard. That then distorted their voices and led to them being completely out of tune. For that reason, I insisted on sitting at the back of any such service away from the speakers and shouting people jumping all over the stage. Perhaps it visibly divided our team in the eyes of the church members as the rest of them sat at the front, but I valued my eardrums.

I felt a bit as if we were only touching the surface spiritually and relationally with some of the church members. A lot of our contact with them seemed to be superficial and they still appeared to idolise us. All of the church messages during our visit were about mission and we were asked to participate heavily in them. I felt uncomfortable that whatever we said carried great weight, even with the pastors, and we could easily influence people's decisions about serious spiritual issues.

One of the pastors conducted an "altar call" for people who wanted to go into full-time mission after one church service. A huge number of church members responded. As the resident missionaries, we were asked to pray for them. Whilst I was encouraged to see their zeal for sharing the Gospel, I participated reluctantly, believing that a serious call to full time mission work could only come from God. It seemed unlikely that so many people from a relatively small congregation could all have been called by God at the same time. I felt that, at least in part, the expectation had been created by the emotionally charged atmosphere and the fact that we were present; the people, especially the youth, wanted to impress or please us. I wondered how all of the prospective missionaries were to be financially supported by the church members, many of whom struggled to find food to eat each day. I had concerns also about the gaps that would be left in the secular workplace which, to my mind, was just as important in terms of evangelism.

I hoped the enthusiastic volunteers realised that the missionary life was hard and not always an exciting adventure. It was easy to see why people living in poverty chased the missionary life that our ship team represented - we were mostly materially wealthy and got to sail around the world to countries that they could never afford to visit. I felt sad that our presence was potentially making them dissatisfied or discontented with where God had placed them, but it was an inevitable consequence of our visit.

Fully recovered from my illness, I re-joined the daily activities of our team just in time for one of the most divisive incidents. During a visit to a local community, we were sitting in a circle outside a house in a public area on some tree stumps in preparation for a Bible study. Suddenly, a Filipino man on a motorbike pulled up next to us and, gunning the engine, asked if anyone wanted a ride. Without hesitation, Bethany piped up "Yeah, alright mate," or words to that effect. Quick as a flash she had jumped on the back of the machine, threw her arms around the waist of the man and was off down the road before anyone could react. Jheanelle's mouth dropped open and she looked as if she was about to have a stroke. The rest of us sat for a few seconds in stunned silence hoping for Bethany's safe return.

When she did return after a quick spin around the block, we managed to make it through the rest of our programme albeit in a tension filled atmosphere.

At one point during the meeting, I asked for the English translation of the Tagalog songs we were singing. I made that a practice; maybe I was paranoid, but I wanted to know what I was singing as it was addressed to God. OM often encouraged people to pray or sing in their own language. When everyone enthusiastically chimed in with the "amen" at the end I was left wondering, how they could agree if they didn't know what was said?

The ticking time bomb went off later when we were back at the church and away from polite company. Jheanelle aggressively confronted Bethany about her motorbike exploits. From her reaction, poor Bethany had obviously had no idea what was coming. It was clear that their cultural backgrounds placed them at completely opposite ends of the spectrum. I had actually found the whole event quite funny and the discussion about it continued to amuse. Jheanelle accurately and zealously demonstrated what Bethany had done and how it had come across to her being from a more conservative background. We were "ladies" in a foreign culture, missionaries representing Jesus, the motorbike man was a potentially dangerous stranger, the mode of transportation might not have been safe and Bethany hadn't asked permission before taking off on her "joy ride." Jheanelle made it sound as if Bethany had behaved as if she were a rough and ready "motorbike chick." I had been concerned about the insurance issue, but no harm had come of it and Bethany had obviously learned that she shouldn't ride on motorbikes in the future! I felt a bit like it was a mountain out of a molehill and that we just needed to move on.

We did move on eventually but only for Nora and me to clash heads about something else. We both had relatively strong personalities and were from opposite church backgrounds. Nora asked us as a team if any of us had the "gift of healing." I sighed knowing what was coming next as I informed her that I didn't believe the gifts were still active. She looked at me in astonishment, obviously having never heard the viewpoint before.

In a similar earlier discussion on the ship, another girl had concluded that I didn't believe in the Holy Spirit when I had reluctantly shared my opinion after being pressurised to do so. I wasn't on board to try to convert everyone to cessationism - the belief that the sign gifts died out with the Apostles in the New Testament period, but I did want to be able to hold my views peacefully and not be told that I was ignorant. I struggled when people who, in the main were a lot younger than me and had been Christians for a lot less time, spoke to me as if they just needed to explain things a little more simply and then I would understand. They didn't seem to realise that cessationism had been mainstream theology in past generations.

On a more positive note, we got on with the practical work. We painted all of the classrooms at the church, which also doubled as a school, a bright blue. We also painted a pedestrian crossing for the street outside the church. I wasn't sure why the church had taken responsibility for the project but it had been planned for a while with all the necessary announcements, colourful banners and photo opportunities. I was slightly perturbed when we were forced to delay finishing the painting to await the arrival of the ship's photographer in order to have some official photos taken. We had actually already finished painting the classrooms, so we had to go back and pretend that we were still working, posing in positions of hard work. I found it difficult not to smile knowing the photographer was at work, but when I made the observation, he laughed and informed me that people always know when they are being photographed. As a photographer, he could tell by a person's facial expressions and behavioural changes the minute they were aware that the camera was on them. So much for natural or unplanned photography; according to an expert, it doesn't exist.

CHAPTER THIRTY-TWO

One Soul Saved; Kuya (Brother) Danny

My most memorable ship story began on 26th April 2012. We were carrying out eye-glass ministry again but I no longer needed to be in charge as the others had been trained. So, having a passion for Christian literature, I had asked to be assigned to a small book table which would sell a few cheap books from the ship. I spent most of the morning at that table with few opportunities for conversation apart from a couple of police officers who had taken some tracts at my invitation.

Then Danny had arrived. Danny was a sixty-four-year-old school teacher who was hanging around the book table. He kept asking me questions about the books like "What is all this about?" I told him it was about Jesus and attempted to answer his many questions. In the end, I asked him if there was a particular book he was interested in as he just kept hanging around and appeared reluctant either to make a purchase or leave. He pointed to a small book entitled "We would see Jesus." I reduced the price from fifty to twenty pesos on the spot wanting him to have it and then offered it to him. I asked him if he was Roman Catholic and when he confirmed it, I explained that I was born again. He told me about an American friend he had had in the 1960s who had been in the Philippines for seven years. He said that his friend had been born again and he spoke fondly about him. I sensed a spiritual hunger in the man and when he asked for my contact details I asked him if he would be willing to talk to a male friend of mine.

When he said yes I called one of the church pastors over and eagerly explained that Danny wanted to talk about Christianity in more detail and that I had thought it would be helpful for him to talk to a man. I waited expectantly as the Pastor made small talk with Danny for a few minutes. He then called Bethany over to tell Danny about the ship! Bethany, having been put completely on the spot, and no doubt wondering why she had been summoned when I was standing right there, struggled through knowledge, help and hope - the three key words for the ship ministry.

Worrying that the conversation was rapidly heading for the superficial, and feeling that it was right to return the conversation to the state of Danny's soul, I waited for an interlude, then intervened to challenge him directly about his need to get right with God. I quoted Romans chapter ten verse nine: "If you confess with your mouth that Jesus is Lord and believe in your heart that God raised him from the dead, you will be saved." Danny listened intently as I was talking and I could see that he was a man genuinely concerned about his spiritual state and ready to do something about it. It was clearly a divine appointment that none of us could've orchestrated. Danny confirmed my thoughts by stating "that is what I needed." His honesty and sincerity made my heart go out to him as he stood there helpless and needing to be guided as to what he should do next. I offered to pray with him, and then with a hand on his shoulder, prayed a simple prayer of commitment, not the 'Sinner's prayer' or anything like that, as I believe that each person needs to come before God alone, to deal with Him directly. It was just a prayer that God would reveal Himself to Danny and that his eyes would be opened to the truth.

Danny confirmed his sincerity by asking for follow up counsel about things that he couldn't discuss with me as a woman. The Pastor then found his voice and from that point on the church were really fantastic. They welcomed him into their midst, conducted one to one Bible studies with him, visited him and really took him under their wing as a new believer. He was even invited to attend a church outing a few days later, although sadly that was the point where I let Danny down as I didn't recognise him on the outing and didn't really speak to him. I rectified that when he also came to church on the Sunday by apologising and I truly felt terrible about it. But it could happen on Logos Hope where we met hundreds of people every day. For the people we met, their encounter with us may have been life changing, but generally for us they were just a face or a name amongst thousands. Danny ended up being a lot more than that but initially I wasn't sure how far he would go with his commitment. Unfortunately, we saw many individuals take that first step enthusiastically only to fall away at the first hurdle - seed that was choked or distracted.

Danny again proved the reality of his conversion by his persistence in attending church even though he had to travel a long distance (and by his failure to allow my inadvertent snub to put him off Christianity.) He informed me that when I had put my hand on his shoulder when I prayed for him it had reminded him of his American friend. He said that I had been kind to him even though I didn't know him and had no reason to care about him at all. I explained that I had been lost once too and remembered the meaninglessness of life then and that my passion was to care for and help those who were still lost. His comments really moved me and reminded me of the impact we can have on people without realising it.

Danny became a regular member of the fellowship at Blessed Church. He got involved in teaching others and evangelising in his own community which was some distance from the church and began helping out practically in the church. He was desperate to spend time with the church members whenever he could and they welcomed him with open arms. Of course, I didn't know any of that until much later. I knew only that Danny was still in the church and I then received a note with his address and contact details and a letter as follows on October 8th 2012:

"Dear sis Natalie, first of all I would like to greet you a pleasant good afternoon or good evening. I hope you are in the best of health. I'm very thankful for the newsletter that you gave me and it really perks me up to be more aggressive in my faith with the Lord Jesus Christ and I would like to thank God because I met you at the eye-glass ministry in our place in Salawag Dasma Cavite. Ever since I accepted Jesus Christ I feel like a new born coz of so many changes in my life. Before I don't bother to read the Holy Bible but now I read it every day. Sorry if it is only now that I was able to write you a letter. At present, I'm having one to one with Pastor Lem Aguirre. He is teaching me on how to disciple and evangelized and we are on the last phase. I guess this is all for the moment and hope to see you again and lastly kindly give my regards to the Logos Challenge Team (God Bless.) It's me Kuya Danny (Ventura)"

The ship photographer later returned to Blessed Church and, whilst there, interviewed Danny on video about his salvation experience. I watched the very long video that accompanied a photo of Danny reading his favourite Psalm chapter fifty-four from his Bible. He said that he had experienced many changes in his life since his conversion, that he wanted to learn more good things from the Bible; that he wanted to join the ship one day; and that if God permitted he would also like to be a Pastor! I was thrilled to hear and see the further evidence of inner change. Danny, in company with other members of Blessed Church, took the long journey to visit the ship and see me but we missed each other. I did write him several notes and emails. Danny obviously felt a special connection with me as I was the person who had first introduced him to Christianity. A year after he was saved, the church members baptised him in the sea and sent me a photograph of the event.

Tragically, when I returned to the Philippines independently in 2014, I was informed that Danny was ill and was in the hospital in Manila. I was in Olongapo (three hours away) at the time, but rushed to the hospital only sadly to find that Danny had already passed away and gone to be with his Lord. It was bittersweet in light of his conversion just two years prior. I was reminded that God's timing is perfect. The church used the opportunity to witness to his family at his funeral. I realised that my entire purpose for being on the ship for those two years may have just been so that I could meet Danny. Is one soul worth a lifetime of witness? Definitely!

> "O God, save me by your name,
> and vindicate me by your might.
> O God, hear my prayer;
> give ear to the words of my mouth.
> For strangers have risen against me;
> ruthless men seek my life;
> they do not set God before themselves.
> Behold, God is my helper;
> the Lord is the upholder of my life.
> He will return the evil to my enemies;
> in your faithfulness put an end to them.
> With a freewill offering I will sacrifice to you;

*I will give thanks to your name, O Lord, for it is good.
For he has delivered me from every trouble,
and my eye has looked in triumph on my enemies."*

Psalm Chapter 54

In memory of Danny Ventura.

CHAPTER THIRTY-THREE

Learning the Lessons

As our team had progressed through the three weeks of the Challenge Team, I found it hard at times not to lapse into robotic conversations when we were conducting eye glass ministry or things of that nature. It felt a bit like sitting at a supermarket cash-desk beeping items through the checkout monotonously. I asked the same questions, "Are you Catholic or Christian?" was a favourite, and quite relevant in the Philippines but I was convicted that I wasn't really using the information they supplied. I may have been congratulating myself for being direct and getting straight into a discussion about God but what was the point if that was as far as it went. I began praying that each person would see their need for a personal relationship with Jesus and that they would come to know that He was the Way, the Truth and the Life. I noticed some people thinking about it afterwards although I still couldn't be sure of their levels of comprehension.

I was also personally convicted every time we ran out of tracts, which happened a number of times. It's easy to look around and blame someone else and sometimes I didn't have control over things like that. But often it was just a lack of organisation which I could just as easily have taken responsibility for as the next person. I began to think more about things like that - carrying tracts and looking for the opportunities. That was important in the Philippines where people had so little materially that a small booklet or colourful piece of paper may have ended up as a prized possession being read over and over again.

When we debriefed the eye-glass ministry I was surprised to discover that the church youth had been counselling people who had been referred for follow up conversations. Some of the adults they had counselled were in their sixties and probably couldn't relate to them at all. I was also fairly sure that some of the youth weren't yet Christians, although others clearly were. I reluctantly raised the issue at the team debrief feeling that it was important enough to discuss. One of the Pastors said that it was a "good point" but other leaders seemed to be totally disinterested in everything that was discussed. It was common practice in Filipino meetings for people to talk to each other, walk around, prepare food, check gadgets and even take phone calls. My British sense of order and basic civility really struggled with the practices.

I wrote in my journal after the eye-glass ministry "I long to be involved in more long term work in a specific country or area. I pray that God will make my future direction clear whilst I am on the ship, but I pray that I will start now by making the most of every opportunity for evangelism. This will involve a change of mindset. Oh Lord, please help me with this and keep reminding me that I can be a positive example for the younger ones on the ship and inspire them to make a difference."

The Challenge Team was drawing to a close; we spent a day at the beach where I realised that I hadn't made as much effort as I would've liked to connect with the church members. It may have been partly due to having been ill or maybe it was just because I tended to find non-Christians relationally easier than Christians! Sadly, whilst we were at the beach a seven-year-old child, Jezebel, from a group that had based near to our group, nearly drowned in the sea. Someone shouted then ran up the beach carrying her; I got a brief glimpse of her lifeless, greying face and limp body. It was awful; judging by her appearance I was sure that she must already be dead. I suggested to the others that we should pray; they concurred and we gathered in a group as she was rushed to hospital. Whilst they were loudly declaring life in Jesus' name, I crept to the back of the group and begged God silently with tears that He wouldn't let the little girl die. He heard all of our prayers and she lived.

A few of the youth from Blessed Church decided they wanted to be baptised in the sea that day so the Pastors started making the arrangements. I was happy to hear that the young people had asked for baptism a while before, rather than it being a spur of the moment emotional whim as it had first appeared. The musicians even took their instruments into the sea to accompany the singing. It was a good opportunity to witness to other groups that had gathered to watch, although when one of the pastors told me that three teenage boys nearby had "accepted Christ" after five minutes of conversation I was a bit dubious. He had also told me that all of the people he had counselled during the eye-glass ministry had accepted Christ. I began to wonder what the statement actually meant.

'Easy Believism' or 'Decisionism' - the practice of encouraging someone to make an on-the-spot decision about becoming a Christian by raising a hand, answering an 'altar call' or repeating the 'Sinner's Prayer,' was extremely common. It wasn't necessarily too much of a problem as long as there was proper follow-up, but in a lot of cases there was none whatsoever. I'm convinced that many of the people who had allegedly 'converted' walked (or swam) away and carried on as if the conversations hadn't even taken place. Sadly, many of the church leaders couldn't see the superficiality of the conversions and the possibility of giving someone a false assurance of salvation. That was the method they had been taught by their own church leaders and they didn't know a different practice. They often didn't focus on the Biblical mandate to count the cost before following Jesus and to be asked to give up everything for Him. There was often little emphasis on discipleship or the asking of clarification questions to check understanding.

We visited one of the pastor's homes. The family told us that due to their financial difficulties the wife had just applied for a job in another country. They had two young children. I was sure that the family had probably sacrificed much for our visit, not just financially but also in terms of their time. Another church family had provided a cook for us for the three weeks and they too were subsequently in financial hardship. Their hearts were in the right place as they believed they were serving God and doing His will but it was heartbreaking to see the consequences. It seemed to me that the most important thing for Christians would be to keep the family together, even if it meant living in less of a house or making other sacrifices. But there was a generally feeling that one half of a marriage working abroad was just part of life for a Filipino.

At the end of the day I wrote "There are so many things that I don't agree with here. I played with Dexter the friendly dog outside and saw loads of cockroaches in a dirty area of the street. Gross. There were people gambling in the house opposite. The whole street was dark and children kept popping in and out of houses even though it was late. The community is much tighter than the West but the poverty is terrible to see. People are so hospitable and friendly; even though they have nothing they will share it with you."

CHAPTER THIRTY-FOUR

Farewell Blessed Church

The final days were upon us and we continued to participate in Church services and activities. On our last full day at Blessed Church we led the main church service as a team. We performed a drama encouraging the church to be involved in one to one evangelism. I agreed to provide an explanation of the drama to the church. I used Acts chapter one verse nine "You will be my witnesses in Jerusalem, Judea, Samaria and to the ends of the earth." I highlighted that we should each be missionaries in our home town initially and that if we don't have a passion for lost souls at home then travelling abroad wouldn't change that. I really felt the church needed to hear that as many of them were anxious to join the ship or to become missionaries without necessarily having heard the call of God.

One of the Pastors gave the main message which was again about mission. He stated that God would equip those who were called into mission work. He then thanked me for quoting the verse in Acts but stated that it meant that sometimes we needed to wait until we reached the ends of the earth. The implication being that everyone would eventually go abroad for foreign mission. At least I could admire their zeal. The Pastors prayed for each of us individually and thanked God for our visit. When my turn came he thanked God for my desire to reach out to the lost. I was pleased that that was what the church would remember about me and hoped that that would always be the case wherever I went!

After the seriousness of the morning session the Filipinos obviously wanted to bring some light-heartedness to the day. We played some more silly games and the youth danced a Zumba dance on the stage wearing face masks with our faces imprinted on them. When we first saw them it was very weird, but after a while I saw the funny side as the fake "me" bobbed and swayed on the stage. The youth had practised a lot and were pretty good which made the experience of watching "myself" even more strange, as I have never been into Zumba or anything like it.

The whole evening then turned into an emotional meltdown with everyone crying and hugging each other. I did tear up when speaking to one lady and also to Danny but, being British, managed to compose myself relatively quickly. The others let it all out with tears streaking down their faces. I felt a bit detached as I had been ill for so much of the time that I hadn't bonded with the Church members in the same way as the rest of the team. Despite that I was included in the array of personal notes and messages that were given to us. Here are some samples;

"Good day! I just want to tell you that you are so lovely and beautiful. I think you should just need a little bit (oh not a little bit, but a FULL SMILE), hahaha...coz you are more prettier when you're smiling. By the way, I'm so happy that God has allowed us to be with you in all our activities this past remaining days. It was so great how God showed his mighty healing power in your life. Hope to see you again! I will miss you Natalie! The joy in my heart that you are all here is always in my mind forever, God bless! Take care always!"

"Salute! Hehe! Just kiddin. You know when I was a child I really wanted to be a police officer! I wanted to be part of the CIA!!! Haha but God has other plans for me, similar to you also, God had called you in a different ministry and lifestyle...I'm really blessed with your life. How strong you are in facing the fears and obstacles in your way...I'm going to miss you."

"Mommy Natalie. Hi my dearest mom (joke) Thanks for being part of my life. Thanks for the happiness you know before I really don't know how to socialize and I'm wasting my time on being sad. I don't know why. I share it to you because I want you to know that I'm so very glad that GOD used your team to teach me to be happy all the time even I saw you slightly smile only. Thanks again mommy Natalie now I finally say that now you are part of my life. Always smile mommy. Because when you are smiling like this you're so beautiful. Love you mommy Natalie, hope you accept me as your daughter (just kidding) I will miss you. Please come back here. Hope you keep this letter as my remembrance to you. Natalie show your teeth always, it means smile always."

I wasn't quite sure what to make of the lengthy outpouring of emotion considering that we had only been at the church for three weeks! I did my best and was touched by some of the words. I came to learn that it is typical of Filipinos to express strong sentiment at an early stage in a friendship; even the men told us that they were going to "miss us." It didn't necessarily mean that they would but it was normal cultural practice to express it in that manner and there were no romantic implications!

We did stay in touch kind-of vaguely with some of the church members via social media and they visited the ship on a few occasions. The social media connection resulted in an amusing conversation some time later between myself and one of the youth after I had seen her Facebook post about wanting to get a tattoo. I was slightly bothered, thinking that she might regret it but initially determined not to intervene. I knew that at least one of our own Challenge Team members who had been to their church had a Bible verse tattooed on her wrist and thought that might be the reason for the sudden interest in getting a tattoo. In the end, I couldn't keep silent as it's not really in my nature, so I sent her a short personal message quoting a Bible verse and encouraging her not to get a tattoo. She responded politely thanking me for my concern but advising that she had been talking about getting a Tattoo broadband stick as that was one of the main Filipino providers. I thought at the time that maybe God was humbling me and convicting me about my self-righteous attitude, but looking back it's pretty funny.

On reflection, the Challenge Team had challenged me personally but I would have liked to have been involved in more structured evangelism and to not have been treated so much like royalty. The people of Blessed Church were extremely hospitable and kind especially when I had been ill. Their church was a great example of a Christian family as they served God together and looked after one another. They truly enjoyed each other's company and demonstrated an active interest in missions and missionary work. There is no such thing as a perfect church. A lot of the concerns that I had had were to do with practices that the church had adopted from within the Filipino church culture. That couldn't easily be changed but I hoped that a careful study of the Bible might bring about some change in due course.

Our Logos Hope team dynamics had been tough and being ill hadn't helped. On returning to the ship, I looked forward to a different kind of challenge. For my next team, I was hoping to be sent to a more primitive place or to be forced to face the trials of living simply for a few weeks. But first I had to brave the ship which was by then in the full throes of dry-dock.

CHAPTER THIRTY-FIVE

Dry Dock Takes Its Toll

We spent a few days at a transfer centre on-shore with all the other people who had returned from their Challenge Teams. A few of us girls watched 101 Dalmatians which definitely lightened the mood. Then the big group of us headed back to the ship for a few weeks' hard work on board prior to being sent out on our next teams. The ship was by that point in full-blown dry dock which meant long (eleven hour) exhausting days with little (if any) air conditioning. Everyone looked haggard on my arrival up the gangway but welcomed the batch of us enthusiastically, and in some cases desperately, as if we were long lost friends. I guess it was a relief for them to see some different faces and they were anticipating the new energy we would hopefully bring to the gruelling work. Many people were ill and everyone was tired; that's putting it mildly.

We were assigned to temporary cabins with random people who we didn't know because our own cabins were out of bounds. It was a bit like living in a parallel universe completely cut off from normal life outside and it began to feel oppressive early on. I felt like a zombie - just going through the daily motions of eating and working and then collapsing into bed, sometimes reading and then sleeping for a long time. The heat definitely took it out of us. I felt sorry for those who worked in the engine department who would be required to live on board for the whole period and who were unlikely to be assigned to any Challenge Teams during dry dock. I struggled with ill health throughout that period. I often left work immediately after completing my necessary duties as Store-Keeper and slept for additional hours in the daytime.

I was also worried about things in England as several of my family members had been hospitalised. I hadn't found out immediately as my mum had accidentally sent the email informing me about it to herself. I only discovered it sometime later when I got annoyed that I hadn't known what was going on earlier. My mum protested, convinced that she had informed me and when I eventually worked out what had happened I couldn't be irritated and had to laugh. My mum is a bit of a technophobe. Sadly, my Gran did eventually pass away during my Logos Hope service but she had become a Christian in the months leading up to her death, an answer to prayer dating back years.

Shortly after our group arrived back on board we were summoned to our first community meeting. The Captain announced that, due to circumstances beyond his control, dry dock would be likely to be extended for three weeks. He said that the news was unofficial and that we hadn't heard it from him! It was the first extension of many, as it turned out, but obviously we didn't know that at the time. That was probably the main reason people survived the eventual nine months. It felt like a race where the finish line was always within reach and sight, but that it just kept being moved. There wasn't a point where it was made unobtainable and so people kept striving to reach the end knowing it was out there somewhere and that they wouldn't have to endure the heat and close conditions forever.

My energy being sapped from living on the not fully functioning ship, where the air conditioning went on and off at will and sometimes even the ventilation was suspended, I couldn't make it out and about. That, ironically, was what I probably needed to do in order to start to feel better but it required too much energy to initiate. I looked for other possibilities to use my time effectively and began writing to a few prisoners whose profiles I discovered on the internet. Some of them were on death-row and I was horrified by their crimes. But having had a heart for prison ministry due to my police work I decided to give it a shot in my spare time, which was a lot at that time. I was thrilled to receive some letters by return and one from a lady called Amber who commented that my letter had "really put a smile on my face and brightened my day." I continued writing to some of the people for several years after I left the ship. I even sent quantities of books and other literature into some of the prisons they were held in. Also, I joined Epalworld - an online community exchanging emails to build friendships.

Obviously, my plan was to share the Gospel with people and I did have some interesting conversations. It seems strange looking back that I was so anxious to fill my every waking moment with evangelism, feeling as if there wasn't a second to lose and that souls were at stake. Undoubtedly, that is true but the urgency, or maybe my motivation, has ebbed and flowed through the years. The passion is still there but I don't think there has been a time since that dry dock period, when I was really feeling so unwell, that I have been so determinedly committed to evangelism. Maybe God was proving that He uses us in our weakness in order that He keeps the glory.

Time also allowed me to do a lot of reading as I wasn't fit for much else after work. I read a book about the work of London City Mission (Waterloo Mission/Webber Street) and a letter that they had received from a member of the public reprinted there caught my eye. I have lost the title of the book so I hope it won't get me into copyright trouble:

"Dear Sir,

I walk past the above premises several times each week. I have become familiar with some of the faces and occasionally exchange greetings with them. That said, once passed by they disappear from your thoughts pretty quickly. However, yesterday morning was rather different. I walked down Webber Street and side-stepped one of the regulars who was face down on the ground, semi-conscious with his hand outstretched towards a beer can. People scurried past, often averting their eyes. They do not consider the 'down and outs' worthy of any attention or indeed sympathy. Then I noticed a young man descend from the stairs of your mission. Watching, as I had stopped to have a conversation on my mobile phone, I initially assumed he was coming to make this vagrant move on. But no. Instead he crouched beside this forlorn figure and stroked his face with tenderness and apparent affection. It was a moving and somewhat shameful moment for me. It made me realise that this person on the street was a real person just like me, albeit perhaps less fortunate. I am grateful for that realisation. I hope that the attached contribution can be used to assist in the good work of the Webber Street Mission, Yours Sincerely……."

I felt conviction on reading the letter and wondered if I would show genuine affection to someone in that state, when not being observed by another. It wasn't long before I had the opportunity to find out.

I was personally challenged by an alcoholic homeless woman by the name of LJ. LJ had spent a lot of time on the ship when it was open and gravitated towards people who had listened to her problems. I had seen Ina from Indonesia hugging her at length in the I-café one day. I had been convicted knowing that LJ smelt terrible as she had often wet herself and rarely bathed or showered. I wondered whether, if I were placed in the same situation, I would be able to see the person inside the broken body and to show God's love regardless.

LJ did start following me everywhere during dry-dock, constantly needing attention, asking me to buy things for her and wanting hugs. If she was refused she became an instant enemy and related it back to her past bad experiences with Christians. It was really difficult to know how best to handle her demands being a non-tactile British person. I just did my best but sometimes I felt that she was deliberately being placed in my path to force me to demonstrate my Christian values. I reluctantly complied, but didn't feel very Christian about it! I supposed I should've been grateful that a few hugs was the extent of it. Some of the guys temporarily became targets for her romantic affection. She named them as her boyfriends and attempted to cuddle them at every opportunity.

Finally, at the point that dry dock had just been extended for the second time I was informed that I would be sent on another Challenge Team. I had high hopes feeling that a lot of the first team had been wasted through illness and so was excited and ready for a new challenge. Mia, my Chinese friend, was not as excited when she saw that she was also on the list having received a promise from personnel that she wouldn't have to go again. Normally quiet and demure she startled us all by announcing, with eyes flashing, that she was going to tell Dan (the personnel manager,) that he was a man of God and that therefore he should let his 'yes be yes' and his 'no, no.' If that didn't work in convincing him to change his mind she had a plan to go to the galley and eat mango which she was allergic to and her last resort was to leave the ship in protest and head home to China! I was glad that others were experiencing the same range of emotions as I was.

Mia often kept me amused; she had gone to the cinema in a large group during dry dock and they had had to choose between the films Spiderman and Abraham Lincoln. They had already seen the former but on starting to watch the latter discovered it was actually entitled 'Abraham Lincoln Vampire Diaries.' Mia didn't know what a vampire was so sat through the first ten minutes or so before walking out when she realised! I found it hilarious as I could just imagine it and her reaction as she stormed out probably leaving her companions baffled. I said that I was proud of her.

CHAPTER THIRTY-SIX

Home of Joy

My second Challenge Team was again in Manila. Others may have been disappointed to be assigned a team within the Philippines as we had been there for a long time already and teams were being sent to other countries. But I was quite happy as I had started to enjoy being in the Philippines and was developing a heart for the people.

My second team would stay at an orphanage called 'Home of Joy' and conduct evangelistic programmes and church activities at a nearby student campus. I was primarily looking forward to the evangelistic aspect. I made sure we had enough Gospels and tracts remembering that we had run out on our previous team. A lot of other teams followed suit which began a run on the Book Hold storeroom, but I'm sure the manager didn't mind.

My new team were all women and there were six of us: Sarah (Holland), team leader Carina (Switzerland,) Sol (Equador,) Eunha (South Korea) and Lucy (Taiwan.) We left the ship very early on our departure date and travelled for four hours on a bus which was always interesting in Manila as it's a bit like being on a race track. It's okay if you don't look out of the window, but definitely don't ever sit at the front of the bus so you can see exactly what's going on, as it can feel like being in a rollercoaster simulator.

Arriving at the bus station we tried to get a taxi to the orphanage but apparently the place we needed to travel to didn't exist. Oh dear. Locals then gathered around offering ridiculous rates to take us somewhere else. Our host had in the meantime sent a text message advising us to walk the remainder of the journey, but we had a lot of luggage. The taxi drivers suggested that they could drive us around searching for the bus we needed. I had been told never to trust a Filipino taxi driver as some didn't see it as morally wrong to try to extort large amounts of cash from an unsuspecting foreigner. They saw it as their entitlement as the foreigner could afford it. In the end, we flagged down a full bus, causing a traffic jam in the process.

We had to pile our luggage at the front of the bus and stand in the aisle causing much annoyance to the other passengers who we frequently bashed into due to the reckless driving. We were charged for an additional two passengers due to our luggage even though none of us had seats. I then noticed some of the bus staff fiddling with our luggage after seeing the reflection in a mirror. It was really all quite stressful and not how I would have hoped our team would begin and, although I was able to share the Gospel with the man sitting in the seat next to me, I was relieved when we arrived at our final destination and were collected by our host!

Our drive to the orphanage was pleasant (well any alternative to what we had thus far experienced would be in comparison.) We revelled in the green surroundings and large modern buildings as we swept past. We were given a snack on arrival which cheered us up and then were seated on comfortable sofas for an orientation which was where things started to go really badly wrong. We were informed that we were to become 'house parents' for the entire three-week period. The regular staff had been sent on a break. Our team would be separated with two of us living with the children in each house and forming part of their families. Each house held between six and ten children including babies. We would be responsible for their care including feeding, washing, clothing, changing nappies and discipline as well as the more practical housework: laundry, dishes, cooking and cleaning. Our day would begin at 5 am and end at 7 pm.

On hearing all of that I was speechless; we hadn't even been asked if we liked children prior to being sent on the team. But seemingly we were to become temporary foster parents for a three-week period. Having worked in Child Protection I knew that the last thing the already damaged and needy children needed was people who would appear in their lives for a short period, form emotional bonds and then leave again. To try to salvage something from the catastrophe I asked when we would be doing the campus ministry, church activities and other evangelism. The response; "Oh you won't have any time for that, there's too much to be done here."

We were handed a long document which turned out on closer inspection to be a contract of employment for our roles at the orphanage. I read the small print and caught a clause which stated that we would be personally and financially responsible for any negligence which resulted in harm to the children. I queried that knowing that none of us had appropriate qualifications or experience for that level of responsibility and was informed that we must sign the contracts. I said we needed time to take them away and examine them and asked if we could come back to it later. The slight concession was granted. We were then shown around the place and to our rooms only to discover that we would be sharing rooms with some of the children, including a teenage boy with special needs. One of us would have to sleep alone with two babies and wake up during the night in order to feed them. It was all too much for me and I felt completely overwhelmed.

We had a private team meeting and I explained to the others how I felt. I said that I wasn't ready to be a parent, didn't want the responsibility and that it was harmful for the children for us to be there for just three weeks and then leave. The rest of the team wanted to give it a week although they also had concerns. Our team leader agreed to phone the ship leadership to find out what we were actually meant to be doing there. The message was relayed that we were not allowed to have responsibility for the children and that we were not there to be care givers. Some further concessions were made but in practice not a lot changed and the ship leadership were reluctant to remove us from the situation probably due to logistics more than anything else. They did say that they would communicate with our host to see if an agreement could be reached and if it couldn't they would "get us out of there."

I became so upset about the whole situation that I started to doubt my reasons for being on the ship in the first place Serious questions began surfacing in my mind. I began to think about ending my commitment after the first year due to my frustrations and the lack of specific evangelism which was what I had been expecting. Everything was such a battle and I couldn't see a way out of the mess at Home of Joy. I felt isolated within the team as the others had decided to try to make the best of things.

Everything was up in the air as two of us had expressed our desire to leave but the rest of the team were happy to remain and take care of the children. Sol had developed serious infected open wounds on her legs although she said she was okay. I was worried as we had been told that that type of thing if left untreated could lead to amputation later down the line!

I withdrew from the rest of the team, still insisting that I wanted to leave and feeling the burden of the demands of the children. I was also bothered that the very young children were being left to watch TV on a mattress all day with no scheduled activities. Eventually the ship leadership relented and agreed to find beds for me and Lucy back on the ship. We were informed that we had to go and see Personnel as soon as we returned to the ship. It felt like a black cloud was hanging over us.

One of the olive branches before we left was that we could lead a youth evangelism programme at the nearby campus. One of our team members dropped out due to the division in the team. The remainder said that as it was my 'thing' I should be the one to lead it and arrange everything. I agreed reluctantly as it was indeed 'my thing.' In the end, it went really well. At the end of our presentation we gave each student a John's Gospel asking them either to keep it for themselves or to give it to a friend or neighbour to try to encourage them to share the Gospel with others. It was a real joy to see them all clutching the Gospels at the end. I was glad we had brought enough literature on that occasion and that we had persisted in obtaining permission for the event despite the traumatic environment.

Lucy and I left after just a few days for the long journey back to the ship, during which we got lost several times after receiving misinformation from a bus driver. I began to wonder if we would ever find our way having ended up miles from the correct path. It was a miracle that we made it really as we had been in the middle of nowhere and just left to make our own way back to the ship. I prayed desperately for direction. We needed to speak to Personnel to resolve things and it was weighing heavily on my mind and heart. On arriving in the general area of the ship after around eight hours travelling, we had to lug our heavy bags for the final part of the journey as no one had offered to collect us. Indeed, really we felt like the prodigal children by that point and were both exhausted and demoralised.

On walking up the gangway and through the ship door I was confronted by Brian who asked me whether I had returned to the ship for 'theological reasons,' as if that was what he had expected of me. I set him straight on that point and, being too upset to talk about it, told him I would tell him about it later.

Personnel met with us straight away and there were a lot of tears and straightening things out. I think the turning point was probably when I showed them a copy of the contract we had been asked to sign; they were shocked and said that they were glad that we hadn't signed it. The rest of the team had settled down by that point and decided to remain at the orphanage. It took me a long time to get over the trauma of that episode, especially the feeling of being abandoned when we were initially told we would have to remain in the situation. It left me reluctant to take part in any further challenge teams.

As a side note to the story, I actually ended up inadvertently revisiting 'Home of Joy' when working as an independent missionary back in the Philippines in 2015. I had joined the annual camp for the homeless people from our church and was accompanying a social worker to see a friend of hers at a "nearby orphanage." Of course, it didn't even cross my mind that it would be the same one. There were hundreds of those places in in the Philippines and I wasn't even sure of the name of the city that I had stayed in before as it had been for such a brief period. I thought it a bit odd when she said it was called 'Home of Joy' but the Filipinos tend to use names like that repeatedly almost as generic names so I wasn't that surprised.

As we drew nearer I felt a sense of horror on recognising the place that I had dramatically left after just a few days a couple of years previously. Typically, I then recognised the staff member who had shown us around on that dreadful day as she tried to get us to sign the unworkable contracts accepting unlimited liability. She was, of course, the 'friend' that my social worker friend had been referring to. I would've laughed at the coincidence on any other day, but it was going to be painfully awkward. On seeing that she didn't immediately recognise me, I determined to make it through the reunion by hiding my face as much as possible and standing behind other people, posts and anything else that could provide cover. Cowardly, you may think, but I didn't want to embarrass my friend who obviously knew the woman quite well. Things were going well as I hovered in the background until we were about to leave. Thinking I had got away with it and avoided the scene that would be likely to be created, the woman approached me making some comment about the fact I was from England. As has been mentioned before, all Filipinos are excessively interested in people from England. "I'm sure I recognise you" she said and then kept repeating variations of that as I hastily backed away commenting that I just had one of those faces and hoping against hope that she wouldn't put two and two together before we had the chance to depart.

    I did feel guilty for misleading her but, as I had been less than complimentary about both her facility and the things that we had been expected to do on the previous occasion, I thought the wisest thing to do was to say nothing and move on. I got away with it, just, but I'm sure the lady was left scratching her head and that at some stage there was a lightbulb moment. On leaving I immediately told my friend what had happened before and she thought the whole situation was hilarious. I was glad she saw the funny side as I had been mortified at the prospect of being discovered and having to provide explanations to both of them for what had gone before. I was reminded that it is indeed a very small world.

CHAPTER THIRTY-SEVEN

Prison Ministry

Having decided that I never again wanted to go on a Challenge Team and refusing the opportunity when it was presented to me, I was forced to resign myself to long-term dry dock work. In the circumstances, I began actively looking for opportunities to get involved in more evangelistic outreach. My first venture was to join a team of people heading to a Women's Prison every Sunday for visitation and to lead a church service. It was managed and led by a local Pastor who had (as I understood) a long-term relationship with the ship ministry. Pastor Tony was an enthusiastic and keen leader of the ministry but he didn't seem to be connected with a specific church at that time. In the Philippines (and elsewhere) many people are given the name 'Pastor' but their actual role isn't always clear. Some of them have even downloaded the certificate from the internet to prove their qualification for the role.

I had spent the morning in a ship church service trying to listen to the main message whilst ignoring the female crew member who had gone to the stage and rebuked the evil spirits apparently taking power back from them, whatever that means. I was keen therefore to do some 'normal' ministry and the jail seemed like the perfect place.

I had been asked to share my testimony. We were nine and the inmates were thirty. It began well with the inmates singing joyfully about the love of God which raised a smile even from me. My testimony went well if a little dry; I realised I needed to focus more on the application otherwise it can be just a nice story that wouldn't convict or help anyone. The main message was also well spoken by one of the guys. The problem arose when it was time for communion, which formed a major part of any service in the Philippines. I had heard of it being administered to non-believers in England by Multi-

Faith Hospital Chaplains, but to see that the practice had spread to third world countries was a bit of a worry. I nudged the main speaker and whispered that I hoped we weren't about to give communion to all assembled as the majority were likely non-believers. Nothing had been said to check their spiritual state or warn them not to take communion unless they were truly trusting Jesus. The Pastor did then mention that but in a culture where every effort is made to please people and to avoid offence I'm pretty sure the warning went unheeded. In any event, all those gathered took the bread and wine offered. I accepted that it wasn't my responsibility and that I couldn't do anything about it.

After the service, there was an awkward moment as the women tried to persuade us to buy their hand-made items. I didn't want to purchase an item that I didn't need just to make them feel better. But the situation became uncomfortable as I wondered how many of the women had attended the service and taken communion all the while thinking about the items they could sell to the foreigners afterwards. It was troubling as they knew that we cared about them due to both the things we had shared in our testimonies and message and the fact that we had attended in the first place.

Back at the ship a few of us chatted about the jail ministry and the limited opportunities for ministry whilst in dry dock. It was suggested that we should seek out opportunities for ourselves and not just wait for them to fall into our laps as that was unlikely to happen. The prison ministry continued although I only went for the first few visits due to getting involved in street children ministry very soon after my first prison visits. After many weeks of Bible Studies, I believe the team ended up baptising over forty women who had professed faith whilst in the jail. I don't know how many of them are still following Jesus but the team had carried out proper follow up due to the lengthy dry dock so I'm hopeful that the conversions were genuine.

I had observed on my first Challenge Team that willing local Christians who, in normal circumstances, would have had other commitments were being drawn into the ministry of the Logos Hope. Sometimes it created hardship for those who gave too much. The lengthy dry dock meant that Filipinos, who should've been supporting their families, and local churches were side-tracked into ship related ministry. A Pastor who spends the majority of his time on the ship instead of in his church because it's a more dynamic and exciting ministry. A family who sacrifice everything to send several key members as volunteers to the electrical team but who are also trying to raise many foster children. Churches who give up their day of rest to come to the ship on Sundays. All of those things bothered me as I felt we should be playing a supportive role in encouraging local churches, not establishing new ministries that the churches would then be forced to take over when we left.

It's a complicated subject as it wasn't necessarily the Logos Hope's fault that it happened. We couldn't exactly stop the locals from being as enthusiastic as they were about the ship ministry. It was a case of "this is God's work, therefore we must abandon everything else and give ourselves wholeheartedly to the ministry." Maybe it was okay for a normal ship visit of about three weeks in each port but I'm sure the eventual nine-month dry dock had some negative effects on those who gave too much.

CHAPTER THIRTY-EIGHT

Help without Hope; The Ultimate Tragedy

Since leaving the ship, ensuring that help and hope are administered together has become one of my passions. I believe the enemy seeks to undermine all Christian Gospel focused ministry by changing it into social justice or action. It was evident on the ship and there was a constant fight to keep the Gospel at the centre. As my one-year mark was approaching some key ship leaders were leaving.

During his farewell testimony, Sam, a ship leader from England, reminded us that we needed to keep our focus on the Gospel; he mentioned that he had struggled with that on the ship. Dan, also a leader from England, reiterated that social action or justice without the Gospel was pointless and advising us to keep 'lobbying' the leadership for tracts. That was because at times the ship itself had actually run out of tracts and Gospel books and we had had to wait for more to arrive although it became less of a problem in my second year. I was concerned that our ship promotional leaflets didn't contain the basic Gospel message and in some cases didn't even mention that we sold Christian books! I raised the issue that not everyone who received a flyer would visit the ship and that therefore we were not making the most of our opportunities to share the Gospel. I was disappointed that despite assurances to the contrary the Gospel message was still absent from the flyers on my leaving the ship.

I had an idea to get more people taking tracts and leaflets out with them on their days off whilst the ship was in dry dock. I took my idea to the leadership thinking that would be the extent of my involvement having made the suggestion. But, of course, they turned it round on me and made me responsible for making it happen, which was fair enough as I had had the idea. I placed a table at the gangway with the literature and ensured it was regularly stocked. Thinking that would be sufficient I relaxed a little and was excited by the enthusiasm of those who began carrying tracts in their bags and handing them out to people they saw in the street. I was even informed that the local non-Christian dry dock workers often read the literature on the table whilst they were having breaks or at the start and end of their shifts.

Unfortunately, not everyone shared my zeal and within a few weeks the table and literature had been packed away in an old store cupboard as the dry dock work progressed and it was considered to be an obstacle or Health and Safety hazard. I had to jump through a few hoops to get it reinstated but was a bit frustrated that others didn't always prioritise evangelism in that way. I guess it shouldn't have surprised me as I had already discovered that some were on board for the work, others for the travelling and to see the world; there were even those who believed that the Bible doesn't teach us to evangelise. I wondered how they had been recruited in the first place!

My evangelism frustrations were levelled by the resumption of our entertaining Ship Family Night after a few months of cessation due to people being away on teams and working too hard. Shamy unexpectedly announced that she would be leaving earlier than planned to continue her studies at home. Uncle Rodney solemnly informed her that he would miss her 'eyelashes' before picking up on a conversation about a kitchen knife and launching into an amended version of "Take my life and let it be." He substituted the 'life' for 'knife' and then changed it to 'wife,' who although dutifully sitting next to him had by that point a rather bored expression on her face. Irene had obviously put up with her husband's diabolical humour for many years. It did raise a laugh from the rest of us, however, and I thought to myself that I would never be able to sing that hymn seriously again.

Frank then added to the hilarity (as he always managed to do, often unintentionally) by looking confused when Rodney was talking about his two children. He then apologised and said that he had forgotten the names of the children having met them a fair number of times already. Rodney made up some really long and complicated foreign sounding names which Frank spent quite a while trying to pronounce before Rodney took pity on him and reminded him of their very simple names, Justin and Marianne. Frank then asked which was male and which was female which set us all off again. We had a visitor to our family that day who, in trying to make polite conversation and learning our assorted originating countries, proceeded to asked Silas whether he spoke German. Silas' responded "Yes" and then under his breath which most of us caught, "most Germans do."

Our family meal was buoyed with a general buzz of excitement from the outset, because we had been told that we would finally be leaving dry dock and sailing on to pastures new and that we would likely be leaving within a few days. 'Crazy Dany', whose nickname had been extended to the rest of the ship, who whole-heartedly agreed with the label, always took things one step further than everyone else. He arrived to join us for dinner late and fell backwards off the wooden bench with his plate of food balancing precariously on his fingertips. One of our number somehow managed to retrieve the plate thereby preventing disaster but, as Dany recovered himself, he informed us that he had just electrocuted himself at work in the Engine Room. Whoever put Dany in the Engine Room in the first place probably has some explaining to do as it was a very risky decision.

The technical personnel got as far as flooding the dock in preparation for our departure, but sadly it was not to be. Water began pouring in through leaks in the engine room. Clearly, we weren't going to be going anywhere for some time.

CHAPTER THIRTY-NINE

On-Shore Book-Fair

Due to our forced continuation in dry dock the leadership began planning further Challenge Teams to try to make sure we were occupied as we entered what was called 'Phase six.' There had originally been just two phases I think. By that point I had largely forgotten my terrible Challenge Team experience and had been comforted when others had returned early from another team. I was no longer the Brit who had led the only on-board Challenge Team rebellion in the history of the ship ministry.

So, when I overheard a manager discussing a team that would be sent to the local shopping mall to set up a mini version of the Book-Fair on-shore I was interested. The downside - Trevor had been assigned to take part in the team and, as I was the only other Store-Keeper, I would have to remain on-board or persuade Trevor to swap. I also felt slightly guilty as I had made a big fuss about not wanting to go on another team and my leaders had respected that. Yet there I was just a few weeks down the line changing my mind and begging to go on one. The fact was that my heart had always been (and still is) in the literature ministry so the team appealed to me far more than any other may have done. But I realised that from an independent perspective I could be perceived as being spoilt or just demanding things in order to get my own way.

Trevor, bless him, received my request calmly, took some time to think about it and then decided that honestly he would rather stay on the ship anyway as he didn't have much of an interest in the mini Book-Fair. I could go instead. I wondered if Trevor was just being nice but I ran into him a few times after our team had moved on-shore and he said he was enjoying his work on-board. He also continued to respond good-naturedly to my teasing after I spent ten minutes one day mocking him for saying that he wanted to go to 'IKEA.' In my mind, it was a representation of Western comfort and culture and he deserved to be mocked having verbalised his desire. But my enthusiasm was quickly dampened when someone else in our group advised me that Trevor had actually said that he had had an 'idea' and that 'IKEA' hadn't even been mentioned. So, I was forced to eat humble pie and hastily withdraw my prior comments whilst at the same time wondering how on earth that had been lost in translation. After all Trevor was from Canada and his accent wasn't that pronounced.

A small group of us went to the movies around that time which was a rarity for me. We had set off in the torrential rain and Trevor's umbrella had immediately fallen to pieces. We took shelter in a doorway and played I-spy to pass the time. We eventually made a dash for the next building and were running single file to avoid the huge puddles when suddenly a crowd of men appeared from a side alley. They just popped out and surrounded us shouting in our faces "taxi, taxi" over and over again whilst gesticulating wildly. They were pointing at the rain as if we hadn't noticed it and advising us that a deluge was coming and that we needed to take a taxi, obviously. Trevor hilariously waved his arms back in their faces as they had been doing to us saying "no, no, no." I pointed out that they were "just doing their jobs" but his view was "and I'm just trying to walk along the road." When we finally reached the movie *Ice Age 4* he continually made remarks throughout, commenting that some aspects were unrealistic until finally I told him to be quiet as it was just animation!

Returning to the Challenge Team, I was advised that all of us would be living on-shore in a house owned by a local charity. I was to be assistant shift leader for one of the Mini Book-Fair teams. Our house was big and it was nice to get a break from the ship, specifically the confinement and conditions in dry dock. I was also hopeful that we would have a bit more freedom because we would be living in a separate house. We were instructed to treat it as a proper Challenge Team with team devotions each day and meetings etc. The house was badly in need of repair. We discovered that early on when my laptop got soaked after water leaked in through a boarded-up window. The water had run down the wall near a socket. The socket sparked every time I plugged a gadget in so I lived in constant fear of electric shocks. But none of that was abnormal in the Philippines so we just had to make the best of it. Which we did.

When we were settled into the house, a few of us went to check out the allocated space for the Book-Fair in the Ayala Mall at Harbour Point, Olongapo City. The mall looked as if it had been newly opened. It was the first time I had been there for any length of time although I was aware that others had been regularly visiting for months already. It felt a bit like an empty hospital as everything was white and many of the shops were still vacant. There were very few people in circulation. I wondered how on earth the shops could even afford to operate with such minimal sales.

The Filipino mall manager Argee showed us around. It was looking likely that we would be given a whole shop to stock. We returned to the ship excited by the prospect of combining selling books with evangelism. Our manager Johan (Holland) stressed the ministry aspect of our team and that it wasn't about selling books but that it was about drawing people into conversation. It was also the reason the shop would be fairly open with relatively few security measures taken. If someone wanted to steal a Bible, God bless them!

I was also happy to hear that we would not be working or opening our mini Book-Fair on Sundays. It was a nice surprise for me as I had struggled with the twenty-four-seven culture of the ship from the outset and felt that we should at least be observing a rest day once a week regardless of which day it was. I had spoken to the Director about it but was given all sorts of different reasons as to why we had to open on Sundays. Unfortunately, most of the reasons related to book sales - that it was the busiest day and Sunday was the only day some people had off work to visit. Even if we had observed Monday as a whole community rest day that would've been better and in some countries we did that. I thought back to when we had arrived in Malaysia and the secular port authorities had assumed that we would be closed on Sunday as our Christian day of rest. There had been a real chance to witness to them through our observance of the Lords Day, but sadly we went ahead and opened on Sundays so the opportunity was lost.

The safety rules relating to how many were required to be in a group and being alone with someone of the opposite gender were relaxed for our team. It was not practical to adhere to them all the time due to the small teams and requirements to walk to and from the ship constantly. Our manager joked that if we developed romantic feelings for each other we should let him know. I commented that the age gaps were too large for that to be a problem for me. At which point a young guy from Germany piped up "Well you never know as my Grandparents are thirteen years apart," before wishing that he had kept his mouth shut as I looked embarrassed and everyone else began sniggering.

The discussion continued as 'Auntie' Irene, who happened to be present, commented that age gaps were "definitely weird when people were younger, such as the difference between someone who was ten and someone who was twenty." She realised her massive mistake immediately. The conversation deteriorated rapidly after that as we joked about marrying rich people then waiting for them to die in order to inherit, or doing away with them if one was tired of waiting. Irene shocked us all by asking me whether I might be able to conceal the evidence of such a crime using my police knowledge. Refusing to answer her question, I asked her instead where Rodney (her husband) was as he usually kept her in line!

During our initial setting-up of the book-fair we obviously had to work long hours carting heavy boxes of books and other essential items from the ship. On one of the trips our Logos Hope labelled van was pulled over by the police. We had been warned about that but assumed it wouldn't happen in a clearly marked van. All of the local people knew that the Logos Hope was visiting and that we were a charity mission ship. The police wouldn't generally pull us over as they were looking for bribes and we didn't have any money. A whole bunch of us were squashed together on the floor in the back of the van, obviously illegal and probably a tad unsafe. But in the Philippines where road rules are not rigidly enforced it hadn't been our priority on setting out. We held our collective breath and then prayed as the police began talking to our driver. I heard our driver offering the policemen a ship tour, maybe he thought it was better than a bribe. But the police had started wandering towards the rear door and were intent on opening it. I'm sure our driver then told the police he couldn't open the door as he didn't have a key! Anyway, the police gave up shortly after that and let us go with an agreement to visit the ship in due course. Maybe the driver had panicked and said the first thing that had come into his head. It's difficult to know how we would act if put on the spot and once the words are out they can't be withdrawn.

We settled into routines at our new house relatively quickly, sharing household chores and the cooking. I entered the kitchen one day and proceeded to reach forward to open a cupboard underneath the sink. I was stopped in my tracks by a rather panicky loud "No, don't, the ants live there!" I turned to face Daniel, the nineteen-year-old German, whose facial expression matched the consternation in his voice. "What do you mean, the ants live there?" I asked indignantly as I opened the door. "Oh" I said, observing the hundreds of ants zipping to and fro inside the otherwise empty cupboard. What a ridiculous situation - a cupboard that had been dedicated entirely to the convenience of the insects who had set up shop permanently.

There were a few arguments in the house, but mostly it was just fun to get to know some new people. The cultural discussions always made for good evening entertainment. Daniel informed us that sheep in Germany didn't say "baaaaa" they said "meeeh." On seeing our blank expressions, he felt the need to enhance his statement but unfortunately began his explanation with "well, when you're being a sheep..." Continuing the sheep theme, I told a very poor joke from childhood "What do you call a sheep with no legs?" but was rather bemused by the answers I received: "sheepless," "handicapped" and "legless." I finally managed the punchline which was "a cloud," but the wrong suggestions had made more people laugh. That, I discovered is what happens when you tell British jokes in an international community, they are totally misunderstood, no one finds them funny and they laugh about something completely unrelated.

We had community devotional times where we sang Christian songs and took turns to give a testimony or thought for the day. It was good and more "real" than many things I'd taken part in since I joined the ship. However, I did have to intervene when a Korean girl repeatedly used the word "safari" instead of "suffering" as she was leading the devotion.

When it was my turn to lead, I was interrupted by a young guy from Thailand who told me that whenever I spoke there was "nothing in his brain." After the laughter died down I realised he meant that his English wasn't yet sufficient to understand or that I was speaking too quickly for him. I tried to slow down and simplify my words but couldn't resist occasionally asking him whether there was anything in his brain that day to check my subsequent deliveries.

In the larger ship community, people were often encouraged by random speeches from the stage that didn't appear to be about anything specifically encouraging or even about ministry. Living in a Christian community involved looking at everything through rose tinted spectacles. But I was more of a realist so I found it troubling and wanted to see some critical thinking in evidence. Stories of ministry always encouraged me though and there were plenty to be had during our on-shore Book-Fair team. The stories came not so much from the mall ministry which only had an average of one or two customers a day in the end, but from another ministry that grew out of it because of the lack of customers visiting the mall - the bridge ministry.

CHAPTER FORTY

The Bridge

The bridge ministry had been started by a small group of us who had been bored and felt a bit useless during dry dock. Tony from Palestine and Nick from Georgia had been the main instigators of the initial idea. We decided to set up a book table on a local pedestrian bridge across a large river and a short walk from the ship. It was one of the main thoroughfares into Olongapo City and was always teeming with people. The purpose was obviously evangelistic, to try to engage people as they passed us. We had been operating for a few weeks on Saturdays when our Challenge Team began. Our ship Book-Fair manager Johan then decided to incorporate the bridge ministry into the Challenge Team. Half of us went to the shop in the mall and half to the bridge each day. Nick and Thabo from South Africa and I became the 'faces' of the bridge ministry and we were there on most days throughout the period.

At the bridge, we had some truly great discussions with Catholics lacking assurance or believing that they needed to earn their way to heaven. I was also confronted one day by a large angry gay man demanding to know whether God accepted gays. I answered that any sexual activity outside marriage is a sin in God's eyes. The man was outraged and poured scorn on me but his partner took a Gospel of John as he did so. Another man told me that he used to be 'born again' but decided that the Bible was using the wrong name for Jesus and was therefore corrupted. He was obviously obsessed with the idea and had allowed it to take over his life and sadly his faith which had died a slow death.

A further man appeared and used shockingly vile language when I asked if I could help him. Nick who was standing nearby calmly turned to face the man and said quietly "Can I ask you, do you have a sister?"

The man said "Yes I do." Nick replied "Good, now would you like it if I used that kind of language in front of your sister?" The man said "No I wouldn't." Nick replied "Well this is my sister, please don't use language like that in front of her." The man said "I'm sorry, really sorry." I was impressed and grateful for the intervention as I had been shocked into silence by the language used. But I thought afterwards that Nick would get himself in trouble as some girls on the ship were borderline feminist and may take offence thinking they could handle it themselves.

I thanked Nick; he was surprised and said that it was normal in his culture and men would never speak like that in front of a woman. He said that he had wanted to punch the man at first. The hostilities obviously faded quickly as shortly after the incident I returned to the bridge table to find Nick and the offensive man wearing silly sunglasses and dancing and singing together. A few days later Nick predictably got himself in trouble by offering to carry some heavy boxes for a German girl who was offended by his offer.

On another day, a white man informed me that he was Catholic but believed he had one thousand and one lives. When I responded to the somewhat bizarre statement I was informed that I had been "trained well" which left me feeling a little frustrated as I obviously hadn't been trained in what to say when sharing the Gospel and was trying to speak from my heart. But I guess when a person believes they have one thousand and one lives there isn't really a sensible starting point so I probably should've just smiled sweetly and said "That's nice" or something similarly bland.

I was grateful to have at least one encouraging conversation that same day with a man named Napoleon who, after I had presented the Gospel to him feeling a little discouraged and lacking faith, announced enthusiastically "So you mean Jesus is like a bridge." And followed that with "So all worldly things, possessions, jobs etc. are useless without faith." Finally, someone who was getting it. I wanted to shout "Hallelujah" and give him a big hug, but I contained myself for his sake.

I spent a lot of time also conversing with the Jehovah's Witnesses (JW) and Mormons who frequented the bridge, also giving out tracts. Although some of them deliberately side-lined our work or competed with us for 'customers.' One Mormon man sharply informed me that he had once been 'born again' but had then found the real truth in Mormonism, before stalking off and refusing to speak to us. Another had been having a conversation with Nick. I had joined the conversation and Nick was telling me that he thought the person believed the same as us and was a Christian. I shook my head and waited for the inevitable. I fired a few basic questions and then watched Nick's eyes widen at the response as he said "Oh my." That was one difference between the Mormons and the JWs. The Mormons wanted us to believe that we were united in our beliefs and we had to be very specific with our questions to ascertain what they actually believed, whereas the JWs were clearer that theirs was a different faith.

One of the JWs did a double take when I showed her John chapter one verse one in my Bible one day. But I noticed that when she read it aloud from my Bible she missed out the crucial words indicating that Jesus is God. I was amazed by the willing self-deception, but a fellow crew member pointed out that the JWs have their own Bible and that her quote was probably from that. She couldn't see the true words because she was so used to reading the false ones. She had become totally indoctrinated into the JW belief system. Unfortunately, at that key moment a street lady came and stood between us and began talking loudly in my face so I lost my opportunity to extend the conversation. Nevertheless, I believe she had been challenged sufficiently.

Another man then approached me and on taking a Gospel from my hand said loudly "my sin is adultery." Rusti had mental health problems but I was alone at the bridge. I took him to meet with a male crew member and on the way he kept asking if he could live with me as he was homeless and I was beautiful. Rusti made a profession of faith and was given a Bible but I'm not convinced that he truly understood what he was doing. It was one of the disadvantages of the short-term type ministry as we didn't have any effective follow up plans. He returned to the bridge repeatedly after that and I made the mistake of asking him one day if he was 'good.' Of course, he replied "Yes, good in bed," before quickly adding that he was joking. I summoned Nick to take over the conversation and before long they were merrily singing Christian songs. I stood at a distance with another crew member who thought it was amusing that

I had unceremoniously dumped Rusti onto Nick. I was just relieved that Rusti had kept his physical distance after one old alcoholic man had kissed me on the neck!

Nick had by that point managed to befriend the manager of Ayala Mall, the guy named Argee who had originally shown us around. In time Argee made a profession of faith and began attending church. He was also helpful in a few situations we faced at the bridge including a man who confided that he was desperate for work. Argee went to lunch with him and offered him a job cleaning in the mall. At first the man took the work gratefully but then decided he found the job boring and quit. We knew that we could only help people to a certain extent and that what they truly needed was saving faith in Jesus, but being able to help practically as well sometimes gave an added dimension to our bridge ministry.

We also learned that cross-gender ministry could get complicated and were often left scratching our heads and wondering whether the person we had just witnessed to was more interested in us or in Jesus. I was one day followed by a Muslim man when I was heading to the ship. I shared the Gospel with him and gave him a Gospel of John. He was listening intently but afterwards asked for my phone number. I had been wondering why he didn't appear to feel any kind of hostility during my earlier speech. It was not uncommon but generally we learned to juggle people and pass them on to their own gender if we sensed a 'special one-sided attachment' was being formed. There were also the random Filipinos who approached us excitedly just to ask if they could add us on Facebook. I found it a bit weird, back to the celebrity culture again, but always said yes thinking it might prove fruitful in the future and that I could always block them if they harassed me. Others were not as willing to share their personal details and probably offended some people unintentionally.

The bridge ministry continued for many months although it turned mainly into an outreach to share the Gospel with street children addicted to solvents who were living under the bridge. Locally the neglected children were known as the 'rugby boys.' You can read the full story about the group of boys in my first book 'They're Rugby Boys, Don't You Know?' My journey on Logos Hope became very much about that ministry and those boys from that point onwards although obviously I had other duties on the ship.

Our Challenge Team ended after the customary three or four-week period although I was allowed to remain for a few weeks longer. I was a bit frustrated that some of the people I had been working with regularly were removed at the point that they had just built relationships with people in the community. At least one was told that he had done enough ministry already and that it was time to let others get involved. It may seem like a fair enough reason but the bottom line was that there weren't people clamouring to join the bridge team. Most who felt jealous of our freedom and who thought they would like it gave up after joining us for a day because it just wasn't their thing or the street children were too unruly or violent. Others didn't know what to say to the passers-by and hid from them. We all had different gifts and our bridge work was a different type of ministry from the work taking place on the ship, but it was all for the purpose of glorifying God. I was sad that some of the most zealous and enthusiastic individuals were discouraged in that way or made to feel that they shouldn't be involved in front line evangelism all of the time.

During our team debrief Wayne from Taiwan stated factually that he had never been involved in street evangelism before as they "didn't do that in his country." Lucy, also Taiwanese, laughingly concurred "yes we never do that" as if their country's failure in that area was something to be proud of. Her jovial, carefree tone about a subject that most people would have considered to be serious set a few of us laughing. Cultural anomalies were again in play. I shared that I had loved the book table evangelism. One of the guys commented that he had learned that he needed to evangelise even when he didn't feel like it and that we shouldn't allow our feelings to control our actions. It seemed that we had all learned some useful lessons.

Eventually, I was asked to return to the ship to prepare for a new role. I was reluctant to leave the exciting bridge ministry but knew that my managers had been very flexible with me and that it was necessary to submit to their authority. Some people also didn't see what we were doing as 'work' in the ship sense, although in my view it was what we were on the ship for in the first place. I could see the other side though as some slaved away for long hours in harsh conditions in the Engine Room whilst we played and built relationships with street children every day.

I heard that our manager had told a fellow crew member that I and several others on our team had "completely thrown themselves into the team." She had responded "But they're all the difficult people." He wisely remarked "Yes I know but I picked them because they're the ones who get things done!" Personally, I took that as a compliment as it's a common trait in the history of missions that some of the most effective missionaries were not always that easy to work with, being single minded and speaking their minds, but they definitely got things done.

CHAPTER FORTY-ONE

Speed vs Detail

I had suddenly been summoned to the personnel department one day and having had a clear conscience couldn't really explain why I felt so nervous. My anticipation increased as the time drew near for the meeting but then dissipated as the meeting was postponed to the following week. When the time finally arrived, I was relieved that I hadn't inadvertently done anything worthy of discipline. They wanted to offer me a new job as Book-Fair Administrator.

I had no idea what the role would involve having thus far worked in the I-café and as Store-Keeper, apart from my brief and largely unsuccessful diversions to the engine room. It would be a nine to five type role at a computer and working alone. The latter appealed to me immensely as you've probably already gathered from reading earlier chapters. I believed the role might allow me further opportunities for evangelism in my spare time and would provide a more regular and flexible shift as I was still suffering thyroid issues making mornings tricky. I resolved to pray about it and to take part in some training with the incumbent administrator before making my final decision.

That was where things nearly went badly wrong. Susan from South Africa and I were totally opposite in every way and clashed constantly. She was extremely detailed in her work and loved beautifully decorated files with everything orderly catalogued. She also loved manuals and training guides and every other lengthy procedure in order to teach and/or learn a job as thoroughly as possible. Me, not so much. I'm the type to avoid every unnecessary process and procedure, to learn on the job without reading training manuals and to minimise bureaucracy where possible. I tended to learn by making mistakes. My problem - Susan was teaching me and I had to abide her methods. I persevered at first and tried to keep my opinions to myself. But I'm also someone who has to understand what I'm doing and cannot learn a procedure rote form without understanding. Susan was the opposite and had virtually learnt everything she needed to do the job by heart. It meant that when I asked questions about why things were being done in a certain way she sometimes couldn't answer them. Instead of saying that she didn't know she told me that I didn't need to know that in order to do the job. It was probably my fault really as I came across as precocious.

I was also being advised by my I-café and Store-Keeper boss Daniel that he didn't think I would necessarily enjoy the new role and that I needed to make sure I really wanted to do it. I had always got on well with Daniel as I felt he was fair and understood me and I didn't take what he said lightly. I also enjoyed my Store-Keeper role but had been having trouble with some of the heavy lifting and more manual work due to my health-related energy levels.

Eventually I decided to take the Book-Fair job but requested I could teach myself with the manuals after several days with Susan which I don't think either of us would wish to recall or prolong. Ultimately it was just a case of totally mismatched personalities and ways of doing things and it was a relief for us both when it came to an end. We talked about and resolved things when we ended up briefly sharing a room together but neither of us wanted to continue the training, so I taught myself.

I was, at the time, also personally being challenged about my longer-term commitments to mission. I wrote "I realised today that I have to make a decision about my future. Do I want to live a simple life in terms of material things and spend every day telling people about Jesus, often standing against the crowd, OR do I want to return to England and my job (or not) and live a comparatively comfortable life with evangelism in my spare time, but always facing choices regarding materialism/money? I believe God may be giving me the choice and I think it's because I often think of the comfortable married life in England with the kids tucked up in a blanket on the sofa watching a family film. I could have all of this but I read in Colossians 3 'set your mind on things above, not on earthly things' and I know this is a decision I have to make. I feel God is calling me to make this decision before I go any further along the missionary route. If I choose the missionary life I must go all out with no compromise as there will always be people trying to divert me from the correct path, most of them Christian".

On reading that extract, I imagine some of you who are married with children are laughing about my apparent naivety and false impressions. I am aware that living in the West is not all comfort and ease and that married life is not necessarily blissful, far from it in some cases. I also strongly believe that Christians are called to evangelism wherever they are living and that secular work presents fantastic opportunities for Christian witness. I do however think that material and monetary temptations are stronger in the West by virtue of a generally higher standard of living. Those were just things that were passing through my mind at that time.

Maybe the spell of personal examination came about due to the visit of my parents around that time whilst we were still in the dry dock. My parents had come to see me and then extended the visit to be part of a round the world trip. They took me snorkelling on a beach somewhere, swimming at a pool and out to dinner, probably thinking I needed a rest from the exhausting work with the street children and evangelism on the bridge. But I found that I missed the work and wanted to get back to it. It wasn't my parents' fault as I had wanted to do different things and had been looking forward to their visit, but my emotions were in a strange place and I couldn't seem to settle down.

My parents came to Worship Night on the ship; it was every Monday evening and led by different bands which had been formed by musically talented crew members. There were good ones and not so good ones. I was glad my parents were not there when a band went rogue and became hard rock verging on heavy metal for the night, screaming into the microphone and pounding out one of my favourite worship songs *As the Deer*. As it was, I think my parents were a little surprised by the liveliness of the evening. It reminded me that I had already adapted to the culture on the ship having been on-board for around a year at the point they visited. I hadn't enjoyed the style of worship on the ship at first but had adjusted as a necessity over time. My parents stayed for a few days then continued their holiday leaving me to return to the bridge and my administrator role.

CHAPTER FORTY-TWO

Book-Fair Administrator

A new batch of recruits arrived: PST Pattaya. They had to be flown in from Thailand as the ship was still in Subic Dry Dock. My cabin mate Ruth had decided to leave the ship as she had become engaged to one of the engineers, Mark; they wanted to get married and were not allowed to whilst serving on-board.

My new cabin-mate was Ana (33) from Brazil. She would be working in the Book-Fair as well as covering for the ship dentist at times as that was her profession. We got on well although I don't think she knew quite what to make of me. She insisted on nagging me about flossing my teeth telling me horror stories about what would happen if I didn't do it. I guess that's the role in life of every dentist. We chatted a lot in the cabin and at one point my Dad had sent me a map to pinpoint where an HSBC bank was in relation to the ship. I asked Ana to find it for me on-shore as she was going out that day. I showed her the map confidently stating several times "Look, it should be only two hundred metres away as the ship is here and the bank here," as I pointed to the locations. I didn't understand why she looked confused as it was a simple business to my mind, until she said carefully "But the ship has to be here, no?" as she pointed to the nearby sea. Both of my points were on land which the ship obviously wasn't. I was never much good at map reading!

On taking up my new role in the Book-Fair, I immediately scrapped a number of, from my perspective, pointless procedures and took short cuts any and every which way I could without compromising the data. Efficient and mostly accurate with the odd mistake: yes, detailed: no. My job fundamentally involved inputting data into an extremely dated system called AREV which was the cataloguing system for the ship Book-Fair. There were numerous memos about the plans to update the system dating back several decades but to date it hadn't happened. It reminded me of Windows DOS for those who remember it. It was the type of system that ended up controlling the person using it rather than the other way round and it felt as if I was constantly battling to get it to do what I wanted it to. AREV was stubborn, but then so was I. The office printer also went to war with me at times and on one occasion printed constantly for four days when I pressed the wrong buttons. Nobody knew how to stop it so we had to let it carry on and put up with the furious beeping.

I was responsible for adding new stock to the system when the containers arrived, updating stock movements and editing and amending items that were already in the system and needed correction. But my biggest responsibility was the printing of the Daily Orders. Every day, once the ship had closed to the public, it was necessary to print a list of stock that had sold on the deck of the ship (deck four) and needed to be restocked from the Book-Hold (deck three.) The Daily Orders only listed titles where three or more copies had been sold. Once the ship had reopened I began fiddling around with the Daily Orders figuring that manual manipulation of the data could be one of the keys to sales growth. There was no facility for automatically increasing the stock on deck for a popular title - one that would've sold more than three copies had they been available for sale. After a while I had learned which titles were popular and manually increased the numbers to be selected from the Book-Hold. Sometimes I got it wrong and they didn't sell but most of the time they did. It saved a lot of time during shifts when it was really busy as it wasn't then necessary to restock in the middle of the crowds. It also made my role more enjoyable as I felt that I could directly influence sales and it was fun to see what happened on each day.

Probably because I had scrapped a lot of admin tasks that didn't seem necessary and a lot of the record keeping, I had a lot of time on my hands. I was therefore allocated an additional role by Andy (England) who became the new Book-Fair Manager shortly after I joined the team. You might remember Andy due to his squeaky voice during our PST training. I was pleased that Andy was taking over as I had always got on well with him and knew he would be a flexible boss and willing to listen to my ideas. Andy asked me to take responsibility for Product Placement in the Children's, Animals, Hobbies and Sport area which significantly covered half of the entire Book-Fair and was easily the largest selling area. I could arrange the deck however I liked and place the books where ever I wanted them. You might wonder why I was even interested in the role, not being notably creative or into 'making things pretty.' But almost immediately I saw that it was about marketing strategy and that if I got it right it would also increase sales. It was a challenge. I needed to examine the habits of shoppers and present the books in such a way that it would draw them to buy.

The problem - I was unable to get on and actually do that as the ship was still in dry dock and therefore all the books were still covered to stop them getting ruined with welding dust. They would also be covered when we finally sailed to Hong Kong and then we would immediately be open so a large reorganisation simply wasn't likely to be possible. So, to start with I wasn't able to do much 'learning on the job' as there was no job. I would have to contain my enthusiasm over the new task for just a little bit longer.

CHAPTER FORTY-THREE

Picking up the Pace

The dry dock work was finally completed after nine months. We set sail for Hong Kong our next scheduled port, arriving on 19th December 2012. A large part of my heart had been left behind with the "rugby boys." Leaving the Philippines had felt like a miracle to most people who had already resolved that they would likely be spending the duration of their commitment on Logos Hope in Subic Bay. The voyage had been rough in places and very slow in others (0.9k!) as engineers had been forced to deal with the problems caused by the newly installed systems during the journey. We spent much of the voyage gazing anxiously out of the window and wondering how far we would actually get, almost anticipating the announcement that we were heading back to the dry dock due to problems in the engine room. Every time there was a loud sound that was unaccounted for we collectively froze as we waited for the explanation, which was usually given via the tannoy to ensure rumours didn't circulate. Living in close quarters it was really easy for a loose tongue or someone with more evil intent to begin a trail of destruction, the fire of which, if not quickly extinguished, could easily lead to panic and/or people making dramatic plans to abandon ship and the ministry. It was a good reminder of the study group in James that I had led and the lessons on taming the tongue!

I remember that it was very cold and miserable when we arrived in Hong Kong and that for the second time we were docked virtually on top of a very large shopping mall. Having struggled with the materialism and commercialisation in Singapore before I had even visited a third world country, you can imagine how I felt having lived in the Philippines for nine months. It was a truly tough time although many crew members had the opposite reaction as they finally tasted civilisation again and realised that life beyond Subic was possible and most definitely preferable.

On a ministry day, I joined a group from the ship that was assigned to present the ship ministry during a church meeting. Obviously, we prepared a programme as usual but we were a little unprepared for the stylish clothes worn by the people and the upmarket building that served as the church premises. Everything was done suddenly and in a rush and I felt a bit disorientated having adjusted to the slower Filipino pace. It felt like there was an atmosphere of excitement during our presentation and our team felt that the people were really catching our missionary vision. But half way through our presentation, when we paused for breath, one of the church leaders asked whether it was time for them to visit the ship with us. We hadn't planned that and it hadn't been discussed but the participants were already donning their coats and heading out of the door and we were expected to escort them. It was as if we had been scooped up by a whirlwind as we followed them and headed back to the ship. They had obviously been excited about that rather than anything else. I wondered if they were even listening to our presentation!

I felt again that although we were very busy in the Book-Fair in Hong Kong that we weren't as welcome as we had been in less wealthy countries. The people had higher expectations of customer service and what they were likely to experience on-board. Some were disappointed as they were expecting a lot more. One man was looking for additional floors or rooms of books, having not found what he wanted, and was astonished when I told him that there was just one floor. Another brought me a book of questions that he had purchased and demanded to know where he could find the answers. I obviously didn't know but then he became angry that we were selling a book of questions without answers. He was ranting about it as if we had sold it to him just to irritate him. Others were complaining about other matters and the cultural stress circulated all around us as we witnessed a father harshly slapping his child in the middle of the Book-Fair. The action upset an Asian crew member so much that he voiced his desire to punch the man in retaliation, but I persuaded him that that wasn't the best course of action. I joked that we should do a customer announcement "Attention all visitors, please don't hit your kids whilst you are in the Book-Fair, it's not very nice."

The atmosphere reminded me a little of working in the police. Although we were still in Asia, material affluence still bred dissatisfaction: the compensation and complaints culture, demanding rights and refusing to accept second best. The people saw us as a business and not as a Christian mission. It was difficult not to succumb to the pressure and to maintain our focus as a community.

I sought refuge in the I-café after some of the exchanges, wondering if people calmly drinking coffee would be more reasonable as conversationalists. I met Penny, a teacher from mainland China. She had travelled to the ship to search for creative teaching methods as her superiors were placing her under a lot of pressure at work. The Chinese (and often Asian) culture dictates that the children must succeed at all costs. Penny had become disillusioned with her country, culture and profession. I shared the hope that I had found in Jesus explaining that I too had been searching for meaning and happiness in worldly things, but that they had always left me empty. My heart went out to her and I prayed that she would really hear my words.

I took part in some spontaneous street evangelism one evening after a girl from Denmark rallied us all during a community worship night. Having begun to share her evangelistic zeal in Danish she realised after a few sentences and a sea of blank faces what she had done and inspired us in English instead. We all headed out for a few hours onto the street. I cornered a Dutchman who had been waiting at some traffic lights to cross the road, so he couldn't really go anywhere. In response to my questions he hesitantly informed me that he didn't believe in God or in heaven or hell. I asked him if he was sure and he responded in the negative before asking me likewise. I said that yes I was sure that God was there and that heaven and hell existed as real places. The man was no doubt relieved that the traffic light had changed but he said that he would think about it. I thought to myself that it was the reason that we needed to 'always be prepared to give a reason for our hope' as someone might only be forced to remain in our presence for a few seconds.

I was glad when we finally came to leave Hong Kong after just a few weeks. We were heading for Taiwan, but we experienced further mechanical problems so had to turn around and return to Hong Kong again. Unfortunately, Hong Kong were not expecting us and had already filled our recently vacated berth. The unexpected stumbling block was to provide me the opportunity I had been not so patiently waiting for in the Book-Fair - every cloud....

CHAPTER FORTY-FOUR

Project Re-organisation

I had mentally prepared for a complete revamp of my section of books as soon as there was opportunity, which hadn't been likely for the foreseeable. On returning to Hong Kong, we were immediately put out to sea at anchor for three days whilst waiting for a new berth to become available. I was itching to get started as, by that point, I had many ideas for improvement swirling around in my mind.

I began by searching the Book-Hold and locating every title that was available. I found a lot of 'lost' stock that wasn't even in the system and got it out on deck straight away. My principle, which went against the grain of normal retail practice, was that the more titles there were on deck, the more choice the shoppers had and therefore the more we would sell. That didn't necessarily work in the real world where shoppers were often overwhelmed by choice and where several spans of one title might draw someone in. But on the ship, it worked well in my section probably because the books were cheap and people had sometimes travelled a long way to see our selection so they wanted as much choice as possible. I squeezed every title onto the Deck by spending days rearranging everything.

Honestly, I was amazed to find the shelves so haphazardly organised in the first place. I could only imagine that during several previous ports which had happened to be busy, most of the stock had sold and the books had just been placed randomly on shelves during the re-stocking process. At least that was how it appeared. The books weren't even in their correct categories let alone in any type of sequence or aesthetically pleasing order. For me it was like a huge jigsaw puzzle that needed completing. I began the mammoth task, preferring to work alone. I took hundreds of books off the shelves placing them in piles on the floor. At times, I looked around and wondered what on earth I was doing as the task was never ending and a bit overwhelming. Andy walked through looking nervous but cheerful at interludes and commented that there were "less books on the floor now." That, when I was still surrounded by book piles in the middle of the chaos. I did have a plan in my head but getting there would take time and determination and it wasn't a tidy business.

I changed the subheadings at the top of the shelves within the categories to make things clearer. Also, I changed a lot of the locations for different types of books, e.g. I made the Children's Bibles more prominent and central and cut down the 'horses' section from three displays to one. In the end, I had probably moved every title of the thousands on deck at least once. After a few days of constant work and long hours, I had all available titles on display and everything was looking neat and tidy. There was just one problem.

I called Andy over to advise him that I had nearly completed 'project re-organisation.' After showing him all the good work, maybe in an effort to prepare him, I informed him of the slight issue that had arisen. I led him to the back of a double display of shelves at the corner of my area. It was totally empty. I had cleared so much space in my efficiency drive that I had run out of titles and had a completely blank display case to fill. I waited for Andy to groan but instead he just laughed and suggested we fill it will toys and games which was a great solution that I wished I had thought of. Problem solved. When the final shelves had been sorted out, I asked Andy whether he had been worried and he admitted that there had been a moment or two as there were "just so many books on the floor!"

After the massive re-organisation, I became quite protective of 'my' titles and knew where every single book was placed despite there being thousands. It was fine in the quieter ports where I could easily ensure everything went back to where it was meant to be. I made sure I was present at the Daily Orders (restocking) which actually most people appreciated. We had a music album of the Christian band Fee. We turned up the volume and set about the restocking as quickly as possible, in time to the music. It's funny how music has that effect, many managers in that type of environment have no doubt found that fast music increases the energy and pace of the workforce; unfortunately the reverse can be true when the music is slow or nostalgic.

Most of the time I could point others to where the titles were displayed instead of them endlessly searching for titles that might not even be on the deck if they had sold out. It could sometimes make the difference between restocking taking one hour and two. Retaining control wasn't as easy in the ports where it was busy due to the visitors not only buying large quantities of books but also removing them from the shelves and replacing them on others or leaving their baskets on the floor having changed their mind or having given up due to the long queues. We could spend hours sorting out the mixed books at the end of a shift which is probably what most crew will remember, maybe for years to come.

I loved the book placement role and saw the administration on the computer as a necessary evil in contrast. I realised though that Andy had given me a lot of flexibility to make changes and effectively take responsibility for my area and that had I had another manager things may have been different. I also knew that if I were to have stayed in the role longer term, maybe for years, the novelty would wear off and I would become bored. The closest analogy is that I've never been one for cleaning things that don't appear to be dirty.

It was also really helpful emotionally as when we left Subic Dry Dock I had been forced to leave behind the street boys to whom I had become so close. The work in the Book-Fair took my mind off them and was in essence non-taxing emotionally. It prevented me having to be public facing which I may have struggled with at that time. I've always been a more behind the scenes person and more comfortable in one to one evangelistic conversations rather than standing on a stage or speaking to large groups of people.

Of course, with all of the positive work, things sometimes went badly wrong. There were several days when the Daily Orders were accidentally doubled resulting in twice the number of books being brought up from the Book-Hold to the deck than were necessary to fill the spaces. Staff were walking around looking confused and leaving small piles of books on the floor next to the shelves when they didn't fit. Then the stock numbers in the system were all wrong due to the mistake. That type of thing always happened when we had just completed an inventory. We always managed to get things straightened out in the end and Andy wasn't really prone to panic which helped me to remain calm most of the time.

CHAPTER FORTY-FIVE

Cautious in Cambodia

We were finally allocated another berth in Hong Kong and were therefore able to re-approach the shore and open the Book-Fair for a few more weeks. I couldn't wait to leave the country to be honest. But I definitely think that was because of the contrast in living standards, having just left the Philippines. Finally, we said farewell to the materialism knowing that it wouldn't be for long. We were scheduled to return to Hong Kong for our annual dry dock just a few months later. We set off on the long voyage to Cambodia, another third world country and more in keeping with my idea of ministry.

Annoyingly, I suffered an allergic reaction after taking malaria pills so I was mostly confined to the ship in Cambodia. The alternative malaria pills listed hallucinations and nightmares as possible side-effects. I didn't fancy taking my chances and swiftly declined the tablets. I was surprised to have suffered an adverse reaction in the first place not being prone to allergies. Continuing the health theme, I spent a fair bit of time calming the fears of fellow crew who feared an epidemic of chlorine water poisoning. Something had clearly gone wrong with the supply and our drinking water began to smell like a swimming pool. It was relatively quickly resolved but that didn't prevent some people milking the effects for all they were worth to get a few extra days off work.

My highlight in Cambodia was our trip to an orphanage with a small team. The main purpose was to give them a donation of water purifiers. We were told not to be too evangelistic with our programme although it wasn't illegal to share the Gospel. Most of those residing in Cambodia are Buddhist. I picked up on the 'too,' and determined that we should at least attempt to share Jesus with the children who might never have another chance to hear about Him.

After my visit to the children's hospital in Malaysia I wasn't sure I could face the heartache of hopelessness again.

On arrival, we taught the house mothers how to use the water purifiers. They were amazed by the purity of the water after it had been filtered, even when it had been filthy to begin with. I saw a small boy, about four years old, carrying two heavy metal watering cans with the handles over his arms. I wondered how far he had to carry them, thinking that they must've been heavy. He grinned cheerfully at us as we passed him. I realised then how helpful our practical gifts could be to many people in countries like Cambodia.

Our brief for the programme had been to teach the children English. I presented the Wordless Book, teaching the children the colours of the book in English as I shared the Gospel. They were receptive and participated in the interactive questions. There was a moment of confusion when it came to the colour green when I asked the children

"How do we grow?" and predictably received the answer "By eating more!"

Of course, the question should've been.

"How do we grow closer to God?"

I'd like to say that that was the only time I made that error but I repeated it later that day when teaching the second group of children. I was the centre of attention at the time and all eyes were on me so I didn't even have the chance to express my frustration with myself. As it was I just laughed and told the astute children that they were right and then rephrased the question hoping for a more spiritual answer.

During the Gospel presentation to the children I had seen in my peripheral vision that two of our team were having an intense discussion with staff members. They had been listening attentively to the things that had been said throughout our programme that day. Afterwards we were excited to hear that a male twenty-one-year-old staff member had turned to one crew member and matter of factly said "So tell me about this Jesus then" Another female member had been asked what she thought about our presentation. The conversation had led to a more in depth sharing of the Gospel and an invitation to visit the ship.

We gave all of the children Gospel booklets before we left. We also gave them school packs containing stationery, basic toiletries and toys. I had tried to get the 'High School Musical' and other worldly stickers removed from the packs. They were always the things the children fixated on and I felt they presented a less than helpful image of Western culture. In the minds of a lot of the Asian children Western culture was the same thing as Christianity. Some of the children had access to Western television shows. The stickers depicted characters belonging to a teenage soap and I just felt it was inappropriate. But I was overruled as the ship wanted to get rid of them and said it wasn't a big deal. Maybe they were right, it wasn't worth arguing about.

Despite not taking the malaria tablets I did get involved in some ministry in Cambodia. However, I had left part of my heart in the Philippines with the street boys and was anxious to see if God was calling me back there in the future. I still had to pace myself in terms of ministry as I couldn't give out too much emotionally. I was probably bordering on burnout. I couldn't recover emotionally because the street children continued to contact me via social media even after we had left the Philippines.

Someone asked me whether I would consider Cambodia as a future place of ministry. Although it was the type of ministry that I had a definite heart for, working with the poor in a third world country with little access to the Gospel, it wasn't the place that God had laid on my heart. I still believed I would head back to the Philippines straight after the ship.

CHAPTER FORTY-SIX

Worldliness in Thailand

Thailand was our next port of call. The capital, Bangkok, was crazily busy in terms of visitor numbers and there was a media frenzy on our arrival. I spent most of my time trying to avoid the numerous TV news cameras that were filming absolutely everything in sight. We had over ten thousand visitors on one Saturday alone. They queued patiently for hours on end in the hot sun on the quayside. The crew were required to find creative ways to entertain them - one of our clowns with a parrot hand puppet squawked at a boy who was slightly too old for that type of thing. He looked at her disdainfully. Watching from a nearby location, I found the interaction hilarious. The boy was obviously totally unimpressed with the attempts to brighten his day, probably thinking that he was too old for that type of thing and that the clown should have known better. A very Western response.

I was extremely busy in the Book-Fair, frantically restocking model aeroplanes and large art packs amongst other things that were selling out as fast as they could be restocked. One of our top selling children's books at that time was entitled *Seasick,* which I thought the media could've made more of. Because the ship bought mixed stock at discounted prices we sometimes found titles that we had to throw away in large numbers due to their content. Usually that would be done in the Book-Hold before the books were even seen by the visitors. They didn't actually reach the public deck. But due to the rush in the port and the high sales, the mixed books had been thrown in with all the others and had ended up appearing on the deck. It was so manic that when I was restocking some areas people were literally grabbing the books out of my hands as I attempted to restock the shelves. I was simultaneously trying to remove the inappropriate titles which were sometimes very inappropriate: tarot cards, voodoo and erotica being among the worst I can recall. But of course, human nature being what it is, my refusal to allow people to have a particular book just made them curious and wanting to get their hands on it even more. In the end, I announced that those particular titles weren't for sale and left the area without further explanation, probably causing confusion. I just didn't have the mental energy to explain to people whose first language wasn't English why those books had ended up on the deck.

Outside of the ship environment, the traffic on the main roads was unusually intimidating. A small group of us ended up in a huddle in the middle of a busy junction. There were motorbikes and cars speeding all around us as, fearing for our lives if we moved one way or another, we tried to figure out what to do next. Shortly after escaping from that predicament we bumped into a disconcerted ship dad whose two-year-old daughter had just pointed at a statue of Ronald McDonald and confidently announced 'Jesus!'

There was a genuine reason for venturing out into the danger zone. We were actually on our way to take part in some evangelism in a Muslim dominated area. It was an unusual idea, the planning and preparation of which had been shrouded in secrecy. I should add that it wasn't organised by the ship but by some individuals who had contacted the ship asking for assistance. I don't think the ship leadership even knew what we were to be involved in. The people organising the evangelism felt that they should use us rather than doing it themselves due to our presence in the area being for a short duration. They didn't want to risk getting in trouble with the authorities as they were working there longer term. I wasn't sure whether there was a need for such secrecy. Evangelism wasn't illegal but, as in most Asian countries, it was generally not encouraged to try to convert someone from another faith.

We distributed small pieces of paper like tracts with a code that could be scanned by a smartphone by those who had them. The recipients watched a short Gospel presentation video which targeted Muslims. Things got a bit difficult when those we approached inevitably asked us what we were giving them; when we explained they didn't want to know. I felt a bit awkward and a little like we were tricking people into hearing the Gospel by using methods attractive to a modern generation. We were giving them an opportunity to show off their smartphone capabilities to their friends. They were not seeking God or the truth, it was being thrust upon them without them knowing what it was. I was also bothered that we had effectively to hide from the police officers who were patrolling in the area. I was astonished that the streets were so carefully monitored - we were moved on several times in just a few hours. Our efforts came to a permanent end when a police officer craftily scanned one of our papers himself and hastily told us to cease our activity.

Afterwards, and on reflection, I felt privileged to have taken part in the ministry. Despite my concerns, I do believe it is important to utilise modern technology and to make the Gospel message relevant. But others in our group had been terrified by the nature of the work and by the police interest, no doubt fearing ending up in a Thai jail with a potential death sentence looming.

I was also part of a team that set up a children's library in a day care facility at an immigration detention centre. I felt we could've made more of the opportunity by providing more Christian books in the selection, and thought again of help without hope.

I decided to get more involved in some ship events in that port. The ship had an events department organising ticketed on-board events that were open to visitors. I shared my testimony at one such event and one of the girls I had spoken to wrote on Facebook "Thanks to our host Natalie, for sharing your life experience and for showing us the meaning of HOPE." I was so encouraged that that was what they had taken away from our meeting.

At an English Café event I met a Buddhist Thai girl named Tak but things hadn't initially gone according to plan. The idea was for a crew member to sit at each table and to mingle with the locals whilst watching a programme on stage at the front of the room. I had already broken the ice with Tak and was chatting to her. But suddenly the music interrupted our conversation and the lights went down - the programme was starting. A local band was introduced to the sound of cheers and shouts. A woman, who I can only guess was the lead singer, began making her way through the tables dotted around towards the microphone on the stage. I couldn't take my eyes off her and neither could anyone else, but for all the wrong reasons. She was wearing a skirt that was more like a belt, an extremely low cut top and her face was caked in makeup. I watched as some of the male crew members averted their eyes whilst others openly gaped.

The other band members appeared and the girl began singing and swaying seductively on the stage. She was singing a Christian song! Afterwards one of my male friends said that he had been tempted to lust. But then had thought that it was okay as she was singing about Jesus, before realising that it wasn't okay at all. I was totally shocked and didn't really know what to do as I was in the middle of a conversation with Tak so I couldn't just leave which would have been my usual response. The music then became louder and more like rock in style. I kept my head down as I considered my options. But Tak obviously noticed and said to me:

"You don't like this music very much do you?"

I said "No, I don't."

She responded "Why?"

Without thinking I replied "Because it reminds me of a time when I was far away from God." It hit me the minute I said it, I had come to Logos Hope to be a Christian missionary, to share with people the hopelessness and meaninglessness of living in the world without God. But, in the middle of that supposedly Christian environment I had been unwittingly transported back to my past life that I didn't wish to dwell on or remember. I knew I would have to do something about that at some point but I decided in that moment to make the best of the situation.

I waited until the programme had finished continuing to make small talk with Tak and the rest of our table. I then invited her for a tour of the ship so that we could continue talking where it wasn't so loud and worldly. I was able to give her a quick tour but she had tickets for another event so I arranged for her to return on another day to continue talking.

On her return to the ship, Tak dined on-board and attended our Worship night; we spent several hours talking. I was amazed to hear that her Buddhist parents had sent her to a Christian school in order for her to have the best possible education. She had been given a Bible by one of her teachers and she still had it. As we chatted, past Bible verses were coming back to her. I encouraged her to seek the truth for herself and she acknowledged that our meeting was not a coincidence.

Having salvaged the opportunity to witness to Tak after initially feeling helpless and a little angry about the position I had been placed in during the English Café event, I decided I had to take the matter further to ensure such a thing didn't happen again. I reasoned that there must have been others who had been concerned and that if they weren't going to say anything I would do it on their behalf. I was chiefly indignant on behalf of the men who had been placed in temptation's path without much chance to flee, apart from walking out of the event and creating a scene. I learned afterwards that at least one guy had done that. I composed an email to the head of the Events Department outlining my thoughts and focusing on the conversation I had had with Tak and how awkward it had been suddenly to feel thrust back into my past lifestyle whilst trying to witness to a non-believer. It was hard to convey the sense of disappointment that I had felt and the isolation as many crew members thought that what had happened was fine.

I received a very gracious reply from the manager who hadn't been present at the event. She said that my message had really convicted her and that she would make sure that the band were not allowed to reappear on the ship during our stay in Thailand. She apologised that I had been put in that position and said that the events team had had no idea that it would be like that as the band claimed they were Christians. I was happy with her response believing that she was genuinely concerned about what had happened and that others had been as well. I then spoke to her in person. She told me that, due to the band's popularity, she had spent the better part of her time for the rest of the port trying to stop the band from being allowed on-board again as others had wanted them. I was relieved that she had stuck to her guns but felt her frustration that our partners on the ground weren't more supportive of our desire to cultivate holiness. The main issue was that there were those who were using culture to excuse that type of behaviour, in effect saying that it was acceptable for Christians in Thailand. I strongly disagreed with that attitude believing that if a culture has fallen into sin then it is an even greater opportunity for the Christian church to shine by being different and taking a stand against it. The worst thing to do is to fall into line with worldly standards and compromise in that way.

Tak sent me a postcard with some crispy fried noodles and sweet sauce; "Dear Natalie, it was great meeting you on the ship and again on the day of the international night! I and my sister really appreciated your kindness taking us around the ship. I wish you enjoy every stop and everywhere you are going to and wish to see you again."

I pray that she will not forget our conversations and that one day she will find hope in Jesus.

CHAPTER FORTY-SEVEN

Fishport Alliance Church

The ship was due for its annual scheduled dry dock which usually lasted for around a month. It felt as if we had only just come out of dry dock but it had actually been several months. There was a sense that no one believed that the Hong Kong dry dock would be completed on time or as planned. That despite having already seen the fast pace and efficiency in Hong Kong which stood in contrast to the laid back and easy going lifestyles of the Filipinos. It was a bit like the boy who cried wolf. We had heard that the Subic dry dock was only going to be extended for one more month, then another month and another. Most of the crew members who had suffered through that dry dock were still on board. It was those people who smiled wryly as the leaders confidently assured us of the steps they had taken to ensure swift progress on that occasion.

As for me, I wasn't going to be affected really as I was heading back to the Philippines for a month-long Challenge Team in Manila. I had known that it would be likely that I would be going on another team and had prayed that if I were meant to return to the Philippines after the ship that I would be allocated one in the Philippines. I had specifically prayed that I would be placed in a team heading back to Subic as that was where my street children were, but I was open to all possibilities. Others thought I was mad as they had had enough of the Philippines and wanted to see some different countries and cultures. I was more interested in longer term ministry plans so I was excited to be included in the team.

The team was made up of Juline, the team leader from Germany; Arnold, assistant leader from Switzerland; Silvana from Brazil; Sunaim from Papua New Guinea and Boyd from Thailand. Juline and Sunaim were from my PST so I knew them a little but not well. I knew enough to know that they were all fairly placid and that I was the exception, as our team leader tactlessly observed during our initial meeting. Our brief stated simply that we would be conducting house visitations during most of the mornings and would be involved in a lot of street kid ministry and other types of ministry. It sounded good and a lot more focused on evangelism than my prior teams had been.

We flew into Manila and began making our way to the church that was to host us for the duration. The heat had hit us like a wave the minute we stepped off the aeroplane but it was great to be back in familiar territory and away from the commercialism and apathy in some other places. Also, I enjoyed the rides on public transport as we bumped along poorly maintained pathways hanging off motorbikes and tricycles with all our luggage squashed in around us. That first hour told me what I had needed to know, I was definitely going back to the Philippines after the ship. I loved it and couldn't stop grinning. I had lost my enthusiasm for a while after leaving dry dock and had really been praying that I would just know one way or the other when we arrived back in Manila. There was no doubt in my mind. I praised God for the clarity and began to feel excited about the future, but I had a Challenge Team to focus on first.

Fishport Alliance Church was situated in a group of houses in the middle of a slum area. The group contained the largest and nicest buildings around and stood in contrast to the wooden shack houses with tin roofs haphazardly positioned along the nearby streets. The people were mostly unemployed or earned a pittance doing laundry or running small shops from their homes selling soft drinks, snacks and cigarettes. Children of all ages filled the surrounding streets playing games that they had made up using items of clothing or pieces of discarded rubbish in the place of toys. Evidence of the most recent typhoon disaster could still be seen in the large areas of flooded rice fields and other crops that had been destroyed. We were told that many had lost their houses and that the church had been overrun with people needing help.

A group of teenage boys with scars and prominent tattoos played basketball in the dust at all hours at the end of the street; they had to shout whenever a vehicle was coming and postpone the play temporarily until it had safely passed. A lot of the men had been in prison for violence or thieving and their group was intrinsically like a gang or fraternity. There were rumours of murder between rival gangs. I didn't feel unsafe and the men didn't feel like a threat to us, maybe because we were foreigners and they were automatically intimidated by us. But I was shocked on hearing some of the more gruesome stories about their exploits and the low value they placed on a human life. I guess I had thought it would be different in a third world country but I was naïve, there was no difference at all. Maybe it was that the things they were stabbing each other over seemed trivial to me but were of a greater value to them as they had nothing materially.

Gambling was in evidence in every direction; whole communities came outside their huts and sat on the dirty ground as they gambled in groups. They played games like bingo; often the children were asked to choose the numbers and watched in fascination as they played or even joined in themselves. I could see generations growing up like that and throwing their lives away on cheap drink and the chance to make a quick buck. Many of the mothers risked their household budget week by week ending up with nothing, but believing they could win it all back. It was a hopeless and senseless business. Those who became Christians and declined to be involved often ended up ostracised by their neighbours and friends and were drawn back into the gambling circles as they were bored and had nothing else to do, also because they didn't want to stay indoors in the dark and their children were outside playing. It was really a difficult dilemma for many.

The church was pastored by a couple in their fifties. The Pastor had a full-time job as an engineer elsewhere and his wife, the Pastora, tended to run things in his absence. Their house was next to the church and some of the more well to do church members lived in the other nice houses attached. Other church members who were employed for cleaning and tasks in the church, or who sometimes gave their time voluntarily, lived in the shack houses on the other side of the street. Immediately I found the distribution of wealth in such close proximity difficult. The Pastor and his wife had a car and a motorbike and spent a lot of time indoors due to both having a form of hypertension.

We were welcomed in usual dramatic Filipino style having spent a considerable amount of time getting down the street and into the church as the kids hung from our arms and tried to engage us in conversation. Sometimes, when we had enough energy, we joined the children in their games and I became attached to a few of the younger ones. I particularly remember a boy aged just two or three called JR who had an affinity for me. When we played tag he always sought to 'free' me from being 'frozen' but because he was so small he had to run towards me and jump really high just to touch my outstretched arm. Inevitably sometimes he got caught by the others when he did that but he always attempted it regardless. The children liked to be swung around and to climb up our bodies as we held their arms. They queued patiently next to us awaiting their turns. Some photos of me and JR were sent to his mother and I was told they had been framed and hung prominently in her house!

The teenagers wanted to play chess and to talk to us in their limited English. They loved teasing me when I made mistakes which happened frequently. For at least the third time I confused 'pusa' (cat) with 'puso' (heart,) solemnly informing the kids that Jesus was living in my cat resulting in them screaming with laughter. I also somehow told them that I liked the cockroach eating my face instead of saying that it was the cockroach that had the predisposition. Despite the silliness, I shared the Gospel with most of the teens during our stay to a greater or lesser extent depending on their age and the availability of translation.

The street chatter began early in the morning and continued well on into the night. It wasn't uncommon to see small children on the street after 11pm and to hear their excited voices as they messed around. There weren't many adults with proper routines and few disciplined their children effectively. Mostly they lashed out in anger having ignored the bad behaviour for a long time and having finally come to the end of their tether.

Our team got down to business, meeting the church leaders and staff then working out where we would sleep. Sleeping became the biggest trial of our stay in the end as temperatures hit thirty-nine degrees and we sweated it out on basic floor mattresses with electric fans. Bathing consisted of a large tub of water and a pail that could be filled and emptied over one's head. The water was always freezing but that was a blessing in the circumstances. Try washing long hair whilst crouched naked in a tiny cupboard sized cubicle and avoiding any spiders or cockroaches that may suddenly appear from cracks in the wall or the drain vents. It was a challenge but somehow we managed it. The guys decided to sleep at times on the roof deck as it was more open to the elements and therefore cooler. Actually, from the roof deck we could survey the whole area including the flooded fields and the roofs of all the shack houses for miles around. It was really beautiful during sunset and we spent time just staring at the surroundings which were so different from what we were all used to. I witnessed small children being bathed in washing-up bowls and many women rigorously hand washing their clothes every day. The gambling could also be seen from the vantage point and the other activities by those who weren't expecting that they were being observed.

Our food, as the title of the church suggests, was primarily fish, fish and more fish. I had expected rice once again to be the staple meal and I was not disappointed in that regard. The church did make efforts to ensure we had fruit and some vegetables but it was nothing like the luxury we had experienced in Dasmarinas City. I was grateful for that though as it felt right that we could really identify with the people we were working with if only for a month.

As had happened on our prior team we were asked to take over and lead all of the programmes and activities for the entire visit. We planned Sunday school meetings and visitations, dramas and skits, songs and special numbers. 'Special numbers' was a phrase used by Filipinos to refer to a song that had been prepared exclusively for the moment. It was hard to keep the Gospel central at times as there was an expectation that the people wanted to be entertained. We realised after we had spent several hours hammering out a short programme that it was a lot more work to keep it focused on the Gospel and to ensure it was coherent than if we had aimed to entertain. Some of our team got fed up when discussing the details and thought we should do less preparation, but most of us realised that it was a huge responsibility and that we had to make sure that the people clearly heard the Gospel from us during our stay.

I don't think it helped that Boyd was asked to carry out one to one discipleship with a man who had just been converted and had become a member in the church. It left our team short-staffed. On the other hand, Boyd did manage to befriend some of the basketball gangsters and joined them in creating and painting a new basketball hoop for the end of the street. They painted "Trust in the Lord with all your heart" onto the board behind the net which should serve as a witness for years to come. It was an odd symbol of God's love in the middle of the violence and bloodshed of gang rivalry.

We often used drama on the ship to get a message across mainly because we were frequently talking to youth and children and it was a good way to make the programmes interactive. It was also a way to remove any language barriers, but when we did that the purpose needed to be clear and the Bible story read and explained properly afterwards. On reflection, I'm not sure how effective that method was for witnessing and whether people did learn the stories, but we tended to use it a lot on the ship and on teams. We performed the same dramas over and over again as they were the ones that crew members were familiar with. Sometimes, as with the Wordless Book, we found that children had seen them before.

We decided that the team would try a new drama from our book that had been provided by the ship. It was an all-age meeting of church members - the drama depicted spiritual warfare. Some of our team represented church members praying to God. As soon as they said the name of Jesus two people dressed all in black representing demons came screaming into the room. The demons in our drama were so loud that people came in from out in the street to see what was happening. The demons were whispering things to the church members and trying to discourage and tempt them, but they were silenced whenever the name of Jesus was spoken. It was a simple message to display the power of Jesus over Satan. Inadvertently we also covered the fact that we shouldn't address demons directly as the characters didn't talk to each other, the church members just prayed when they felt under attack or discouraged and that was sufficient to banish the demon.

For Sunday School, we received over one hundred children of all ages. There were no classes and not enough room for them all to sit down. It was mayhem as the children fought and jostled to see what was going on at the front and the assistants tried to calm them down. There were a few gigantic pillars in the middle of the room that obscured the views of some of them. Culture dictated that they all wanted to get as close to the front as possible so we ended up with a kind of mob. We chose children to act Bible stories like David and Goliath and Daniel in the Lions' Den and explained the stories as the children acted them out. Sometimes we acted them out ourselves. We played trust games - children fell backwards and trusted a leader to catch them. Until someone dropped a child then we decided to stop that. Our take-away point ended up being that humans would fail and let them down, as had been evidenced when we dropped the child, but that God was consistently faithful. I'm not sure about the theology but the point was made.

We began to feel exhausted as we trekked from place to place always followed by hundreds of children. At first, we could just plan one programme and repeat it in three different ministry locations as there were different groups of children. But then they started following us from one place to another and loudly commenting when they had seen it before or telling the others what would happen next. We just didn't have the time to plan additional programmes as our schedule was jam-packed and the heat was oppressive. Between events mostly we collapsed on our mattresses and went to sleep.

CHAPTER FORTY-EIGHT

Various Visits

Our first team conflict occurred within a few days of our arrival, although it wasn't really a team issue. We had been placed in small groups led by some prominent church women. Our aim was to carry out visits to the people living in the nearby streets. Great, evangelism, I thought. But no, we were going to hound the church members who had stopped attending the church. Whenever we passed a house without knocking and I asked about it I was told that the house wasn't part of the church network or that it was owned by a Muslim or Buddhist so we wouldn't be calling. The ladies appeared to be afraid of the consequence of calling on someone of another faith and shied away from it, although it is perfectly legal in the Philippines. I was disappointed but felt compelled to submit to the leaders. I did chat to a few of the forbidden people in the street if they happened to come out at the right time, but then it felt as if I was holding up the rest of our group.

One of our group's first visits, which I'm sure I will always remember, was to a woman and her children, including a teenage boy. The woman had called the boy forward as the group of about six of us piled into her very small house and sat around on small wooden benches or on the floor. The boy looked moody and sullen. I was embarrassed when one of our ladies began outlining the history of the family in front of us. I could tell that the family understood at least part of what was being said and it was being relayed in a derogatory manner mainly in relation to the teenage boy. After we had heard the life history and the vast array of sins the boy had committed I was asked to 'share' with the group. I told them a little of my testimony and explained the Gospel. The mother, we had been told, was already a Christian. I had to ask for what I had said to be translated as, although they had said they understood, I could see from the blank looks on their faces that they were just being polite and didn't have a clue what had been said.

On my insistence, the lady with our group spent a few minutes speaking to the teenage boy who nodded at the end. Then she said to me, "That's it, he's accepted Christ. Are you going to pray with him now"? I froze, not knowing what to do. We were being hurried along as we had other visits to conduct and couldn't afford to dawdle. The statement had been made in a dull monotone as if that kind of thing happened every day. Actually, as mentioned in earlier chapters, in the Philippines shallow conversions are frequently seen due to 'Easy Believism' being widely practised. But it was the worst example of it that I had seen and I had never been placed in that position before. They were all looking at me expectantly, waiting for me to pray a 'Sinner's Prayer' with the boy and welcome him into the family. But I had seen no evidence of comprehension from the boy and wasn't even sure what had been said during the discussion he had had with our leader.

It had become an awkward 'catch twenty-two' situation. If I questioned him too thoroughly I would shame and embarrass our leader who had already clearly claimed that he was professing faith having explained the Gospel to him herself. If I prayed with him as it was I felt that I would be offering false assurance. I decided to tread the line and began asking supplementary questions. The boy just nodded to everything I said and no one was translating for me. I had once again to ask for translation which was provided reluctantly. When I began asking him about Jesus it was clear that the poor boy knew nothing about what was going on and was just saying yes to please his mother who was anxiously gazing at him throughout. As that began to be exposed the woman leading and translating became angry as she obviously sensed that I wasn't happy with her efforts.

It's difficult to explain how offensive my actions actually were in that type of shame culture, but I could feel the tension in the air. In the end, I had to stop asking questions as the lady began translating things wrongly to cover her shame and I felt we were getting nowhere. We prayed for the boy before we left, me being convinced that he was in the same spiritual state that he had been when we arrived, but maybe slightly more intimidated by Christians who forced their way into his house and demanded that he made a commitment on the spot, having highlighted his sins to all and sundry in advance. What a disaster. The church lady then went around telling everyone that the boy had been saved and how great it was that the missionaries had gone there as they had been praying for him for a long time. I was glad to hear that they had been praying but it felt almost as if they had somehow set up the conversion to take place during our visit.

We held an emergency team meeting and I described what had happened to the group and how I never wanted to be put in that position again. Of course, I was labelled difficult again, although our group leader did share my concerns and express some empathy. The other groups hadn't had my experience in their teams and the team members who had been with me didn't think it had been that much of a big deal. I did go on a few more of the visits but similar things kept happening and in the end I asked to be excused from them. Also I found it hard to make sure I was prepared for each visit as the church ladies often turned to us and asked for a message or testimony randomly as if we had words of inspiration on the tips of our tongues at any and all moments. It was again a drastic misunderstanding of the role of a missionary and an expectation that we were somehow on a higher spiritual plane, that we had come down from somewhere lofty to bring God's message in a new and special way to the people.

CHAPTER FORTY-NINE

Gambling Never Pays

Having opted out of the small meetings to rally the backslidden church members, I didn't want to waste my time. I had been bothered by the gambling dens and the visibility of the vice from the outset. Being an ex-gambler myself, I knew how addictive and destructive it was and wanted at least to ensure the people involved heard the possibility of a different way through Jesus. I came up with a bold plan to create a tract with my gambling testimony and what the Bible says about gambling. I would then get it translated into Tagalog and print copies for distribution. I also found a basic Gospel tract entitled 'The driver, the convict and the skydiver' on the internet which I hoped we could use as well.

After initially looking at me as if I were barmy on hearing my desire, the Pastora suggested that one of the youth leaders could translate the tract for me. I had befriended an older teenage student who lived in the street opposite the church. When I informed her of my dilemma and my plan for the tract she said that she had printing facilities inside her wooden shack. I found it hard to believe but it turned out to be true. She faithfully printed hundreds of copies of my tract and agreed to accompany me for the distribution. This is what was contained in the tract:

"Bingo....what does God think?
- God has given us work as the normal way to get the money we need (Eph 4:28; 2 Thess. 3:12; Prov. 31).
- When a person cannot work, the second choice is prayer (Phil. 4:6, 19).

- All my income belongs to God and I am not free to use it as I wish. I am a steward, and should use it for God's purposes (Psa 24 :1)
- Christians should meet the needs of their family (I Tim. 5:8)
- Christians should share with others, particularly other believers with needs (2 Cor 8-9; Gal. 6:6-10; 3 John).

God uses money to accomplish important purposes in my life:
- Meet basic needs (Matt. 6:11; I Tim. 6:8).
- Build character (Phil 4:10-13)
- Give direction, by providing or withholding things.
- Helping others through me.
- Show His power through miracles.

Am I looking to God or to gambling for my needs?
- Greed and covetousness which are motives in most gambling are sin (Ex. 20:18; I Tim. 6:9; Heb 13:5)
- Proverbs warns of disaster for people who want to get rich quickly (28:20,22).
- Money that is gained easily is lost just as easily (Prov. 13:11).
- Money gained the wrong way breaks up families (Prov. 15:27).
- Gambling is addictive and your example may cause others including your children to become addicted to it (I Cor. 8:9, 13).

The Bible says to "redeem our time". Our few days here on earth are so short and precious, in relation to eternity, that we ought never to waste time but to use it only on that "which is good and helpful to us" (Ephesians 4:29).

Can we honestly, in good conscience, ask God to bless and use the particular activity for His own good purposes. If there is room for doubt as to whether it pleases God, then it is best to give it up. "For whatsoever is not of faith is sin" (Romans 14:23).

Even if a particular thing may not hurt us personally, if it harmfully influences or affects someone else, it is wrong. "It is good neither to eat flesh, nor to drink wine, nor any thing whereby thy brother stumbleth, or is offended, or is made weak... We then that are strong ought to bear the infirmities of the weak, and not to please ourselves" (Romans 14:21; 15:1).

Remember, finally, that Jesus Christ is our Lord and Saviour, and nothing else can be allowed to take priority over our conformity to His will. No habit, or recreation, or ambition can be allowed to have control over our lives. "All things are lawful for me, but I will not be brought under the power of any" (I Corinthians 6:12). "Whatsoever ye do in word or deed, do all in the name of the Lord Jesus" (Colossians 3:17).

My Story

I am 31 years old. I am a visitor to the Philippines as a Christian Missionary. I have spent over one year in the Philippines in total and have grown to love the people and country. I would like to return to the Philippines as a long term missionary next year (2014.)

Whilst in this area I have seen many things which make me sad and one of these is the gambling which many people are involved in including Christians. This saddens me not only because I believe it is wrong and a waste of time but also because I too was a gambler and I know how addictive it is.

It started when I was a child, I used to gather loose change to put into slot machines in the hope of making more money and whenever I was near to the machines I would always play them even if I was meant to be doing something else. Sometimes I would be there for hours. Most of the time I lost my money but sometimes I would win and this made it worthwhile.

As I got older and began working I had more money to spend and my habit became more dangerous. I began using more expensive machines and gambling more money. Then I started using the internet to gamble. I would use casinos online, scratch cards, the lottery and bet on the horses, football and anything else available. Most of the time I lost but occasionally I would win which made it worthwhile. Ironically my winnings would often be placed straight back into the machine or casino to try and make more money and then I would lose it all. As long as I had money left I would keep playing in the hope that I would make more money which never happened! Sometimes I would play for a whole day or many days in a week. I spent most of my spare time gambling the money that I was working for. At the height of my addiction I placed one thousand two hundred euros (seventy thousand pesos) on one blackjack card and lost. This is an example of the extremes that I went to, but I was gambling like this on most days and I was restless when I wasn´t gambling. It was the only thing that I wanted to do and I wasn´t interested in anything else. All of my time was taken up with this activity and I would isolate myself from my family and friends in order to gamble.

I loved the excitement of placing the bet or spinning the wheel or choosing my numbers but the thrill would only last a few seconds or minutes and then I needed to spend more money to get the same effect. It was exactly like a drug. The more money I lost the more I had to spend to try and make the money back. If I ran out of money I would go to the ATM and get more money. I would make promises to myself about how much money I was willing to lose but I would always break these and spend more trying to win back my losses. And when I won I would forget about the huge losses and tell people about the win. The reality is that I lost thousands of pounds and wasted months, maybe years of my life in this way.

Maybe you are reading this and thinking that you would never spend large amounts like I did or that you haven´t got enough money for gambling or bingo to become a real problem in your life. Please remember that I started with small money too and consider what would happen if you received money unexpectedly...where would this go? I mean you could feed the family for a whole month or you could gamble the money and feed them for two months...right? OR you could lose it all. Honestly add up the wins and losses in your life so far and make a decision TODAY to never again spend a single peso gambling. You will find great freedom when you make this choice.

If you would like to know more then please email me or contact me on Facebook. Maybe you are wondering how I broke free of this addiction and others. The short answer is that I confessed my sin to God and trusted in Jesus Christ as my Lord and Saviour. When Jesus died on the cross He died for all of my sin including the sin of gambling and I am no longer controlled by it. I made a decision eight years ago to never again gamble and I have been able to stick to this with God's help through prayer. Nothing is impossible with God."

I felt a bit unsure of myself as I took the lead and marched into the middle of those streets of avid gamblers giving out the tracts. I stopped and spoke to those who asked what we were doing. Most people took the tract eagerly as they did most bits of paper wondering if there was a freebie inside or planning to keep it as a reminder of the day the white person came to their village. Some of the men asked if my phone number was on it in front of their wives which irritated me immensely. But their wives just grinned as if it was the funniest thing in the world for their husbands to have said. The distribution certainly created a stir pre-eminently in the local bar where the tracts were given to all of the men drinking and playing snooker before we made a hasty exit.

At the end of one street a group of ladies invited us to join them as they sat eating and drinking in the sunshine. We did so and obviously they wanted to know all about me as a foreigner. I spent time answering their questions and explaining the Gospel to them whilst the girls who were with me sat shyly and quietly by my side taking it all in. The girls loved to be involved in that type of activity but I think it was more that they liked to spend time with me, the foreigner. I don't know if they would've had the courage effectively to condemn the activities of their friends and neighbours in a manner like that if I had not been there. But I was pleased that they had accompanied me regardless of the reasons and hoped they would learn - evangelists in training! Being a foreigner and short-term visitor was to my advantage; I wasn't there to build long term relationships, only to share the Gospel and to link people to the church. I didn't need to worry too much about people being offended by me provided they read the tract and received the message. Really, I just wanted to get people thinking about their vices and to make it clear that it was not God's way and that they had a choice not to partake. I was also shocked to see at times some of the church members involved in those types of practices; I hope my presence convicted them as well.

I don't know how much of a difference the intervention made. Normally I wouldn't advocate trying to change people's behaviour prior to conversion but I felt that in that case (where whole communities had succumbed to the sin and where it was difficult for individuals to stand against the crowd), if they did convert then it would be worth it. The only visible positive result from the tracting that I became aware of was a lady who had been attending a cult church and had decided, on reading the tract, to attend the church that we were connected to instead.

Afterwards I was encouraged to receive a letter from the teenager who had printed and distributed the tracts with me. She wrote 'Dear Ate Natalie. Thankyou Logos Hope Team for visiting our church, for your Christian Mission. I want to thank you for sharing your life to us. As John 12 vs 35 says "Then Jesus said to them 'A little while longer the light is with you. Walk while you have the light, lest darkness overtake you; he who walks on darkness does not know where he is going." I know that a long time ago you walked in darkness, you walked to find your own happiness but as time goes by you realised that you're on the wrong path, that you didn't find peace in what you are doing. I know that God let that moment happen to you because he want to give you a lesson, a lesson that most of the people will serve as their guiding force to change. Repentance is never too late and look at you right now, you're a new person that Jesus use you as His servant to share the Gospel to the people needing it. Thankyou Ate Natalie for the time we shared together with JR and Charmie when we were giving out the 'Driver, the convict and the skydiver" to the person that we didn't know at all. I'm hoping that the paper you made for them will help in order for them to know more about Jesus. Have a safe trip Logos Hope Team! More power and God bless! :)

CHAPTER FIFTY

Poverty and Ignorance

We were accompanied everywhere we went by women who volunteered in the church. Many of them were simultaneously trying to raise families and work full-time jobs just to put food on the table. Jocelyn was one of the volunteers. In her early forties, Jocelyn was always at the church and rushing around after us. She was always cheerful and helpful. She volunteered to accompany me on a long journey to visit some of the street boys from Subic in rehab one Saturday - they had ended up in Manila. Our team really had no idea about Jocelyn's personal struggles due to poverty as she selflessly served us day after day.

We were eventually invited to visit her home which was just opposite the church. She had held off inviting us due to being embarrassed about her living situation. She was living in one of the wooden huts which had been extended to form two stories. I assumed that the whole structure belonged to them knowing that Jocelyn had a husband and four children. I was shocked to discover that they only really had access to one room. The room was about two metres squared (if that.) She informed us that the six of them slept in that room but that there wasn't enough space for them all to stretch out because the children had inevitably grown bigger. The room was stiflingly hot during our visit and there was just a tiny open space near the roof serving for ventilation. It wasn't possible to stand up properly in the room, I had to stoop and when I sat down I couldn't stretch out my legs. There was no real furniture present.

I felt tears building when she told us that her children had cut themselves on the electric fan which had to run whenever they were in the room for obvious reasons. There was no cover on the fan so sometimes they injured themselves when they were asleep. It was really a terrible situation and I couldn't quite believe that nothing had been done to help the family considering the comparative wealth of some of the neighbours. She informed us that they had been saving money from her husband's salary for a long time in order to build a further room extension but the recent flooding had caused such a lot of damage that all of the money had instead had to be spent on repairs.

We discussed the situation as a team and decided that we wanted to gift Jocelyn the money that they had lost in order to build the extension which they had been praying about for fourteen years! I wouldn't advocate throwing money at things in most situations in foreign cultures but we had got to know the family, they had helped us a lot and it was really a way to say thank you to them. They had not asked us for anything and they could not finance it themselves. We ensured the money was given through the church and that we saw pictures of the project as it was completed.

One of the reasons Jocelyn had invited us to her house in the end was because she was sharing the space with her relatives and their children. Her elderly mother and father lived in an adjoining room and they were not yet Christians. She regularly prayed for them in the church meetings, principally for her father who was losing his eyesight. She was desperate for them to be saved. I was in evangelism mode and the usual fears of offending people or being rejected didn't seem to apply in that situation as we would be leaving after just a few weeks. I had asked Jocelyn whether she had clearly shared the Gospel with her parents and was astonished when she said that she had not and that she couldn't as she was too shy. Later on learning more about the culture I realised it was also a lot to do with the hierarchy and the respect for elders that is part of the fabric of Filipino society. It would be considered totally disrespectful to confront one's parents about their personal faith. But more than that, Filipino culture considers its citizens Christian from birth (very much like the Western culture used to do,) so to suggest to one's parents that they might not be Christians or that they need to change their beliefs and practices would be highly offensive.

Our team was not in that position and were uniquely qualified to share the Gospel, not because of any special skill or title but purely because we were foreigners and therefore automatically respected and listened to. I offered to share the Gospel with Jocelyn's parents and was humbled by her overwhelming gratitude before I had even done anything. Her eyes lit up and she was so excited. I felt the pressure of her anticipation but I knew that I couldn't do anything in my own strength. We prayed prior to our visit and then cautiously climbed the rickety ladder-like stairs to get to the room where her parents spent most of their time. I introduced myself and the others who accompanied me and then shared the Gospel with Jocelyn translating. They listened intently to everything that was said and I knew enough to realise that there wouldn't be any spontaneous response due to cultural shyness. We prayed in the group and then left the house after promising to gift them a large print Bible due to their collective failing eyesight. What had been a simple thing for me to do had been priceless to Jocelyn who as a true believer wanted nothing more than for her parents to be saved.

I thought about it a lot afterwards. It seems like an obvious consideration for Christians who are faithfully praying for their unsaved relatives, but I think you would be surprised by how many are not sure whether their relatives and friends have even heard the Gospel. I found on the ship that sometimes people hadn't even thought about it. They hadn't considered that they might be the only person connected to that friend or relative who knew the truth and was able to share with them. Surely that is the starting point. How can they believe if they have not heard?

It may seem like an emotionless transactional approach to dealing with people: on finding out that someone is praying for a non-believer, always to ask them whether they have clearly heard the Gospel and then to offer to share it with them. But if we really believe the Bible as we claim to, that is the method that God has chosen by which people can be saved. Our failure to share with them is evidence of a widespread lack of faith or unbelief. Do we really believe that the Gospel message will truly save people from an eternity in hell? If so we should have more confidence and ensure that everyone who comes across our path hears it. Instead we apologise for our message and the offence it causes or we water it down to make it more palatable or we obscure it with comedy and entertainment.

In recent years, I've started thinking more and more of people in terms of whether or not they are saved as that is the only thing that really matters. When someone dies I wonder if they were saved - if not, I feel real sadness even if I don't know them and if they are, relief and thankfulness. As Christians, it should be our focus; what can be more important than where someone spends eternity? We should take confidence and trust that God's Word will not return to Him void but will accomplish all that He desires and always be prepared to give a reason for the hope that we have. (Isaiah chapter 55 verse 11 and 1 Peter Chapter 3 verse 15)

CHAPTER FIFTY-ONE

Cultural Oddities

It's probably not very politically correct to say that another culture is odd, strange or bizarre but I'm sure the Filipinos would also use words like that at times to describe things about the Western culture. They probably wouldn't go as far as to include it in a book or even to speak it out loud due to cultural shyness but they definitely think it and probably whisper it among themselves.

I was returning from a ministry commitment and was walking up the street where the church is situated, having emerged from an alleyway at one end of the street. I was just fifty or so metres away from the church when I saw a child who looked to be aged about four sitting in the street outside a house. The child caught my eye because not only was she filthy dirty and swarming with flies but she had large infected scabs on her shaved head. Her eyes were full of fear and she didn't seem to belong anywhere. I remembered that I had seen her a few times before when playing with the other children and that she had always looked similarly neglected.

Although it was a poor area the other children were always dressed in clean or at least freshly washed clothes and they were given regular baths. The little girl therefore stood out to me. I was due back at the church and knew that it was really none of my business, but concern for the child welled up in me and I knew I was going to have to say something. I asked the adults nearby whether they were planning to give her a bath. In a Western setting abuse may have been screamed at me for daring to interfere, but in Asia the foreigner card allowed me to involve myself initially. I wasn't sure how far I would be permitted to go though and knew I needed to tread carefully. It was also taking place just down the road from the church where we were staying and I needed to avoid upsetting any local people as they all knew we were staying at the church and that we were missionaries. Many of the people and nearly all of the children attended the church. Maybe I was more outspoken as I knew we were leaving to head back to the ship that day so the situation was more urgent and I was more willing to take a risk.

A woman came out of the house as I stood there waiting for a response to my question. A crowd started to gather including people whom I recognised from the church. I wasn't yet sure if they were in favour of my intervention or not. I asked again whether someone was going to give the child a bath and the woman who had appeared said somewhat flippantly "later." I knew that in the Philippines that meant "never"; it's the same as their use of the word "tomorrow." Their culture doesn't allow them to refuse directly as they shy away from confrontation so they use vague time declarations to fend off any awkward questions. I wasn't satisfied with that and said that the child needed to be bathed immediately because she was covered in flies and really very dirty and that her wounds were likely to deteriorate if they were not cleaned. It was really just highlighting the obvious as they could already see the state she was in. She was also looking more miserable by the second but I think that may have been due to terror from my presence, also the fact that all of the attention was focused on her. She was aware that we were talking about her by then.

I received a similar brush off to my initial attempt and decided to risk forever offending the people for the sake of the child as I suggested that I give the child a bath myself in the street. I asked for soap and water. After a short pause where everyone gawped at each other wondering if I was seriously going to do what I had said, small pieces of soap began to materialise from nearby dwellings. The whole situation had created an impossible cultural dilemma for the people - they couldn't refuse me as a foreigner as that would've been seen as extremely rude but to allow me virtually to assume the role of a neglectful parent by washing one of their own children in the street thus getting myself dirty was also unthinkable. Nevertheless, a bowl appeared and the lady who I later learned was the child's aunt brought water from the house. I called the increasingly terrified child over and spoke gently to her asking for her name and other simple questions. I asked those gathered to explain that I was going to give her a quick bath so that the flies went away and that she might feel better afterwards.

At first, she didn't want to take off her clothes but the others gathered, having recovered from their collective stupor, took up the cause and encouraged her. She stepped into the bowl of water and she was assisted to remove her filthy clothing. I disguised my horror at seeing her whole body covered in infected sores and open wounds similar to those on her head. I wanted to cry but knew that I could not. She watched me with wide eyes probably wondering what I was going to do to her having created the big fuss.

I wasn't sure what to do next as I didn't want to get involved in physically touching her too much for obvious reasons. Fortunately, by that point other ladies had gathered and were entering into the spirit of things. They began soaping her down and helping her wash. I took more of a back seat and asked for a towel and clean clothes.

I then turned to the Aunt and asked why the child was in that state and where her mother was. I was told a long and sad story about neglect and prostitution. It was clear that the Aunt didn't appreciate having to take care of another child in addition to her own and didn't approve of the mother's lifestyle. Her own children were clean enough and playing in the street. I felt the anger rising knowing that that type of indifference meant that the poor child would likely never be taken care of. She would always know that she was different for reasons she didn't fully understand and that she couldn't do anything about. I asked the aunt whether she even loved the child and got a half-hearted response.

By that point I could tell that the local women and children were on my side and that the state of the little girl had obviously been bothering them as well. They commented about the lack of care and the shame being brought to them as a community. I told Aaliyah who had told me shyly that she was four that Jesus loved her. The aunt proved that she was at least capable of some human kindness by bringing her a clean and pretty white dress to wear. It hadn't initially been obvious that she was even a girl due to her shaved head, but I knew that parents sometimes did that to protect the children from head-lice which were a common affliction.

Deciding that my job had been done, I made the aunt promise me that she would give Aaliyah a bath or shower every day and try to keep her clean. I then wandered back to the church. Jocelyn emerged from the crowd as I left and fell into step next to me. She said that she knew the family and the situation and that she would ensure that Aaliyah was not neglected.

It's always the same people doing all of the work and I knew that Jocelyn had enough to do already with her own children and work schedule. But I gratefully asked her whether she could take responsibility for buying some medicine if I got her the money. Of course, she agreed. On reaching the church I went inside, leant against the wall and cried. I had held it in knowing it was necessary to get things done but the state of Aaliyah and the lack of care and compassion towards her had really hurt me. I had struggled not to cry throughout the incident.

After a few minutes, I composed myself just in time to be manhandled out of the church by some of the older ladies. I had made the mistake of joking earlier in our trip that I wanted to find a husband and that maybe they knew of some suitors. I had given them a verbal list of requirements. If I had known how seriously they would take it then obviously I would never have said anything like that. I had wrongly assumed that as they were Christians they would take it with a pinch of salt, knowing that God controls things and that generally match-making doesn't go according to plan. I was aware that during our stay they had been canvassing church members and arranging for me casually to meet their sons. One such son had even ended up preaching for the first time at an event that we were present at which was afterwards highlighted to me by many different women. They pointed out that he had leadership capabilities and was what Filipinos considered 'good looking.' The poor guy had stumbled through his message shaking like a leaf.

Still struggling with my grief from just a few minutes previously, I didn't really know what was happening as I was marched behind the church along a short path and suddenly found myself in the entrance to a small dwelling. A man was asleep on the sofa and to my embarrassment I saw that he was just wearing a pair of boxer shorts. There were a few other people in the house who started in surprise on our arrival. The half-naked man also jumped awake as the church ladies announced that we were there to pay a visit and that I was going to sing and pray for the man on the sofa as it was his birthday.

Mortified, as it dawned on me that it was all as a result of my earlier unwise comments, I greeted the man who was rubbing his eyes and looking confused as his mother poked and prodded him knowingly. They then began a joyful Filipino rendition of Happy Birthday in which I was forced to participate, after which I had to pray for the stranger. Immediately on concluding I apologized profusely for my rudeness advising them all that I had a plane to catch and must leave straight away.

I dashed out of the door covering my flaming cheeks and not really believing what had just happened. I made my way back to the church and found everyone packed and waiting for me. I told them what had transpired and of course they thought the whole thing hilarious. I was relieved that it had happened just as we were leaving, thinking that I might end up being married off to a random stranger if I were to stay any longer.

As we said our final goodbyes and drove slowly up the street in our convoy of vehicles, all of the people came out to wave us off. In the distance, I saw Aaliyah dressed in the pretty white dress; she was waving cheerfully and smiling. Crouching next to her was her aunt, who had her arm around Aaliyah and was pointing me out to her. It was a beautiful transformation and memory as we left to head back to the ship. The medicine worked wonders and within a month I was receiving pictures of Aaliyah without any visible injuries, still wearing clean clothes and free of that dull unloved child aura. I hoped and prayed that it would continue to be the case and that she would one day find true hope in Jesus.

CHAPTER FIFTY-TWO

Island Adventure

My favourite part of the Challenge Team was when our team paid an impromptu four-day visit to another island, Talim. It was an unexpected bonus as we hadn't been informed about it in advance, although I'm sure our hosts had been planning it for a long time. The excursion took place soon after we had arrived at Fishport and before we had had a chance to settle in. We travelled in a small wooden boat for several hours to reach the island. I was struck by the many wooden shack huts that were visible on the coasts of the other islands that we passed. I wondered whether they had a Gospel witness and began to feel excited about the prospect of one day returning and sharing with the people on those islands. There was something special about those lost people living primitively having survived numerous catastrophes. They were living aimlessly without a hope or future just waiting for the next typhoon or flood. Any religion that did exist was a formal, dead, Catholic faith full of superstition and a God who desires to punish not save.

We arrived at the island and were greeted by a Pastor and his wife who lived there. They had been sent from the mainland church in order to plant a church on the island. They had been there for several years already and had made a good start. A group of islanders gathered regularly at their house for worship services including a Bible study. The children appeared at their house at all hours of the day and night and played in their courtyard which was spacious. They had been going door to door to share the Gospel and pray with people in the community. They knew most of the people whom we came across during our stay.

I was concerned that Easy Believism was again present as the Pastor's wife told stories of one person and another person having 'received Christ.' It seemed that in order to be recorded as a non-believer by the zealous evangelists in those communities, the person would have clearly to deny Christ. Clearly in a shame culture that wasn't going to happen as it might cause offence, so it was easy to see where the inflated conversion statistics had originated. Having become accustomed to it I tended to ignore the proclamations and look for evidence of saving faith. If it wasn't present or the person couldn't explain adequately what they believed I would give them a tract and share again with them.

Despite their naivety, which was obviously due to the methods they had been taught and their training, the couple's hearts were in the right place and I admired their willingness to give up their home comforts and live on an island that was so isolated. They had chosen the island due to its lack of Gospel witness - there was just an old abandoned church building that had belonged to the Catholics. The ministry was twenty-four-seven and the people had a lot of practical needs. Medical treatment was far away and most of the people couldn't afford to take the trip when it was required. It was difficult to convince people that God was the answer and that prayer would be the most effective tool in the absence of anything else.

We stayed in an extremely luxurious house near the sea, probably the only really nice house on the island. I was a bit bemused as I had expected a simpler experience but I was also grateful for the hospitality and the good food which was frequently served. The owners of the house had been befriended by the Pastor and his wife on their arrival. The lady was a Christian but the man wasn't. He sat outside gambling with cards whilst she chatted with us. They had hundreds of dogs. It was almost like a pack of hunting dogs that followed them everywhere. Monkeys were also dotted around.

One of the chief amusements in the Philippines is to sing karaoke loudly and out of tune at all hours of the day and night. I had thought that coming to the island would put an end to that type of thing so was somewhat surprised to see a large karaoke machine standing in the courtyard at the entrance to the family's house. The teenage daughters took turns singing and we were persuaded to take part for a little while. The family had quad bikes and other such vehicles which the boys in our team enjoyed taking for a ride.

Boyd and Arnold managed to get the man of the house chatting one evening over an innocent game of cards after we had prayed for an opportunity to witness to him. He admitted that he knew that there was a difference in the lives of his wife and daughters and that his life was empty and meaningless without God. He drank quite a bit as well. But he just wasn't willing to take the step of faith, which was sad. The contrast between the man and his wife was stark. He was living a materially prosperous life and had everything he could have wished for, but it had fallen short of his expectations and he was miserable. It was unusual to see someone who wore their emotions externally as he moped around depressed and desperate day after day. Maybe living in the midst of Christians and being reminded of his fate on a daily basis kept the things of God in mind and riled his conscience. Whatever the reason, he definitely wasn't at peace and I hoped that it wouldn't be long before he found it.

Perhaps the relaxed atmosphere and material luxuries were a bit too much for some of us as we lolled on our backs on the floor outside listening to music and sharing stories having been stuffed totally with food. I had already fallen asleep in the boat on the incoming journey and had awoken to discover to my embarrassment that one of the older ladies travelling with us had spent the whole of her boat trip fanning me to keep the flies away. The island sapped our energy, it was probably the heat if nothing else.

But after our initial lethargy it was time to do some ministry. We discovered when we joined the Pastor and his wife for the visits that most people were relying on their good works to get to heaven. I had with me an evangelistic 'smart card.' It contained a thumb print on which a person could hold their thumb for fifteen seconds. If it changed colour it indicated that they were good enough to get to heaven. I was amazed by the number of people who voluntarily submitted to the test. One lady confidently asserted that she would be in heaven but as she was holding her thumb on the card she began to become agitated and said "I don't think I'm good enough," several times. It was as if the weight of her sin suddenly became a reality to her as she waited for the outcome. Obviously, the colour of the card never changes. On the back of the card is an explanation taken from the Bible explaining that no one is good enough to get to heaven and that that was why Jesus had to die. I talked the lady through it and left the smart card with her as a reminder.

We met a frail old man without teeth sitting alone in a chair outside his house. Not wanting to intrude we called out to a younger man inside the house asking whether it was okay for us to chat with his father for a while. The man shouted back that he didn't care as he was trying to watch TV. I was surprised to see a TV on the island. As we shared the Gospel with George and prayed with him, his worried face changed into a smile and he said "Jesus is my God." I felt moved with compassion for the very old man who was not long for the world and was glad that he appeared to understand the significance of our message.

As on the mainland there were hundreds of children and we spent time with them and held Sunday school meetings and classes for them to attend. Jason, a young boy of about seven, had oozing infected sores on his legs. I was worried that if he didn't get them treated he could end up needing amputations. The islanders were completely ignorant about things like that and even the Pastor and his wife didn't know what to do. My first aid was extremely basic but I knew that whatever first-aid I could give would be better than nothing and I had dabbled with things like that when helping the street teens in Olongapo. It sounds wrong in some ways but experimentation was welcomed by the parents who knew that we would do our best to help the children. Clearly in Western society if you start administering medicine to a stranger's child in the street you would probably be carted off to the nearest police cell or psychiatric institution, but the people there trusted us and relied on their basic instincts which told them we were 'friendlies.'

I tried to give myself a confident air but inside I was petrified as I found some band-aids, gauze, alcohol, cotton wool and cream. I sat Jason down and cleaned his filthy wounds with the hastily gathered medical kit. I wanted to weep over the state of his legs and feet, more so as he must've been in agony as I scraped and opened the infected scabs, but he didn't cry. In fact, at first he just looked terrified of me, with wide frightened eyes transfixed to my face, can I trust the foreigner who is hurting me? I'm sure that's what he was thinking and I was wondering the same thing myself due to my cluelessness. Arnold assisted me after a while and distracted Jason as I finished cleaning him up. He immediately went back to play afterwards, jumping around happily with the other kids, which was a relief. I prayed that his sores would heal and that I hadn't made things worse.

Jason was with a band of others on which we used colourful face paints when explaining the Gospel. I had the idea when I saw that the colours of the paint matched the colours needed for the Wordless Book. Instead of using the book which they had already seen, I marked their arms with the colours in a row explaining what each meant as I did so. The kids loved it and began going around and telling each other what each colour meant. It was great to see as they were sharing the Gospel with their friends and family almost as a game. But the Gospel was being shared regardless of the method and that was exciting.

After a whirlwind four days, we had headed back to the mainland. I had felt my heart stir during the trip and wondered if something similar might be part of my long-term future. I loved the simple living and ministering to a people with no Gospel witness. The idea of being a light in a small community like that and getting to know each person to show how God could help them and change their lives really appealed. As we sailed back I looked at the small communities on the other islands in a sort of daze thinking that one day I would like to come back and continue the work that had been started in that place. There were many more souls there and frequent disasters meant that their days could be numbered.

CHAPTER FIFTY-THREE

Streets Paved with Vice

Our Challenge Team having come to an end we had been subjected to the usual round of emotional Filipino farewells before heading back to the ship. The interesting thing that time was that the team were more realistic about the relationships they had formed. The others commented that they wouldn't be able to stay in touch with everyone they met whilst on the ship and they knew that the likelihood was that the locals would forget us as soon as the drama of our visit faded. They would then return to their lives as before. It was actually my preference as I didn't want people to become dependent on us emotionally, materially or even spiritually as was possible in cases where people only came to church to see the foreigners or to listen to and watch our programmes. It's sad but that was sometimes the reality.

The team had been great and I think we had all learnt a lot. It had been a lot more ministry focused than my other Challenge Team to Manila the previous year. But that might have been because I had managed to keep myself more focused on ministry and when the opportunities weren't there I had determined to create them. I was able to do that with the help of the street teens in the area who were more than happy to follow my lead and just appreciated me spending time with them.

On arriving back in Hong Kong, we were relieved to discover that the dry dock had that time gone according to plan. It was announced though that we would be heading back to the Philippines to visit two ports that had had to be cancelled during the super long dry dock in 2012. There was a collective groan when the news was announced as most people were really fed up with the Philippines by that point. I was one of the only people who was happy about it. We set sail for

San Fernando in the Philippines but on arrival discovered an engine problem. I then heard a rumour that we might end up back in Subic for repairs but didn't really believe it. The leadership kept referring to an 'unnamed' port in the Philippines. But many crew were afraid that if we ended up back in Subic we would stay there forever. When it was finally confirmed that we were going back people congratulated me as if I had won a personal victory. I had already decided that I wanted to work there in the future and I was keen to see the street boys again.

In San Fernando, I took part in bar ministry in the red-light district. I hadn't known what to expect because it was my first time participating in that type of ministry. I was surprised that the male crew members were allowed to join us. We walked along a street which was end to end with bars. Outside each bar were approximately three scantily clad and heavily made up girls. Hanging around were a few men including on many occasions the bar owners or the man managing the girls. It was terrible to see the vice being practised so openly.

I was amazed that we could walk up to the girls and start a normal conversation with them. The men could see that we weren't clients and probably guessed that we were religious groups and that our aim would be to persuade the girls to leave their lifestyle. Despite that they didn't try to interfere but allowed us to chat. It must've been either because they were holding the girls by using threats and intimidation and knew that they weren't going anywhere regardless or because for cultural reasons they were afraid to approach us as foreigners. The shady characters often looked weak and pathetic as they hung around. It made me angry to know that they were keeping the girls in subjection and humiliation.

Sometimes our presence did deter potential customers but it was obvious that we were fighting a losing battle as there were just so many girls and bars that a punter could disappear down an alley and reappear further along the street to find a whole new load of girls to choose from. That is unless they had any conscience at all and were ashamed to take part in those things in front of us, which most of them weren't.

I chatted to one very attractive girl with piercing eyes. She had drawn my attention because she looked a bit less made up and not as self-confident as the other girls. She also looked young. Evelyn was twenty-one and had come to the area having travelled by boat for a few days because her family was in financial difficulty. She honestly believed that she could sell her body for six months to pay off debts and get enough money for college and that then she would go home. Her family had no idea what she was doing or where the money she was sending was coming from. I begged and pleaded with her to give it up making it clear that there would be long term emotional and physical damage, that what she was doing would affect her for the rest of her life and that she wouldn't just be able to walk away. I think she knew it and maybe deep down had already decided not to leave, but I just became desperate to help her. I asked her to consider leaving and swapped Facebook details with her. On leaving I prayed for her and hoped that she would change her mind as she had said that she would consider leaving if a job could be arranged for her.

I tried to add her on Facebook but finding there were thousands of people with the same name I added every single person with that name and spent hours checking each one who accepted to see if it was the Evelyn that I had met. The next evening I was working on the ship when suddenly Evelyn appeared alongside a male crew member as a ship visitor. The crew member had been taking part in bar ministry in the same location as I had been and had also spotted Evelyn and decided she really didn't belong there. They had started talking and he had offered to pay her the going rate for the night if she came back to the ship! I wasn't sure about his approach but was glad she was there in any event. We hatched a plan to arrange for Evelyn to meet us in Subic, our next destination. We wanted to get her away from the bad influences that surrounded her and give her time to think things over. Ideally, she would have been willing to head home to her family, but the long journey and the thought of explaining things to her parents put her off. I would pay her fare to get to Subic as she wouldn't be allowed to travel with us on the ship. We would then use some of our prior contacts to see if we could get her a job there. I was specifically hoping that Argee, the mall manager who had become a Christian during our bridge ministry, might be willing to help.

I was once again frustrated that we really didn't have any long-term plans or follow up ideas for the people in need whom we met.

We didn't have strong enough links with local churches to refer people, particularly those who would need significant support. In a perfect world, all churches would automatically be willing and grateful to receive someone new into their midst but I often heard "our members don't know how to deal with that type of person/issue/ situation" and "we don't have capacity to begin a new programme right now" or "yes of course we can make contact...in a few weeks when the Pastor is free." The lady really needed immediate help and although we did our best in the circumstances we fell short of what I would have liked. Having initially agreed to travel to Subic to meet us Evelyn changed her mind at the last minute choosing to remain in the dark world of prostitution for the time being. I had to let her go knowing that God was in control and that she had heard the Gospel and maybe would respond when the time was right. Due to that experience and others, I was realising more and more that my heart was in longer term relationship building - sharing the Gospel from the outset but then helping someone practically with the next steps if they decided to follow Jesus. I was keen to leave the ship and begin the longer-term work but I still had a few months to go.

CHAPTER FIFTY-FOUR

Scared to Skype

The few of us who were excited to return to Subic Bay awoke anxiously to find that we had docked in exactly the same berth as we had been in previously. It had not been planned but the berths had been changed at the last minute which added a touch of the surreal to the proceedings. When I wasn't dealing with the street boys, who had by then become my preoccupation whenever we were in the Philippines, I took part in street evangelism. We were instructed not to restart the bridge ministry as we were only going to be in Subic for a few weeks and a market had by that point been set up across the bridge in any event so there wouldn't have been anywhere to set up a book table. We walked around with tracts and Bibles encouraging people to visit the ship as we shared the Gospel with them.

It was in a park near to the ship that I met Jasmine, a married Filipino lady in her twenties. She was sitting on a grassy area having a picnic with her mother and two children. I used the Wordless Book to share the Gospel with them. I prayed with the family and gave them a Bible that I had actually brought to give to someone else who had thus far failed to turn up for the prearranged appointment. I asked her to promise me that if I gave it to her she would read it, thinking that then if the other person did turn up I wouldn't feel so guilty and could bring another one from the ship. God's ways are higher than ours as the other person didn't show up - the Bible was obviously intended for Jasmine and her family!

Jasmine hadn't said a huge amount although I had spent a fair bit of time with her family and could see that she was listening and absorbing what I was saying. She later sent me a message on Facebook which read, "Wow…just wanna thanks for the things uve shared about Jesus and thankyou for the prayer. Hope u will have more people to touch and share about Jesus...When I got home the day u talked to me and realize that no matter what happened just have faith in God and in Jesus Christ...thank you Natalie, I will never forget u and I am reading the Bible u gave to me just like what ive promise to u. hope we'll see each other again. Now I'm confident to tell u that if I die I will go to heaven no matter what happened just have faith in God and trust Jesus Christ with all our hearts." She also posted on her public wall "Live life with faith in God trust him with all ur hearts and soul....follow Jesus and you will be saved."

What encouraged me most about the exchange was Jasmine's clear focus on Jesus. It was difficult in Filipino culture to take the focus off us as foreigners, but Jasmine had clearly received the message and was just grateful to the messenger rather than using the message to try to form a bond with the messenger because they are a foreigner and they might be rich or to parade them round as a status symbol of some sort. Yes, honestly, it did happen and sometimes it was difficult to detect exactly what a person's intentions were until we were already taking part in the parade!

I stayed in touch with Jasmine and invited her to church after my ship commitment had finished and I had returned to the Philippines independently. I had tried linking her up with some church members before but she was always too shy to take the plunge. When eventually I obtained her exact address and researched churches in her area I discovered that the church that I was attending was literally a few hundred metres away from her house! She accompanied me to one of the services where I put her in touch with some local women.

Over the past few years Jasmine contacted me a few times about issues in her life and she struggled to attend the church I had recommended. But I continued to believe that she heard and understood the Gospel that day in the park and so I continued praying for her. When she contacted me with a serious crisis after I had moved away from her area I reached out to another church that I had become familiar with and asked them if they could support her. I explained her situation and that I believed she had made a profession but had failed to grow as a believer. The church immediately took her under their wing, conducting a Pastoral visit and follow up visits, taking her to their church and making her feel welcome. The Pastor sent me a text message thanking me for the ministry opportunity. I couldn't quite believe it. Wow, what a change from the excuses and deferrals that I had become accustomed to. I think there is a lesson there for all of us about what it means to be involved in a church family.

Subic, on that occasion, proved to be a short visit and before long we were heading to Puerta Princesa, another Filipino port which we had missed due to the long dry dock. I took part in Eye Glass ministry in a male prison and was encouraged to see that the prisoners were more interested in the Gospel literature that we had brought with us. I recalled my experience in the women's prison and the complaints about the style and type of glasses and all the tricks that had been used to try to con us into giving more than was due. It was a joy therefore to see the men quietly slipping away to corners of the large room and eagerly reading the small *Gospel of John* and *Book of Hope* (a Christian magazine) that we had distributed.

Inside the prison, I met Ed, a sixty-two-year-old Englishman. He told me he was hopeless and wanted to end his life. He claimed to be a Christian but there was obviously something missing. It was unclear exactly why he was in the prison in the first place, it related to tax fraud I think. The main problem was the lack of certainty regarding an eventual release date or even a clear timescale for the court procedure. He denied having done anything illegal, but being an ex-police officer I knew to take that statement with a pinch of salt. Having spent a lot of time trying to encourage him and failing, I agreed to try to send him some ship books to relieve the boredom. I hoped that it wouldn't cause division amongst the prisoners if I were to do that but he was the only Englishman there (the books were written in English) and I told him that he must share them around, which he promised to do.

I wrote Ed a letter and sent it to the prison with a selection of Christian biographies and theological books, including *Taming the Tiger* by Tony Anthony. Anthony had ended up in prison after becoming a Christian and used his time inside to evangelise; I hoped it might inspire Ed not to waste his time. I felt quite pleased that I had thought to include the book as it seemed very relevant to Ed's situation; I believed that God may have prompted me. However, several years later, the book became the subject of a scandal in the Christian world due to the falsehoods and inaccuracies apparently contained within. Maybe my spiritual discernment was not as sharp as I had hoped. In the end, I realised that it wasn't an absolute disaster - I prayed that God would use the book to challenge Ed as I had given it to him in good faith.

I was a bit startled when later down the line I received a Skype friend request from the Department of Corrections in the Philippines. Cautiously I asked who was behind the important sounding title, mentally reviewing my connections and wondering what on earth it was about. Of course, it was Ed who, although still in prison, had somehow managed to get regular access to Skype, probably by bribing the officials with some of my books! I didn't Skype with him because he was constantly asking me for material things and by that point we had already moved on to another country. I did connect him with a local church and requested that the Pastor paid a visit, but whether or not that was followed up I couldn't tell you.

I met so many people on the ship and through the ship ministry that it would have been impossible to keep contact with all of them. There were a few special cases and people I would remember, usually due to their response to the Gospel. Even when people became Christians I wasn't really able to remain involved in their lives as we were always on the move. I learned that God uses His people to move people that one step closer to Him and that we are all links in the chain. It was God's way of keeping the glory for Himself, leading people to trust Him and stopping people becoming dependent on us personally. It was a tough lesson for a person like me who didn't like to do things half-heartedly, but I was learning.

CHAPTER FIFTY-FIVE

Winding Down

On leaving the Philippines for the final time, we returned briefly to Malaysia where the law had tightened in the area of religious freedom since our first visit as we were solemnly informed that we were 'forbidden' to evangelise. I often wondered why we even visited countries with those laws and why the authorities let us in. I'm sure they knew our intentions and we did honour their instructions according to the law of the land. We were told that if we wanted to break the law to share the Gospel we needed to return and do that independently and not risk the entire ship ministry in the process. I understood that but it was frustrating at times.

For a ministry day, I was asked to share my testimony with three classes of school children without mentioning God. That was a challenge as my testimony doesn't exist without God. I spent hours in preparation and finally resolved that I would focus on encouraging the children to search for the truth with all of their hearts to investigate for themselves and not to give up until they found the truth. I necessarily substituted truth for God and felt a bit of a fraud as I did so but I didn't really want to be the cause of the ship being impounded and the end of OM's fifty-year ship ministry so I had to comply. I handed out copies of my testimony to each child at the end with my contact details in case they had further questions, maybe once I had left the country.

I was somewhat dismayed though at the end of the programme after I had repeated my carefully worded lesson to three full classes of a total of one hundred and twenty students in quick succession. One of the teachers said to me that a lot of the students were Christians and that it would have been fine to say a bit more about

God! So much for my careful planning and for the information we had been given for our preparation.

In one of the countries we visited towards the end of my commitment, some crew decided to perform a 'Christian Flash-mob.' I had never heard of a flash-mob. Apparently, a group of people would suddenly, unplanned and unannounced, descend on a public location to perform a skit, drama or song in order to attract an audience. The group didn't generally provide explanations afterwards and the activity could be extremely random. The message had to be effectively communicated via the performance. At the end of the act they dispersed quickly, usually leaving a bewildered crowd of people. It was the surprise element that was meant to be uniquely exciting.

Because the crew were attempting a Christian version we would give out tracts and try to provide an explanation for any onlookers. Logos Hope's attempts went seriously wrong for several reasons - the area chosen was too big and wide so the music couldn't be heard; the performers didn't make enough noise at the beginning of their act to get the attention of people in the area who didn't seem to notice that anything was happening; the dancers hadn't practised sufficiently resulting in the formation being badly out of sync; and the dance selected didn't seem to bear any relation to Christianity or anything remotely connected with it. The result was that the majority of people who ended up watching were fellow crew members wanting to see what a flash-mob actually was (which is why I had gone.) In hindsight, a performance like that should probably only be attempted if a group has a very special skill and something unique to offer that will draw a crowd. I'm not sure that the practice could effectively be utilised by Christians.

But, after the disappointments, I was cheered up by a beach day for the Book-Fair team where I was able to swim out to some distant rocks and relax watching the sunset as I read a book. It was good to relax as earlier on I had taken part in games which proved to be a bit wild in the end. Beginning on all fours, I had to balance on my hands with my legs supported by the person behind me who was also balancing on their hands. There were four of us in the people snake and needless to say it didn't work as, on moving forward, I fell on my face in the gravelly sand getting a mouthful in the process. Not very dignified you might think.

My time on Logos Hope was drawing to a close. It became a wind-down period and a small group of us spent a couple of evenings watching the BBC's *Sherlock* in the Book-Fair life-boat, which helpfully had a large screen. One of my friends from our *Sherlock* group, Jenny, provided a final comedy moment. There had been an older man Jack on board who was acting as the Chaplain; he was often in the company of a similarly aged lady. The man left the ship and we heard on the grapevine that he had married. The lady returned to the ship independently but everyone just assumed that she was the one who had married Jack. We were having a conversation one day with the lady and Jenny was talking to her about Jack. The woman looked a bit confused and eventually said that she had known Jack for a long time and that yes they had been friends but that he had married another woman. Jenny exclaimed "Oh, I'm sorry, I thought he'd married you!" Ouch....

Some of my friends and other crew had already used their seven annual leave days for beach holidays. I had used a few days to travel to the locations of the Filipino street teens but I hadn't taken a proper vacation since the visit of my parents in late 2012. On arriving in Phuket, Thailand, our last but one destination, I decided to join friends for a four-day beach and touristy break. We stayed in a pretty nice hotel and went snorkelling and swimming after sailing to an island. I ended up in a sand and mud fight with two of the girls and got totally coated in the stuff which they found entertaining. It was nice to be able to swim in the sea without fear of illness or death due to the absence of both pollution and jellyfish on that occasion.

I was sad to see the vast array of superstitious beliefs that were diligently put into practice by the locals on a daily basis. The most visible was the food that was laid out in pretty dishes in different locations or in front of statues and idols. The food was an offering for the numerous gods that cluttered up the place. At first I found it amusing wondering why people didn't realise that their gods were not real when they didn't eat the food they were given and it began rotting on the pavement. But in time I moved through fascination as I saw how sincere the people were, and then sadness as I realised they were totally enslaved to it. Even those who couldn't afford to eat themselves would probably still sacrifice to their gods. It was necessary when walking around always to be careful not to accidentally kick or tread on an offering that had been left in the street as they were everywhere. I had visions of an irate Thai man coming running out to the street to apologise to his gods or berate us for our carelessness. But fortunately, we were not placed in that position.

It was great to take those days out for rest and relaxation and to think about my next steps as my return to England was looming. Back on board after our short vacation in Thailand, we completed our final sailing to Sri Lanka and I took part in my final days of ministry. I visited a rehab centre where I shared my testimony, and a girls' home, where I heard the most enthusiastic singing in two years!

Arriving in Sri Lanka had been a bit surreal as it was the port from which I would finally depart. In some ways, it felt like those of us about to leave had already left. Many of us had saved our days off for our final moments on-board so we were no longer required to work. There were a lot of people wandering around reminiscing, doing not a lot and just saying goodbye to people. People (not me) were also taking numerous selfies with every possible item and person on the ship. There was still one final momentous hoop to jump through and, still being afraid of public speaking, it was something that I had been dreading virtually since my arrival on-board.

CHAPTER FIFTY-SIX

Goodbye Logos Hope

It was time to prepare something profound for my farewell testimony. I had listened to several already and by the time I came to read mine most of PST Penang had already left the ship. They began to leave a few months prior to their end of commitment citing the beginning of school years in their home countries or dry dock burn-out. I was tempted to leave early as well but wanted to fulfil my two-year commitment.

It was interesting to see the different attitudes towards the opportunity to speak in front of the entire ship's company for five minutes. Some made jokes or ran through long lists of the names of the friends they had made whilst on-board, inevitably elating some who weren't expecting to be on the list and offending others who found themselves curiously absent. Some used it to bash all the leaders over the head with things that should've been said privately. Others ran through vague spiritual experiences and statistics of souls they had been involved in saving. The shy ones even occasionally declined to take part knowing they would be a bundle of nerves unable to contribute anything useful or be understood due to their shaking. There was even one guy who spoke for five minutes all about the environment and didn't mention God at all. The most tragic stories were the odd one or two who had somehow managed to lose confidence in God on-board and were returning home having effectively realised that they were non-believers.

I thought a lot about the speech believing that I needed to take it seriously, wanting to influence those who listened for good but also to inspire change in the areas that needed it. My emotions were raw having dealt with so many issues during my time on-board and it would've been easy to join the 'list of things wrong with Logos Hope' club. But I knew that had I begun in that vein I would lose most of the audience within the first thirty seconds. Also, I wanted to highlight some positive experiences I had had. I decided in the end to choose one major frustration that could be changed and then to focus on the positive aspects of the ship's ministry.

When the day came, I was very nervous but less so because I could simply read my speech from a piece of paper rather than it being off the cuff or memorised. This is what I said:

"I worked in the I-café at first where I had some good conversations but it was hard as I had little patience. The team was incompetent especially at weekends when random galley members came to "help" us without a clue how to do things and we had to teach them whilst serving ten thousand people. I also worked as storekeeper, enjoying the physical work and laughing at Trevor as I would see his legs sticking out from aisles in the storeroom when he fell asleep on the floor.

Dry Dock Subic changed my life. Every day for many months we manned a book table and shared the gospel. Myself, Nick and Thabo were the regular team. A group of street teens were sniffing glue nearby due to hunger. Over time we built friendships, shared about Jesus, gave food, went to hospital to deal with various ailments and gave clothes. I forgot to tell the team about this, so Nick confronted a load of kids wearing book fair uniforms and asked if they had stolen them and they said "yes." The standard response when they don't understand. Arlene joined us so we could finally communicate properly. Some of the older boys started working and the younger ones left the street going home and back to school.

Marlon (twenty-one) seemed a little crazy and I was slightly afraid of him but told him "Jesus loves you." He questioned "Jesus loves me?" and then repeated it in a mocking tone but then he disappeared. His friends said he was working and had changed. On returning to Subic I saw him transformed. He said he realised God loved him, so he had given his soul to Him and was attending a local Baptist church.

We began a feeding ministry for those staying off drugs. This triggered the worst behaviour and we became the target of violence, stealing, swearing, drug taking in front of us and other things which broke my heart as they were hurting themselves to hurt us. Every day we forgave them and started again prompting the question "why do you always forgive us?" Our response "because of Jesus."

My favourite day: eleven very excited boys visited the ship for dinner and the Jesus movie. Many crew helped and everyone smiled and make them feel welcome even though their behaviour was terrible. They kept escaping and running around the ship unescorted and we found jam and other food hidden on them. I saw logos hope wrist bands for days afterwards! But they watched the movie avidly. At the front were Ismael (fifteen) and Aiman (ten) the two Muslims. During the movie Aiman said excitedly to Ismael "this is where Jesus is in the tomb for three days!" he remembered from an Evangecube!

A local family took some of our boys in but when the ship left they ran away ending up in rehab in Manila where we visited. Some will return to the family next year and there is evidence of genuine faith. Joven's T-shirt had the print "God loves me" at the rehab centre. A huge thankyou to everyone that helped, listened, prayed or gave money.

I also had two great challenge teams in the Philippines. Last year Danny, a sixty-four-year-old school teacher, became a Christian after conversation during eye glass ministry. He started evangelising in his community, was baptised in April this year and wants to be a missionary.

After Subic I worked as Book Fair Admin and product placement much to the annoyance of those doing daily orders as I reorganised everything. I wanted the Christian Children's Books and Bibles to be more central. Thank you Andy for being a great boss and for your flexibility.

Other Highlights: C Days, thank you events! My cabin mates and friends, especially my prayer partner Mia. The Hui Ship family - Many Tuesdays I have been in pain from laughing too much, normally at something Frank has said or done!

Struggles: I have struggled with MANY things theologically and otherwise but my biggest frustration has been the missed opportunities to use literature in open countries. We have few paper tracts and often run out of literature. Why isn't the gospel on our fliers and why don't we use Christian literature for C Days/Challenge Teams/Help and School packs? We can give material things to people but without Jesus they will still go to hell. Help and hope must go together. I pray that someone will take on this responsibility full-time and make distributing literature a focal point for all crew members.

Future plans: The video "tears of the saints" reminded me that nothing is more important than where someone will spend eternity and that the price for a soul isn't cheap which is why people should count the cost before deciding. Proverbs 24:11 instructs us to "Rescue those being led away to death and hold back those staggering towards slaughter." Strong words, yes, but non-believers are literally staggering towards an eternity in hell. This is an emergency as the gospel is only good news if it gets there in time!

With this in mind I will resign from the police, where I had been working for ten years, when I go back to England on 15th September. I hope to return to the Philippines this year to work amongst people with little/no access to the true gospel. I will also reconnect with the boys. On challenge team in Manila I stayed at a house church plant on an island. They were evangelising door to door and helping the community. I was inspired by this and would like to be involved in something similar one day. Please pray for the right church partner as I will return independently without an organisation."

On reflection, although my speech drew a laugh in places and wasn't intended to offend anyone, I probably wouldn't word some of the things in quite the same way now. But I thought it was important to represent things as they actually were rather than seeking to Photoshop them to perfection.

As I was rushing down from the platform, feeling relieved that it was over, I was approached by one of the ship leaders. He had been standing with the Assistant Director at the back of the room listening to my comments and said that they had discussed my speech. They had heard what I had said about the Gospel literature availability and how it was distributed. He said that it had been a hard word for them but that they would make changes. I was humbled and grateful for the acknowledgement and commitment.

I had been building up to the leaving point for quite a few months and was beginning to feel as if the walls were closing in. Living on a ship for two years can be tough. It feels like a parallel universe - that you and your fellow crew mates are the only people who exist.

Indeed, one of the weirdest things I found when I got home to England was that everywhere I went I kept mistakenly thinking I saw ship crew members in the street. My mind had just become so used to seeing the same people that I saw them everywhere even though it was virtually impossible for them actually to be there as they were from completely different countries.

There were numerous end of commitment events on-board and farewells for all the different groups, clubs and even countries. I showed my face at some of them and avoided others, not really being the social type and definitely not enjoying the superficiality of some of the farewells. I had been known to slink away without saying goodbye at all whilst everyone was busily hugging each other, but decided I should at least make the effort as I had made some good friends.

My flight was at 6am but we left later than planned as someone who needed to accompany us was asleep. On the way to the airport we were stopped by the police who wanted a bribe. The negotiations went like this:

"There's something wrong with your vehicle."

"Um, no I don't think so."

"We need to take some details from you."

"Sorry we don't really have time as these guys have flights to catch."

"Maybe you can come to the police station?"

"No I don't think so."

Until thankfully one of our number realised they had left their laptop on the ship so we managed to persuade the police to let us go back the way we had come. We then took a different route on the return journey. All of the delays and inconveniences were blamed on me as I had shouted "freedom" a little prematurely.

Keen to be reunited with my family, particularly my sister who had had a baby whilst I was on the ship, and totally shattered, I wasn't really in the mood to get into deep conversation. I found myself sandwiched between a talkative American lady and a curious Indian man on the plane. I shared the Gospel, answered their questions and exchanged contact details with both of them. The difficult moment was when the lady became interested in my conversation with the man and started loudly interjecting because she was drunk. Fun times!

Epilogue

Prior to my service, and even to some extent whilst I was onboard, I had thought that Logos Hope was a training ground for those who wanted to be long-term missionaries in the future. That may well be true for some people but, as a slightly older recruit, I needed to be spiritually prepared to enter the Logos Hope environment. I needed to be willing and able to stand up for the truth where necessary and to learn to trust God and lean on Him more. I needed already to have a consistent daily devotional time, to know what I believed and why. I needed to be willing to challenge cultural practices that weren't biblical and to be willing to stand alone where necessary. None of those things should have been a surprise to me as that is what the Christian life is like and no one can live it for us. We make choices each day about whether to conform to the behaviour of those around us or to stand out as a light for Jesus. I just didn't expect that to be the case whilst serving on a Christian missionary ship - I was naïve.

I want to be clear that a lot of my struggles were not on or directly related to the ship itself. A lot of the things you have read happened on teams or at places other than under the direction of the ship leadership team. Some of the things that did happen on board were the result of the sin of individuals which will happen in any environment and cannot therefore be attributed to the ship's leaders. I have omitted some of them as I don't think it would be helpful to include them here, other than for shock value. There were things on which I felt the leadership should have taken a stronger line and those I have highlighted.

My overall conclusion after several years of reflection is that I'm grateful for my experiences on Logos Hope as I believe they taught me spiritual lessons that I couldn't have learned in another way. God had a purpose. I have tried to document the lessons I learned in the narrative but conclude here by re-emphasising some of the bigger ones.

- Take the time for proper preparation when teaching others in any capacity. It is a big responsibility and they may only hear the Gospel once. Take it seriously - pray and really search the Scriptures to make sure that what you are teaching is biblical. Encourage others to do the same. Arrange translation and other practical matters in advance, don't just rely on the Spirit because you are not adequately prepared. (2 Timothy 4:2)
- Be as direct as possible with the Gospel in the context you are in. Remember that it is the method by which God has chosen to save people. Don't water it down or tone down the message - How can they believe if they have not heard? (1 Corinthians 1:21)
- Small things are important to God, be faithful in them and then you might be given bigger things. One soul saved is worth a lifetime of ministry. (Luke 16:10)
- Don't be discouraged by what others are doing or saying and don't follow the crowd. Choose your own path with God by following His Word. "Choose for yourselves this day whom you will serve but as for me and my house, we will serve the Lord" (Joshua 24:15). You will stand before God alone one day and give an account of your life; your friends and family will not be standing with you.
- Are we trusting in God or in men or people? To whom are we ultimately responsible? (Psalm 118:8)
- You cannot buy a soul or force someone into the Kingdom. The price was too great and we are given free will for a purpose. (Psalm 49:7)
- Help without hope is the ultimate tragedy. You can prolong a person's life and make it temporarily cheerier but what of their soul?
- There is no break from being a Christian. You are a witness all the time and everywhere you go. Sometimes we can be tempted to separate ministry and put it in a box but the way we live our lives impacts those around us whether we are taking part in planned ministry or not. Some of the best contacts and conversations I had were not part of planned ministry. We need to be open to the leading of the Holy Spirit and always be ready. (Hebrews 12:1)
- Simple living - maybe all of us in Western countries will be judged by God for living lives of comparative luxury. We don't know

what standard God will use. We need to think about that specifically when serving amongst those who have little.
- Communal living can be tough, especially when there is a mix of different cultures. It would have been possible to spend all of my time on Logos Hope in conflict with others instead of getting on with God's work. I learned to try to choose my battles - to take on only the most important spiritual issues for the sake of truth and to compromise on lesser issues to foster Christian unity.

Would I encourage others to join the ship? A few years ago, I may have said 'No,' but time having passed and reflecting on my experiences I would say now that an individual must go where God calls them. For some people, it may be to Logos Hope, for others it will be somewhere else. The important thing for anyone to consider when joining the ship ministry is whether they are adequately prepared for the experiences. If God calls you He will equip you; that must be your confidence as you take that step into the unknown. I hope by reading about my experiences you will know a little better what to expect when joining the 'Largest Floating Book-Fair' in the world or any other mission field. So, yes, go to Logos Hope and serve faithfully but first check your calling and second check your spiritual resources. Are you ready for the challenge?

THE END

If you have enjoyed this book, feel free to contact the author at natalie.vellacott@gmail.com and reviews are always appreciated at Amazon and Goodreads. Thankyou!

Farewells and Birthday Wishes

On returning to England I was finally able to read properly through all the letters, cards and other notes that I had received in the last months on board. It had also been my birthday just before I left which I hope explains some of the comments. I thought it would be a fitting end to share some of them here, a lot of them relate to my ministry with the 'rugby boys,' which, as already mentioned, was the subject of a previous book. I have listed the main reason I knew the person and the country they were from. Please keep in mind that I wasn't some sort of saint on board which might be the cumulative effect of reading all of the messages - people who didn't like me weren't exactly going to write farewell notes to tell me that. It was a Christian community where people tended to try to encourage each other and see the positive side. There was also a tendency towards excessive displays of emotion, especially when saying goodbye to people. The final note from my cabin mate is probably a more realistic picture!

"Dear Natalie, it was really special to have chatted with you, even for a brief moment. Thank you for sharing what is in your heart. You have been a blessing not just to one but to many boys/girls, especially the 'rugby boys.' Will keep you in my prayers as you continue to seek the Lord's best will for you after your time on-board. You are always welcome to call our office/email me for any future concerns. Keep up the good work- For His glory"
 - Leader of OM Philippines

"Natalie, you've been an inspiration to me with the kids, your love for them, dedication and perseverance is admirable. Thank you so much for all you've been doing. Keep me posted and enjoy the rest of your time on the ship."
 -Leader of Line-Up (South Africa)

"Thanks for your good example in our family, of the importance of sharing God's word and taking every opportunity to do that. You're like Ranseal varnish- 'does what it says on the tin' in your Christian faith. Thanks for being unreservedly focused on evangelism and being pro-active to help make that a focus of Logos Hope! It's been a blessing to have you as a sister and I've grown to appreciate your dry humour. Thanks for your Ranseal character in being a woman of integrity, you are who you are. Your love for the street kids in Olongapo is inspiring and I thank God he enabled you to be involved in this ministry. I'll pray for you!
-Ship Family Member (Ireland)

"Natalie, it was great getting to know you, to see all the love and energy that you put into your passions. Seeing the boys coming off the street was amazing. To hear how their respond to you even greater. Thank you for being an example of Jesus compassion. And I enjoyed your efficient work very much. God bless you and provide while you're following his way back to the Philippines."
PST Penang (Germany)

"Natalie V, you will make my time in Fishport unforgettable and I'm so thankful for the things that I learned from you. I hardly know anybody that has such a passion to bring God's children back to him and having compassion at the same time. May nothing take this away."
Challenge Team Leader (Germany)

"Natalie, thanks for being my first best friend on-board. I will miss you but I know that you will do amazing things where God calls you. Keep in touch. Hugs and prayers. Thanks for being one of my first friends forever"
PST Penang (Fiji)

"Thanks, I remember when I was working Book-Fair. You are master to know where the book is. Thanks for hard working"
Book-Fair (China)

"Dear Natalie, thanks for being an enthusiastic evangelist in our family. Thanks for all you do, especially your heart of love and compassion for the people God has brought into your life. Our prayers are with you as you take the next step into the future with the Lord as your counsellor and guide. Love and prayers."
-Ship Parents (Singapore)

"Natalie, you already know how much I love you right? I'm really thankyou that being real sister in ship. You're being with me when I feel tired, so I want to say 'salamat po!' (thankyou in Tagalog.) For 2 months, I'm going to miss you. It was big blessing to me spent time with you as same ship family. It was privilege to me to get to know you. Thankyou for your intimate love to me."
Ship Family Member (South Korea)

"Dear Natalie, I'm really glad I got to know you and serve Christ together. You passion is challenging and encouraging. Thankyou for allowing me to join in your ministry. I love the Philippines and the people we met. May God bless you and the work you do! Ingat (take care.)
Co-worker (Australia)

"Hey Natalie, thankyou for being such a good example. Your involvement in ministry shows me that I want to do more and motivates me to go on. Your strong and radical opinions let me think about mine again, which makes me grow. I'm sorry if I don't always seem so thankful. You are a great sister! Ship family wouldn't have been the same without you and it was great! I will pray that your preparation for the Philippines will go well and I'm excited to hear what God will do through you. Please send me your updates. God bless you"
Ship Family Member (Germany)

"Dear Natalie, thankyou so much for your patience with me, my English and love for details. Thankyou for your trust to share with me and your honesty. I am glad that I could better get to know you and your heart for the kids and evangelism. Your stories and newsletters touched my heart. My prayer is that God will provide the best things

for you and guide you the right way. I am sure God has great plans for you and He will use you for ministry. I pray that you'll have patience and trust to 'be found' by the right husband. Nothing is impossible for God and it is good to know that He has everything under control!"
Book-Fair (Germany)

"Hey buddy, thankyou for everything being a good friend! I enjoy serving our Lord Jesus with you, keep burning for Jesus. God bless you!
Bridge Ministry (Georgia)

"Love you and gonna miss you. Thanks for everything. Thanks for your hard work." And "Thanks so much for our time together on-board and in Book-Fair and specially in our Challenge Team where I could get to know you better. Your amazing testimony and see your passion for sharing the gospel and reaching out to the poor. Keep going and keep trusting in God. He will lead and guide you in the future. God bless you"
PST Penang (Denmark)

"Hey, it was always very funny how you treated me during Daily Orders you made me feel like a kid. But I really appreciated your work. It was a great joy to see you down during Daily Orders"
Book-Fair (Unknown)

"Hey Natalie, my big sister, I'm just a little happier when I see you and I wanna thank you for being everything you are in our family. God bless you so much!!! I've really come to love and appreciate you more and more over the time. God bless you and I pray he will always keep your heart as it is. Some maybe don't like it, but who cares. God bless"
Ship Family Member (Germany)

"Happy Birthday my sister. I am really glad to know you big sister Natalie. Thank you for been fun with me and teach me how to speak good English. Thankyou very much I will miss you a lot...your brother."
Ship Family Member (Taiwan)

"Thankyou Natalie for working hard in the Book-Fair. May God bless and guide you as you continue this journey with Him. Hug. PS Thankyou for the good advice you gave. You have really been an example to me during this time. Your passion for the street kids. Willingness to serve those who are the lowest ones in this world. May the Lord bless your future ministry, God speed."
Book-Fair (Switzerland)

"Thankyou for always being willing to direct the blind. You will be missed."
PST Penang (Hungary)

"Natalie, you're wonderful. I've enjoyed the time I spent with you very much, even if it wasn't a lot. You're so straight-forward and very practical. Do you know how incredible that is? I hope the things I've learned from you will stick. All the best- may God bless you and give you His peace."
Co-worker (USA)

"I've really come to admire you over the past few months. I MEAN THAT!"
Book-Fair (Sri Lanka)

"Dear Natalie, I have always been impressed by your dedication and the effort that you put in everyday. You are truly a role model for us and you have shown us how to be a humble servant. I also have to say that you are really good at putting all these mixed books back onto their shelves. I certainly can never do that! Take care and may God pour his blessings onto you everyday!"
Ship Volunteer (Hong Kong)

"Natalie, beautiful woman with a heart for lost people, a passion to share the truth. Please keep on going. God will show you the way and make your steps firm. You will not get tired but will be filled with light and strength God gives. Thankyou for being part of my life. I really enjoyed your company in On-shore Book-Fair. God bless you."
Book-Fair (South Korea)

"Natalie, I hope and pray that this letter finds you well. I just wanted to say that I thoroughly enjoyed talking to you and our short conversations. One of the biggest things that stuck out to me was how you said you could not wait to be thru with your 2 years here on the ship. Yet every time I saw you, you were working as hard as you could, even on your day off. To me this is a testament to how you love the Lord and work as if you're working for him. I was greatly encouraged by this. I just want to thank you for being a light every time I saw you. I also want to encourage you to press on and continue to serve the Lord with all that is in you. I can see you're an amazing woman of God and I hope you continue to serve with such a great heart. In Christ"
Short-term Visitor (USA)

"Dear Natalie Vellacott, your humility humbled me a lot. I really admire your character and I will miss seeing you around. And I must say that your heart for those kids in Subic humbled me. When I met you I thought you were so serious but then I realise how nice and funny you are. Be bless in your future plans serving the Lord, I will be praying for you. With love."
PST Penang (Chile)

"Thankyou for being my big sister and taking the time and effort looking after me during my time on-board. I felt so welcomed and settled in very quickly. You have given me inspiration to be a good big sister to me little sister."
Little Sister (England)

"It's a blessing to see a girl who loves the Lord and relies on God as you do. Keep on for the rest of your time and keep on delighting yourself in God's timeless truth. From your brother in Christ"
Co-worker (Ireland)

"Natalie, It was amazing to see how God has been using you in our two years. You are really an example for me of living the Gospel out and loving like Jesus. May God bless you as you rely on Him. I look forward to hearing what God will do through you in the years to come."

PST Penang (France)

"Dear Natalie, It's a blessing to know you in my life. I learn a lot from you. You are such a strong woman (positive way) but your heart is so full of compassion for others. I see how you changed a lot in these 2 years. Amazing God! Thankyou so much for being a good friend to me"
PST Penang (Indonesia)

"Natalie, thankyou that God made you the way you are, your passion for literature and passion for children. Not sure how the Book-Fair would be without your hard work, we are all so grateful for you. Keep walking in the light, God bless"
PST Penang (England)

"Thankyou for correcting me many times on how I should behave. You have been a good mum and you really helped me to grow and mature on-board. God bless"
PST Penang (Scotland)

"Dear Natalie, thankyou so much for everything. Thankyou for your encouragement everytime we're talking. Thankyou also for your help, you know what I mean. Hope to see you again, I will surely miss talking with you. If you are planning to go to Olongapo just let me know, if I'm free, I will surely accommodate you. Always take care and God bless. You're always in my prayer."
Ship Volunteer (Philippines)

"Dear Natalie, I am thankful for you being part of the weekly prayer. You have a great zeal in helping people and bringing them to Christ. May your strength always be the joy of the Lord. God bless you!!"
PST Penang (Germany)

"Happy Birthday Natalie, thankyou for your great and wonderful example"
Director and his wife (Germany)

"My dear friend Natalie, Happy Birthday!!! I really thankful that I could get to know you on the ship, you're honest, passion, integrity, love for people, always encourage me a lot. Thankyou for being my prayer partner. I really love to pray with you. You're so good to me, thankyou. I also love the passion you have for God. Not so many girl have. Keep in touch."
Prayer Partner (China)

"Natalie, thankyou so much for everything over this last 2 years. Thanks for all of the discussions over a cup of tea, it's been great to get to know you and to see God at work in your life. I pray that God will truly bless your future ministry and pray that everything will go well with moving to and working in the Philippines. Many blessings." And "Sherlock Holmes was awesome."
PST Penang (England)

"God bless you Natalie! Thank you for your hard work and commitment on board, even when it was hard to be here. Thank you for sharing your heart...letting others be inspired by your passion for the boys in Olongapo. May you know the Lord's grace and guidance in your future steps! Any blessings
Assistant Director and Family (South Africa)

"Natalie Vellacott, Wow! What a challenge you have been and still are! Girl, I praise God for you. You have been my clapper boy many times and also an amazing friend. I'm really blessed that you are my friend Natalie and have seen how God has shaped you so much during this time. He really broke your heart for what breaks His and I am in awe of that. Continue to do the work He has given you and don't forget to sit at His feet in-between. Don't miss what He wants to teach you about Himself. You are a blessing to me and I love you. I look forward to your newsletters from the Philippines."
Challenge Team Leader (Jamaica)

"Happy Birthday Natalie, thankyou for so many great conversations" and "It has been such a privilege serving on Logos Hope with you! I know it wasn't easy for you but I'm proud of you for sticking with it until the end! Thanks for all the great conversations

we've had, for praying for me, for inspiring me and for showing me that with God it is possible to literally transform lives. God bless"
Book-Fair (USA)

"Hi Natalie, Good day!! I just wanted to thank you for the good times we had. Thank you for teaching me to forget the things that matter least and remember the things that are close to God's heart. My one month (almost) in the I-café with you is one of the best days of my life. Thankyou for your patience, for your kind heart and your prayers. Thankyou for teaching me how to make popcorn! It's the first thing I learned in the I-café. I almost forgot, thankyou for teaching me manners. Hahaha. God bless you!!! I hope we see each other again..."
I-café (Malaysia)

"Natalie, I am so glad I was able to get to know you better. You are such a wonderful woman. Stay strong and look at the positives. I will miss you so much. God bless"
I-café (USA)

"Natalie, It has been a good time with you! I really thank GOD that he put you into our team! Even though we are very different, I could always talk with you openly and honestly. Thankyou for your listening and for giving advice! And we've had some crazy times as well - remember when we were in kay-kay at the jelly-fish beach and were all grumpy haha and then ended up in this nice swimming place and another time when you just poured water over me or the funny times in the choir! Hey keep going - don't ever lose hope - the ship's time is a special time! I'll pray that you will have an amazing time on the ship and also for a good friend, GOD will put aside you! I'll miss you!"
I-café (Germany)

"Here's wishing you a Happy Birthday for today. That will make you 36 years younger than me. So that if you married me you would in all probability become a 'widow' in your mid 40's."
In an email from UK

"Natalie, I don't know what to say...I think God worked a lot in our lives in this time together here? Ok...at least for me...I haven't read your letter yet. For me it was very good to know you, a little bit but it was good, it was my challenge too but I learned to like you and I'll miss you but just a little bit ok? I'll be praying for you and your future husband.....no, that's time for everything (Ecclesiastes) and God knows what is better for us. Sleep tight and don't let the bed bugs bite."

Cabin Mate (Brazil)

Natalie's Story

I became a Christian at a young age primarily due to having been raised in a Christian home and being surrounded by Christianity. As a teenager there were times when I was really serious about my faith but I often became distracted. During a more serious faith phase at the age of seventeen, I was baptised, but just six weeks later fell away from God in dramatic fashion.

I subsequently spent six years immersed in the "party lifestyle", succumbing to many activities and bad habits that sought to replace God, including an abundance of alcohol, cigarettes and gambling. I moved from one non-Christian relationship to another in an attempt to find the happiness that eluded me. I became more and more miserable, attempting to ignore God but knowing deep down that He was there and that I was under His judgement because of my lifestyle choices.

In the year 2000, I began a degree course in Law and Criminology, but dropped out after just six weeks to join the police, thereby fulfilling a childhood dream. In 2002, my younger brother James (who was a Christian) was tragically killed in a car accident at the age of just eighteen. My parents clung to their Christian faith at this time, but I became angry with God for allowing this to happen and resented Christians for judging my lifestyle.

In April 2005, after many other problems and a long struggle, I faced up to the fact that I was miserable and that my life was a total mess. I had recently witnessed my younger sister, Lauren, going through some of the same struggles. I then saw the resulting contentment when she turned back to God. I knew that I was carrying the heavy weight of my many sins around on my shoulders. I sometimes woke up at night in a terrified state, believing I was going to Hell because of the things I had done. I knew that God was waiting for me to repent of my sins and turn back to Him, and that He had been patiently waiting for a long time. I lived in constant fear that time would run out and that I may have tested God one too many times.

Eventually, like the prodigal son in Luke chapter 15, I realised I couldn't continue as I was and I came to my senses. I said sorry to God for my many sins and asked for His help. I believed the promise that "everyone who calls on the name of the Lord will be saved."

I abandoned my sinful vices immediately and began regularly attending my former church, Worthing Tabernacle. Two Bible verses became very important to me as a result of my experiences. The first is found in John 6:67-68: "'You do not want to leave too, do you?' Jesus asked the Twelve. Simon Peter answered him, 'Lord, to whom shall we go? You have the words of eternal life.'" (NIV) These verses remind me that seeking anyone other than Jesus is a total waste of time because He is the only one with the words of eternal life that can offer hope for the future. The second verse is from Mark 8:36: "For what shall it profit a man, if he shall gain the whole world, and lose his own soul?" (KJV) This sums up my life experience as I tried seeking happiness in the world but foolishly risked losing my soul in the process.

God already had His hand on my life, due to my Christian upbringing, former beliefs and the fact that many people were praying for me regularly. All of the glory for the change in my life goes to God as I wasn't capable of turning my own life around having tried and failed many times.

The Wordless Book

Just in case there are any non-believers reading this, I would like to explain how to become a Christian and how you too can be free of your sin and reconciled to God to spend eternity in Heaven with Him one day.

During my few years of missionary service, I was taught a tool to explain the Gospel. It has been effectively used by millions of people around the world. It is called the "Wordless Book" and consists simply of five coloured sheets of paper, or material each representing part of the message of salvation found in the Bible:

YELLOW

This represents Heaven. Do you want everlasting life in Heaven? The Bible tells us that the streets in Heaven are paved with gold. It also tells us that God is light and that in Him there is no darkness and that Jesus (God's only Son) is the light of the world. Heaven is God's dwelling place and the Bible also tells us that no man has ever imagined the wonderful things that God has prepared in heaven for those that love Him. Heaven is forever.

BLACK

This represents sin. What is wrong with the world? More importantly, what is wrong with me? Being honest, we need to face the bad news in order to see the value of the good news. The Bible says that all people have sinned and fall short of the glory of God and that the wages of sin is death. God is holy and cannot have anything to do with sin. God is righteous and just and, therefore, cannot just overlook our sin and forgive us because this would make Him unjust. Our sin separates us from God's love permanently. All sinners are destined to spend an eternity in Hell under the wrath of God. Hell is a truly terrible place where people will long to die because of their torment but will be unable to do so. Hell is forever. This is the bad news.

RED

This represents the blood of Jesus. Why did Jesus need to die? God loved us so much that He provided a way of for us to be reconciled to Him and to escape the torments of Hell. He sent Jesus, His only son, to live a perfect life here on Earth. It was necessary for a penalty to be paid for our sin. Jesus' purpose in coming was to die for the sins of the world so that anyone who who believes in Him can get to Heaven. He died instead of us so that we could be free from the guilty sentence hanging over us because of our sin. He died on that cross and then rose from the grave just three days later, proving that He had defeated sin and death once and for all. Jesus' death acted as a bridge between guilty sinners and God, allowing all who trust in Him to be forgiven of their sins and to live in Heaven forever with God.

WHITE

This represents being washed clean from sin. How can be we sure of God's acceptance? Think of your life as a white sheet. Every time you sin, even in a small way, a black stain is left on the sheet. When a person becomes a Christian and turns away from their sin, God promises them a new start. He says that he will remember their sins no more. When God looks at the life of a Christian, he sees only Jesus and His righteousness instead of the sin.

GREEN

This represents growth. How should this change my life? All true Christians will grow spiritually over time. In order to grow, Christians should regularly read the word of God (the Bible), pray, attend a church, spend time with other Christians, and tell other people about Jesus and His sacrifice for them. These things do not save people. There are no "divine scales" weighing good and bad deeds as a determining factor for entry to Heaven or Hell. No human can ever do enough good things to get to Heaven, as the standard required is perfection; this is why Jesus had to die. The things described here are the grateful response of a Christian who has been rescued from a life of sin and death and has been reconciled to God for a life of hope and an eternal future in heaven.

This Series

Street Kids, Solvents & Salvation
Bringing hope to the hopeless in the Philippines
Natalie Vellacott

A MISSIONARY IN MANILA
NATALIE VELLACOTT

True Stories

Christian Fiction Short Stories

Christian Choose Your Own Adventure

Printed in Great Britain
by Amazon